EDUCATION AND DRAMATIC ART

To this day, *Education and Dramatic Art* remains the only fully worked critique of drama education in schools. Provocative and iconoclastic, this new edition brings the argument up-to-date and locates the author's proposals for a curriculum based on the making, performing and appraisal of dramas securely in the evolving culture of schools.

The first section of the book traces the origins and fortunes of drama in schools in the context of changing political times and argues that by neglecting the customs and practices of the theatre, drama-in-education has often kept from the students it professes to empower, the very knowledge and understanding necessary for them to take command of their subject.

Part two examines the developmental and pedagogic claims of drama-in-education. Theories of knowledge and meaning and assumptions about schools drama's power to establish a moral and social agenda, are all called to account.

Finally, *Education and Dramatic Art* proposes a multiculturally-based, theoretical structure for the teaching of drama which pulls the theatre and the classroom together and offers teachers the foundation for a broad and balanced drama curriculum with its own distinctive body of skills, knowledge and understanding.

David Hornbrook is Arts Inspector for the London Borough of Camden and an Associate Fellow of the Central School of Speech and Drama.

EDUCATION AND DRAMATIC ART

2nd Edition

David Hornbrook

London and New York

First published 1989
by Basil Blackwell
Oxford

Second edition 1998
by Routledge
11 New Fetter Lane, London EC4P 4EE

Simultaneously published in the USA and Canada
by Routledge
29 West 35th Street, New York, NY 10001

Typeset in Palatino by Routledge
Printed and bound in Great Britain by
Biddles Ltd, Guildford and King's Lynn

British Library Cataloguing in Publication Data
A catalogue record for this book is available from the British Library

Library of Congress Cataloguing in Publication Data
A catalogue record for this book has been requested

ISBN 0–415–16884–8 (hbk)
ISBN 0–415–16885–6 (pbk)

CONTENTS

Part 2 Drama-in-education: interpreting the text

Part 3 Towards dramatic art

CONTENTS

PREFACE

As the announcer on BBC radio's *Saturday Night Theatre* might have said, a decade has now passed since the manuscript of the first edition of *Education and Dramatic Art* dropped through the letter box of Basil Blackwell Ltd.

It is a rare privilege for an author to have the opportunity of re-visiting a published text, particularly a polemical one, and of making changes that reflect not only the passage of years but also reaction to the original. When I first sat at my screen in the mid-1980s to write a critical account of drama in English schools, I had little idea of how it would be received or whether my own growing disenchantment with the class-room remedies I was dispensing to would-be teachers in the name of drama was widely shared.

At the time, I suppose, I was driven mostly by intellectual curiosity. It just seemed to me odd that a set of simple classroom techniques based upon spontaneous make-believe should be able to inspire such a fierce, almost religious, dedication among a small group of teachers and advisers. My sifting of twenty years or so of trade journals revealed not a word of criticism, either of the practices of drama-in-education or of its proponents; it was as if one was researching a cult rather than a relatively minor part of the school curriculum. And yet I could not help noticing that all this fervour stood in marked contrast to the almost complete ignorance of the custom and practice of drama in schools on the part of everyone else. Indeed, I still find it impossible to speak to actors and directors about what goes on in schools by way of drama, or even to members of the drama faculties of universities, without a lengthy, explanatory preamble. Some secondary headteachers I meet in the course of my work as a school inspector, even those commanding flourishing drama departments, have very little idea of what is going on in their drama studios.

Education and Dramatic Art was the first sustained critique of drama-in-education and when it was published in 1989 it inevitably caused a few ripples. Responses to the book ranged from the hysterical 'How *dare* you criticise Dorothy!' variety, which I had expected, to supportive reviews from closet apostates, which were a pleasant surprise. What I did not foresee was that my polemic would come to take a place on the reading lists of prospective drama teachers, or that it would be regarded as representing a particular view of how drama should be taught. As the years passed I began to see that by offering an alternative to the prevailing orthodoxy, the book had possibly, in a modest way, *changed things*.

Perhaps this is an exaggeration. Change is not wrought by individual authors although individual authors can articulate change and these articulations may, in turn, help others to hurry it along. Whatever the causal balance, faced with the preparation of a new edition I was aware that the context in which the shifts of history had placed the old one could not be ignored, for it was this context which would determine the usefulness of its successor. Thus, while my curiosity about the strange freemasonry of drama-in-education remains and while the thrust of the new book is still a challenge to the rootless subjectivism of its ortho-doxies, I began the revising task in the knowledge that some, at least, of the changes of emphasis I proposed ten years ago had been realised. I was clear, too, that this slow but continuing metamorphosis was occur-ring in an educational landscape quite different from that of the mid-1980s and that this new geography would also have to be reflected in the new edition.

One of the principal questions I had asked myself in the 1980s was what effect the drama methodologies so extensively advertised in jour-nals, conferences and in-service training sessions had actually had on classroom teaching. My conclusion then was that the gap between rhetoric and reality was a disturbingly large one. My visits to schools revealed custom and practice looking not so very different from that which I had experienced when I began teaching in the 1960s. 'Predominantly', I wrote, 'children get into groups, pile up chairs, make up improvisations, show them at the end of the lesson'.

Ten years on, it is evident that events outside the drama studio have had some impact on the way affairs are conducted within it. The intro-duction of a statutory curriculum together with pressures from all parts of the political spectrum to raise students' achievement across the board have forced some rethinking. While my inspection visits show that schemes of work for drama often still feature elements from that curious lucky dip of drama exercises invented in the 1980s – terms like 'forum theatre', 'freeze frame' and 'hot seating' have become part of the *lingua franca* of secondary drama – I also see a growing willingness, especially among younger teachers, to tackle the important question of what young people should be learning *about* drama and to worry rather less about techniques designed to help their students learn *through* it.

So there is cause to be optimistic. Also, for all the anxiety created by the 1988 National Curriculum for schools (in which the subject failed to appear), drama remains buoyant. In 1992, the Arts Council of Great Britain estimated that seventy per cent of secondary schools in England and Wales employed drama specialists and every year nearly twice as many 16 year olds are entered for national drama examinations as are for music (a National Curriculum subject). Meanwhile, across the country school productions continue to flourish and there remains a huge commitment to extra-curricular drama. Although curriculum provision for 5 to 11 year olds is still patchy, class performances are a feature of the daily life of the primary school.[1]

As for drama specialists themselves, they are still, without doubt, most impressive classroom performers. In marked contrast to some other areas of the curriculum, the drama teaching I see in schools is characterised by responsiveness and flexibility and the drama lesson can be the stage for a formidable range of teaching techniques. Classes are invariably lively with opportunities for independent learning, discussion and work in small groups with teachers making good use of open questions and genuinely listening to students' replies. As a result, students invariably respond well to what is provided and, in my experience, levels of concentration, motivation and enjoyment in drama lessons are usually high.

While all this is most encouraging, there is still a long way to go before we will be able to say with confidence that drama in English schools is supported by a curriculum as coherent and rigorous as that of, say, music education. The sophisticated pedagogy, in other words, is often not matched by a corresponding clarity of purpose. This acute disjunction between form and content becomes apparent as the hypnotic effect of the pedagogic pyrotechnics wears off and one is left asking the question, *What are students actually achieving in drama?*

Many drama lessons are based on the exploration of themes and issues of various kinds through role-play. At their best, and when dealing sensitively with subjects such as 'Bullying' or 'Homelessness' or 'Attitudes to HIV', these topics may be legitimate vehicles for the teaching and learning of drama. In my experience, however, where there is this emphasis on issues, clear objectives to help students progress in the subject of drama are rarely set or followed through. Assessment records often emphasise social and behavioural outcomes – attentiveness, concentration, working well in groups – rather than the progressive acquisition of drama skills, knowledge and understanding. As a result, the range of opportunities suggested by the examples in the National Curriculum for English – understanding direction, being able to portray and interpret a character, knowing the characteristic features of tragedy, comedy and farce – is often unfamiliar territory for students before the age of 16. Similarly, I find little evidence in secondary schools of students writing plays in drama lessons or of students' scripts being performed, despite the National Curriculum requirement that students should be participating in 'the writing and performance of scripted drama' in their primary schools. It is perhaps an inevitable consequence of this muddle, that for all the hard work and fine teaching, drama in many schools remains characterised by low teacher expectations.

One of the last acts of the old drama team of Her Majesty's Inspectors under Roger Williams was the publication in 1989 of *Drama 5 to 16*.[2] In the document's first introductory paragraph, we are reminded that drama is 'a practical artistic subject', ranging 'from children's structured play, through classroom improvisations and performances of specially devised material to performances of Shakespeare'. While *Drama 5 to 16* embraces all the many manifestations of drama in schools, including the use of drama as a learning method in the context of English, the picture it unambiguously paints is of an arts discipline with its own particular associated skills and ways of understanding. Drama, it argues, 'encompasses the art of the theatre and involves some of the technologies or the applications of the sciences, as in designing and making scenery or controlling sound and lighting'. And it highlights the 'public aspects' of the subject, emphasising the way 'performing and sharing work with others, provide important links between schools, parents and their communities'.

It is in the spirit of *Drama 5 to 16* – also, now, approaching its tenth birthday – that I offer to readers this new edition of *Education and Dramatic Art*. As before, in examining the paradoxes of drama-in-education I shall try to make sense of them against the background of a wider and fast-changing historical scene. My modest aim remains to offer drama teachers ways of recognising, legitimating and developing what is best in their practice, in all its rich potential, so that curricular objectives may be articulated with more confidence and clarity. As I wrote in 1989:

> while the form of this book is unapologetically theoretical, it is not a book which itself proposes a pedagogic theory. It aims to be descriptive and interpretative rather than prescriptive and definitive. In that over-worked aphorism, it starts where teachers are, in the everyday experience of their classes and out-of-school drama activities, and it attempts to bring to all that enthusiasm, integrity and expertise, a structure whereby we may better understand both what we have been doing and where we might go.

David Hornbrook

November 1997

ACKNOWLEDGEMENTS

I am grateful to the following for giving permission to reprint material: Heinemann (USA), for D. Heathcote's `theatre' picture (reprinted by permission of Dorothy Heathcote and Gavin Bolton, Drama for Learning: Dorothy Heathcote's Mantle of the Expert Approach to Education, Heinemann, a division of Reed Elsevier Inc., Portsmouth, NH, 1995); Hutchinson, for N. Morgan and J. Saxton's assessment table from Teaching Drama; `A mind of many wonders..' and for B-J Wagner's Tomb Drama extract from Dorothy Heathcote: Drama as a Learning Medium; Hodder and Stoughton, for R. N. Pemberton-Billing and J. D. Clegg's Picnic in the Country from Teaching Drama; Batsford, for B. Watkins' Air Disaster from Drama and Education. I would also like to thank London Drama and NATE for permission to reprint the Patchwork Quilt flyer (and to point out that the course advertised was still available at the time of publication), London Drama for the Drugs Lesson from K. Taylor's Drama Strategies: New Ideas from London Drama, (and to point out that the original idea for this book grew out of the work developed by Islington Drama Teachers), and Professor Patrice Pavis for permission to reprint his questionnaire in Appendix 2. Finally, my thanks to Lynette Leggett and Sheena Masson and all the children at Rhyl Primary School for a wonderful evening at the opera and permission to publish their flyer.

PART I
DRAMA-IN-EDUCATION
TELLING THE STORY

1

THE PLOT

The rise of drama-in-education

NOBLE SAVAGES IN AN ENGLISH ARCADIA

Theory, and the challenge it implicitly presents to empiricism and 'common-sense', is viewed, like ideology, with some suspicion by groups traditionally disposed to favour practical ways of doing things. For fifty years or so there has been a small but eloquent faction in English education which has committed itself to the practical way with some single-mindedness. Believing in the power of make-believe to awaken empathy and understanding in young people, its members have dedicated themselves to the use of drama as an educative instrument. The discourse associated with this distinctive alliance of drama and pedagogy has come to be known as *drama-in-education*.

Modesty of ambition has not marked the advertising of drama-in-education's portfolio; in 1995, a prominent advocate described one of its techniques as 'the best possible form of education',[1] and there was a time when some enthusiasts really believed that drama-in-education was so significant that it would one day assume a place at the core of the school curriculum. History, as we shall see, has not dealt kindly with these pretensions. Nevertheless, close observation of exemplar lessons followed by affirmative analysis has helped to sustain believers' faith in the transforming power of their methods and confirm them in their conviction that the processes of drama-in-education are radically enlightening. Meanwhile, although debates about the relative merits of this or that form of empirical verification have multiplied, the theories that lie behind the classroom practices and the claims made for them have remained obscure.

In fact, the distinctive discourse of drama-in-education may be traced to a series of inter-connected assumptions associated with the progressive education movement. This movement, in turn, has its origins in the revolutionary spirit of late eighteenth-century Romanticism, so that in Jean Jacques Rousseau's model of pre-civilised man (*sic*), his noble savage imbued with natural goodness whose infallible guide was his

3

feelings, can be recognised the ghostly prototype of the paradigmatic student of drama-in-education. It is worth noting, in the light of the unfolding argument, that Rousseau's noble savage in a significant sense epitomised the ideal family man of the bourgeois imagination: a responsible and considerate husband and father inspired with a natural kindliness and possessed of all natural wisdom – a point which has not escaped feminist critics.[2]

The autonomy of consciousness advocated by Rousseau, with its extension into a universality of moral feeling where the source of moral rectitude is seen to reside, not in the hands of the gods and their earthly representatives, but in the authentic examination of our 'true and uncorrupted conscience', lies at the heart of the challenge that was to be offered to conventional ethics by Romanticism. This view of human nature is, of course, in marked contrast both to that of the traditional Christian account of original sin and to that of the seventeenth-century English philosopher Thomas Hobbes, whose argument for a strong state was based on his belief that, in nature, our lives would be 'solitary, poor, nasty, brutish and short'. It is from Hobbes' individualism (through Adam Smith) rather than from Rousseau's that modern economic orthodoxy derives, an opposition that will be shown to have had no small influence on the moral and political imperatives of our study.

The Romantic idea of a subjective morality accessible through an awareness of our true feelings has permeated thinking about school drama. It has long been supposed that students engaged in the spontaneous improvisation and role-playing of the drama lesson can lose themselves just sufficiently for their 'deeply felt', and by implication, *genuine*, morality to reveal itself. While 'in the unreality of the classroom', wrote one practitioner in the 1980s, students 'may adopt an intellectual posture of accepting the notion of shades of opinion, what surfaces in drama is their real feelings'.[3] Romanticism and drama-in-education both share a commitment to a private world of sensation where cognitive endeavour may be safely confined to knowledge about what one truly feels.

Rousseau also had strong views about drama. His polemic against Jean Le Rond d'Alembert,[4] who had suggested that the city of Geneva might improve its amenities by building a theatre, reveals not so much a puritanical dislike of pleasure but, rather, a perception of theatre art as leading to the falsification of the self. To be sure, the cramped, odorous playhouses of eighteenth-century France can hardly have been places of moral or spiritual self-enhancement. For Rousseau, committed as he was to the authentic voice of conscience, the actor on the stage deliberately distanced himself (*sic*) from the universality of moral feeling, thus diminishing his own authenticity by 'counterfeiting himself', by 'putting on another character than his own'. He proposed instead the replacement of those 'exclusive entertainments which close up a small number of people in melancholy fashion in a gloomy cavern', with open-air festivities of communal participation. 'Let the spectators become an entertainment to themselves; make them actors themselves; do it so that each one sees and loves himself in the others.'[5] Again, we will see clearly reflected in drama-in-education Rousseau's deep-seated suspicion of the entire apparatus of theatrical illusion as well as his enthusiasm for the home-made authenticity of participatory drama.

While it might fairly be said that real feelings and personal values have no more a place on the stages of Shaftesbury Avenue or the South Bank than they did on those of eighteenth-century Paris, we should be careful of making too easy a distinction between the 'false' world of the theatre and the 'genuine' world of human interaction. Also, although we often speak confidently of our *real* feelings, it is not altogether clear how we can reliably make a distinction between the feelings we have, such as we may intelligibly say of some that they are true and of others that they are false. And who is to mediate between your morality and mine when our 'true and uncorrupted consciences' lead us to different conclusions? As an inheritor of these paradoxes, drama-in-education has had some difficulty disentangling itself from the deep contradictions of its Romantic legacy, as the following chapters will show.

If not in its playhouses, historically England did provide more fertile and stable ground for the seeding of these particular products of Romantic naturalism than the turbulent politics of nineteenth-century France. Without the home-grown images of political despotism that inspired the liberationist visions of their European counterparts, English Romantic artists turned instead to attack the economic despotism of the Industrial Revolution which they saw as callous and philistine. The expanding working-class ghettos of the new cities were the antithesis of naturalism, their inhabitants as far from ideals of simple pastoral nobility that it was possible to imagine. Against the bleak, dehumanising townscapes of industry the English Romantics fielded, not a class-based politics of revolution, but the sensibility of the radical individual. Human liberation was to come about not as a result of class struggle, but through love, creation and self-expression. There was to be a revolution of feeling, a new self-awareness, leading to a nobler, more progressive, humanism.

Established to further this aesthetic, the first English progressive schools were patronised by members of a prosperous and comfortable new social class who, in their revulsion with the industrial squalor brought about by their forebears' indiscriminate wealth-making, sought to insulate their children from its less attractive consequences. Schools like Abbotsholme (1889) and Bedales (1893) provided idyllic pastoral environments, far removed from the material and moral pollution of Blake's 'chartered streets',[6] where the sons and daughters of the *rentiers* could happily indulge in pre-industrial pursuits. The education they received eschewed the institutionalised brutalities and regimentation of the traditional English public school, and fostered instead the cultivation of individual sensibility. Progressive school teachers aimed to liberate the spirit of their students, allowing them access to the uncorrupted conscience of Rousseau's moral and aesthetic universe. In this respect they saw themselves as educational facilitators rather than teachers in the conventional sense, offering opportunities for the growth of learning in place of the imposition of knowledge.

It is here that the radical spirit of drama-in-education has its source. Its apologists have traditionally been the champions of a humane, child-centred individualism in education, believing, sometimes passionately, in the liberating powers of self-knowledge. Most would probably still consider themselves to be 'progressive', in the widest sense of that word, favourably comparing their digressive practices with what they see as the narrow, conformist pedagogy of other areas of the curriculum. True Romantics, they are likely to entertain a deep suspicion of society's institutions and of hierarchies of all kinds, regarding themselves as the allies of their students rather than their instructors.

ART AND THE PLAY OF LIFE

There were, of course, no theatres in Arcadia. Virgil's young shepherds and poets were in as little danger of being corrupted by the 'intemperate madness' that Rousseau perceived in Aristotelian catharsis as were the boys and girls of Abbotsholme and Bedales. Although theatre as an institution was disapproved of, art itself, defined by Romanticism as pre-eminently the expression of an inner creative process, had by the end of the nineteenth century assumed a predominant place in the education of the liberated consciousness. Indeed, the idea that personal autonomy is fostered by art is fundamental to all progressive education. Children put paint on paper or make shapes out of clay with no avowed intention of ever becoming painters or potters, but because the very practice of art is seen as a way of nurturing a child's imagination and creativity.

The experiments of the Austrian art teacher Franz Cizek, who opened free classes for children at the School of Applied Art in Vienna in 1898, provide a pertinent example of the way in which these new ideas about art in education began to take shape. Young people came to his studio to paint and draw as the mood took them. Cizek, always encouraging, made a point of never interfering or attempting to correct their drawings; from time to time he would randomly select work for display. An archetypal early progressivist, Cizek aimed through his classes to awaken the unconscious art which he believed lay in everybody. The colourful walls of today's primary and infant classrooms are evidence of his continuing influence.

Drama's eventual guarantee of a place in this aesthetic owed no more to conventional theatre practice than Cizek's art classes did to the academies. Rather, there was an understanding among early progressivists that the innocent make-believe of children's play was a form of highly beneficial 'natural' education in itself. In 1911, Harriet Finlay-Johnson described how she had transformed this simple ideal into practice in her village school in Sussex. 'Why not continue the principle of the Kindergarten game in the school for older scholars?'[7] she wrote in *The Dramatic Method of Teaching*.

> am I quite wrong when I say that childhood should be a time for merely absorbing big stores of sunshine for possible future dark times? And what do I mean by sunshine but just the things for which Nature implanted (in the best and highest part of us) an innate desire – the joy of knowing the beauties of the living world around us and in probing its mysteries.[8]

It was Cambridge schoolmaster Henry Caldwell Cook, however, who, by fusing play ('the only work worth doing') with the idea of the player on the stage, became the first to describe a comprehensive programme for what we now might recognise as drama-in-education. Because he considered that 'acting out' motivated his boys to a more profound understanding of dramatic literature than could be achieved by formal teaching, Caldwell Cook encouraged the performance of plays, both in the classroom and later in what must have been the first purpose-built drama room, which he called 'The Mummery'. Groups of boys were also encouraged to write material of their own for performance.

The Play Way, published in 1917, its heady progressivism expressed in the author's idiosyncratic *Boys' Own Paper* style, completely reflects the reformist spirit of ideas about art and education abroad at this time.[9] Caldwell Cook's ideal school, his 'Play School' of the future, was characteristically to be situated in the country away from the detrimental influences of city life, and governed by a kind of Athenian assembly of all its members. Singing, Drawing, Acting and the writing of Poetry, would dominate the timetable alongside crafts like Carpentry, Weaving, Printing, Bookbinding and Gardening. Discipline was to be founded on mutual trust and understanding, based on the observance of 'right conduct':

> We must let ourselves live fully, by doing thoroughly those things we have a natural desire to do; the sole restrictions being that we so order the course of our life as not to impair those energies by which we live, nor hinder other men so long as they seem also to be living

well. Right and wrong in the play of life are not different from the right and wrong of the playing field.[10]

By superimposing the morality of English team games onto the free spirit of Romanticism, Caldwell Cook was unwittingly rehearsing the ethical conundrum which we have already visited and which continues to haunt drama-in-education. At what point does our right to do 'those things we have a natural desire to do' give way to the demands of 'right conduct'? In a world where the values of the public school playing field are by no means universally accepted, who is to adjudicate?

It was the advent of psychoanalysis, and in particular the attention given by post-Freudians to the developmental significance of children's play, that finally legitimated a form of drama within the 'inner-world' concept of creativity favoured by educational progressivists. By the time Harriet Finlay-Johnson was preaching 'the gospel of happiness in child-hood',[11] Karl Groos had already identified play as practice for adult life,[12] and it was not long before a succession of post-Freudian psychologists were elevating the play of young children to a dominating position in theories of early learning. The plausibly scientific recognition of play, with its 'naturalness' and intrinsic 'let's pretend' element, as a route to intuitive wisdom, enabled the teleological gap between self-authentication and acting to be convincingly bridged. Now the fantasies of an innocent child, acted out in the playground or street, could be represented as a *real* drama, rich both in creativity and learning. Through the offices of psychology, drama had been transformed from the frivolous diversion described by Rousseau to an essential ingredient of a child's balanced development. By the 1930s, this perception had even reached the corridors of England's Board of Education.

> Drama both of the less and more formal kinds, for which children, owing to their happy lack of self-consciousness, display such remarkable gifts, offers further good opportunities of developing that power of expression in movement which, if the psychologists are right, is so closely correlated with the development of perception and feeling.[13]

By the outbreak of the Second World War all the guiding principles of drama-in-education were in circulation. Endorsed by the child psychologists and psycho-therapists of the 1930s and 1940s, drama was now in a position to make its mark on the school curriculum. It was to present its credentials not in the form of a body of theatrical skills and practices, but as a quasi-therapeutic process, dedicated to the perceived aesthetic and developmental 'needs' of the young. With their acceptance, drama-in-education may be seen as the crowning achievement of English progressivism. The universality of moral feeling and the primacy of the subjective, the authentication of the self through the exercise of the creative faculty, the need to play: these are the field's cherished tropes. They encapsulate its humanity as well as its naïveté, implying a vision of a better world, but, as we shall see, lacking both the epistemological and cultural foundations upon which such a vision might be built.

WELL-DEVELOPED PEOPLE

In Great Britain, the Second World War gave new impetus to thinking about education. There was a widespread feeling that a new and fairer society should be built from the ruins of one where classes of forty or more were not uncommon and where 5 per cent of all children were officially classified as under-nourished. Even Winston Churchill recognised the public mood. 'I do not think we can maintain our position in the post-war world', he wrote, 'unless we are an exceptionally well-educated people.'[14] The 1944 Education Act upgraded the old Board of Education to a Ministry, raised the school-leaving age to 15 and set up a system of state primary, secondary and further education. With the founding of the Educational Drama Association a year before the Act became law, and the appointment of Peter Slade as the country's first drama adviser, the historical climate was set fair for the ideas of Harriet Finlay-Johnson and Henry Caldwell Cook to advance from the educational fringes into legitimacy.

Drama, recast in therapeutic form, seemed perfectly to encapsulate the idealistic mood of this time of national renewal, a fact that was not lost on educational policy-makers. An internal report from the new Ministry of Education in 1951 applauded the fact that drama was now 'an established and worthwhile part of school life',[15] and by the time Slade's *magnum opus*, *Child Drama*[16] was published in 1954, the philosophy which inspired it had a firm hold on educational thinking across the country.

Meanwhile, the raising of the school-leaving age together with the post-war population bulge were creating an urgent need for more teacher trainers. Through the 1960s, the number of full-time teacher-training courses offering qualifications in drama rose from six to over one hundred. To cater for this vast expansion, former schoolteachers with drama backgrounds ranging from English and amateur dramatics to licentiateships from the speech and drama academies found themselves swept into the new or enlarged teacher-training colleges on a wave of progressivist enthusiasm and entrusted with the initiation of students into the mysteries of Child Drama.

Like Cizek and Finlay-Johnson, Peter Slade believed that the creative activity of children should not be measured by adult standards. For Slade, Child Drama was 'a high Art Form in its own right'.[17] A true progressive, he stressed the importance of non-interference in what he saw as the natural creative process, suggesting that the teacher should instead 'guide and nurture', perhaps drawing a group's attention 'to some little piece of beauty they may have missed'. (For a good example of the teaching style of this period, see the 'Picnic in the Country' lesson in Appendix 1.) He emphasised the distinction between the spontaneous processes of classroom drama, 'drama in the widest sense', and the theatre 'as understood by adults'.

> Of course theatre has its place. It can be wonderful and beautiful, but it is only a small part of Drama, and we shall not get the balance right unless we see this quite clearly; and, unless we do see, it is difficult to understand the supreme and innate culture of Child Drama.[18]

By elevating classroom drama ('part of real life') in a way which sought not only to distance it from general theatre practice ('a bubble on the froth of civilisation')[19] but also to invest it by implication with a superior moral status, Slade inherited the aesthetic of Rousseau's Romantic Naturalism and inscribed it irrevocably in post-war thinking about drama in schools. It was a little piece of dogma that was to have a profound effect on the subsequent history of the discipline.

A further characterising feature of the Sladian aesthetic was also to lay up problems for the future. Like Rousseau, Slade believed in the primacy of self-expression and the discovery of moral truth by inner reflection.

> in this drama, two important qualities are noticeable – absorption and sincerity. Absorption is being completely wrapped up in what is being done, or what one is doing, to the exclusion of all other thoughts. . . . Sincerity is a complete form of honesty in portraying a part, bringing with it an intense feeling of reality and experience. [20]

This established early on the emphasis on the active and spontaneous participation of students in dramatic games and improvisations, familiar enough to those who have seen classroom drama in action, but which ever since has inhibited judgements about students' progress in drama and which has led, as we shall see in the following chapter, to a tendency, in the absence of any other acceptable criteria, to assess students on their level of *acquiescence*. Paradoxically, despite his enthusiasm for spontaneity and his injunction not to criticise, Slade, like Caldwell Cook before him, was in little doubt about the rules of 'the play of life':

> pointing out the need for cleanliness and good manners will often help them [the lads in the school] to grow up and be more acceptable to the young women . . . Girls do not take kindly to rather ragged, rough-mannered clowns who spoil the drama period.[21]

In terms that Aristotle might have understood, honour is due to those with clean hands and good manners!

For all the sentimentality and internal contradictions of Child Drama, there is no doubt that the pioneering work of Peter Slade in the years following the war enthused huge numbers of young teachers and succeeded in establishing drama as a force in state education. The Newsom Report of 1963, which expressed its concern over the education system's apparent failure with the less able, gave much credence to the psycho-therapeutic role of drama in countering the 'social maladroitness and insensitivity' of 'less gifted' students. Art, according to Newsom, and drama in particular, should be regarded not as a 'frill', but as a way of helping young people to come to terms with themselves. 'By playing out psychologically significant situations' said the Report, children 'can work out their own personal problems'.[22]

The idea that drama-in-education has much to do with the psychological adjustment of young people to their social circumstances figured prominently in the rash of handbooks which followed the success of *Child Drama*. Probably the most notable of these was Brian Way's *Development Through Drama*. Published in 1967, in the wake of the Plowden Report's endorsement of progressive education in primary schools,[23] *Development Through Drama* provided just the right mix of theory and practical advice to stimulate and inspire a second wave of young drama teachers. [24] Way reinforced Slade's distinction between 'theatre' and 'drama', but largely abandoned the latter's idea of Child Drama as Art in favour of a comprehensive theory of personal development. Believing, along with the child psychologists, that play is practice for adult life, and hypothesising that it is an instinctive need artificially suppressed after early childhood, Way saw school drama as a means of restoring the 'natural' developmental processes which play encourages.

> Fully developed people will seldom make poor or uninteresting drama, even though it may not be brilliant ... drama, far from being new, is closely interwoven in the practical implementation of both the spirit and the substance of every Education Act that has ever been passed, especially the idea of the development of the whole person.[25]

In the 'whole person', the unique 'human essence' for whom Way's drama lessons were to be a gradual nurturing process, we can clearly see the ghost of Rousseau's noble savage, that decent, law-abiding liberal humanist, sensitive, tolerant, imaginative and reflective, fitting in well to the social environment, who yet manages to be creative and original – within acceptable limits. Through the mid-1960s and early 1970s, book after book professed to demonstrate how drama-in-education developed 'self-confidence', or encouraged 'personal awareness and an awareness of others', or taught students how to co-operate in groups, or fostered qualities of 'tolerance and understanding', or helped children to become more 'self-disciplined'.[26] Just about the only thing classroom drama made no claims to do, and by this time many teachers would have been puzzled to have it suggested, was to equip young people with an understanding of actors, theatres and plays.

LEARNING THROUGH DRAMA

As books offering menus of 'ideas for drama' proliferated, those drama teachers who found themselves dipping into themes such as 'Conflict', or 'The Family', or 'A Fairground' were generally content with the assumption that so long as their students were sufficiently 'absorbed' in their improvisations then they were, *pace* Brian Way, 'developing' satisfactorily. They saw no need to contextualise the work and believed that any attempt to improve the performance skills of their classes would inhibit their students' 'natural creativity'. Often students were led through imaginative exercises of one kind or another, or, more frequently, encouraged to play energetic games before collapsing into small groups to make up plays for performance, time permitting, at the end of the lesson (see the 'Air Disaster' lesson in Appendix 1). Buoyant on the high tide of progressivism, such scepticism as there was about these practices could be dismissed as straightforwardly reactionary, with the confident (some might say, complacent) assumption that more traditionally minded teachers expressing worries about the noise and apparent anarchy of the drama class, would, given time, become aware of its assuredly self-evident value.

There were some dissenting voices, but, after brief defensive flurries and a general closing of ranks, their concerns receded into obscurity.[27] One of the handful who took the trouble to reply in print to the questions raised by David Clegg in *Theatre Quarterly* about what was going on in schools in the name of drama was a lecturer at the University of Newcastle who was herself about to rise to pre-eminence in the field. In a letter published in 1973, Dorothy Heathcote agreed with Clegg that school drama was suffering from a tendency to create 'high priests', unthinking allegiance to whom was ossifying practice. She said she shared his worries about teacher training, and argued that it was necessary to prepare drama teachers 'who can stimulate commitment' and 'follow it through to meaningful learning'.[28]

The change of approach indicated here was significant. Those who had seen Heathcote at work in Newcastle could hardly have failed to be aware of her dominant, directorial relationship to the unfolding drama, or of her willingness, on occasions, to become a participant. They would also have noted the extensive time she allowed for debate, even for writing, intrusions which amounted to a conscious challenging and shaping of young people's ideas (see the 'Tomb Drama' in Appendix 1). All very unsettling for drama teachers brought up on the strict non-interventionism of Child Drama.

Heathcote believed that the teacher's aim was to use drama 'in the way in which it will most aid him (*sic*) in challenging the children to learn'.[29] By using the motivating energy of dramatic play to support pedagogy she sought to redefine drama-in-education as a *learning process*. Through the sensitive agency of the teacher, Heathcote argued, the imaginative world simulated by the spontaneous acting out of events would reveal to a class new insights and understandings. 'Drama for understanding' or 'drama for knowing' became key concepts in a new language of 'authenticity', 'negotiation', and 'universals', whereby it was argued that by manipulating dramatic improvisation, students could be led to an 'authentic experience', a so-called 'deep knowing', of the essential truths of the human condition. Rather than being the subject of pedagogy, drama-in-education became a sophisticated form of pedagogy itself.

There were many drama teachers at this time understandably willing to see Heathcote and her new methodology as potential saviours. By the mid-1970s, the long march of drama-in-education had come to a slow halt as national contraction replaced the huge post-war expansion in education. By the early 1980s, the number of specialist initial training courses in drama teaching had fallen to only seven. While this to some extent reflects a more general cutback in teacher education, the relative drop in drama courses was particularly severe.

The dissection and analysis of Heathcote's methodology came to mark out the parameters of acceptable drama in schools, helped in no small measure by the charismatic qualities of her remarkable presence which began to bewitch the increasing numbers of drama teachers who came to watch and participate in her workshops – two early converts described her work as 'breath-taking'[30] – and by 1979, a eulogistic account of her techniques was on the shelves of English bookshops.[31] For those inspired by Heathcote's innovative way of working the old handbooks of themes-for-drama now seemed paltry. New collections of lesson ideas by drama specialists with ordinary school experience attempted to translate Heathcote's idiosyncratic skills, such as 'teacher-in-role', into manageable techniques for the classroom.[32]

At the same time, and rather less happily, a fierce sectarianism gripped drama-in-education as ranks closed around the new methodologies. Panegyrics flowed from the pens of Heathcote devotees during the 1980s, ranging from the worthy to the unshamefacedly messianic, but all united in their devotion to the words and deeds of their mentor. A decade after her retirement from Newcastle in 1986, past accounts of

Heathcote's drama workshops were still being dissected and analysed by her admirers for the wisdoms they might offer up.

In reality, for some at least, the return from Damascus proved to be a sobering experience. The newly-converted not unnaturally attempted to imitate Heathcote's techniques back in their classrooms, but, confronted with the frustrations of their 50-minute lessons and the daily battles of the school, many teachers saw themselves as failing to live up to her exacting standards. For others, the Heathcote 'revolution' simply passed them by. Overall, despite its persuasive methodology and its very considerable claims on the curriculum, evidence suggests that this latest manifestation of drama-in-education was rather less successful in engaging with the day-to-day practice of drama teaching than those which had preceded it. The legacy of Peter Slade and his Romantic forebears continued to exert a powerful influence in the classroom throughout the 1980s and 1990s, more often than not shaping the reality of school drama if not the discourse used to described it.

2

THE PLAYERS
Witness and revelation

I will give power unto my two witnesses, and they shall prophesy one thousand and two hundred and threescore days.

(Revelation 11.3)

MYSTIFICATION AND DRAMATIC MIDWIFERY

Although the radical seriousness represented by techniques such as 'teacher-in-role' blew through the aimless games and improvisations of the 1970s with the promise of a new purposefulness, this alone does not explain how the personalities of Dorothy Heathcote and her colleague and admirer, Gavin Bolton, came to be woven into the peculiar fabric of drama-in-education in the 1980s or how their message managed to shape the discourse of the field for well over a decade. Despite the fact that Heathcote had never held a post in a school – both she and Bolton had been members of university departments for many years by this time – the domination of the stage by these two high-profile performers was complete. At least as influential as Peter Slade had been for an earlier generation of drama teachers, they succeeded in inspiring in their supporters a loyalty to the idea of drama as a cross-curricular pedagogy that for some came close to religious devotion.

In 1954, Peter Slade had painted a vivid picture of the magical world of Child Drama, which he claimed should remain for the child 'a realm of mystic secrecy'.[1] Subsequent literature abounded with similar sentiments. 'In creative drama work … [we] soar into the world of magic and mystery – the world in which our most private and peculiar selves obtain that which enables the metamorphosis from "existing" to "being" to happen.'[2] By contrast, in her early writings, Dorothy Heathcote speaks of what she does with an appealing clarity. Here she is in the same year, 1967, and in the same journal, describing 'dramatic improvisation': 'Very simply it means putting yourself into other people's shoes and, by using personal experience to help you to understand their point of view, you may discover more than you knew when you started'.[3]

15

As the years passed, this refreshing directness was replaced by a more convoluted style, where insights into her methods became mixed up with excursions into her private and idiosyncratic bibliography. The result produced an effect hardly less mystifying than that which had so characterised the writing of her predecessors. This is all much in evidence in a published interview some twenty years later. She explains:

> If theatre is anything to anybody, it is thick description, and if theatre is to be used for perception, perception will only come through thick description, this laid upon that, provided that slow incrementing of one experience on another is filled with – filled with joy.[4]

On occasions, presumably in the cause of clarification, Heathcote would resort to drawings. Here she is in 1995, again attempting to throw light on what she means by theatre.

> I can sum it up in this way: the human face is usually possessed of a mouth, a nose, two ears, and two eyes, with surrounding bits to join these elements together. The bits that join and surround create the communicating system of the face. Theatre has many 'communicating faces' that surround and give a variety of shaping to a few operant laws:[5]

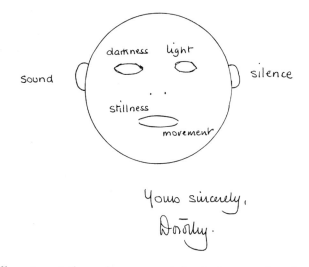

Ernest Gellner is not the only commentator to have pointed out that in order to reap the spiritual benefits offered by mystics and therapists we must suspend our rational disbelief and submit ourselves to their greater wisdom. In dependent relationships of this kind, he says, 'critical considerations become assigned to the realm of symptoms, of the reducible, while *assent* is part of the endorsed authenticity'.[6] Far from alienating teachers, Heathcote's elaborately figurative approach played a major part in her ascension, enveloping the woman who had once deplored the creation of 'high priests' with an aura of pedagogical magic which served both to deflect criticism and to reinforce her mystical status. Devotional acquiescence began to characterise the discourse of drama-in-education during this period, the strident assentiveness of the language used to describe Heathcote and her work transforming potential analysis and explanation into simple expressions of allegiance.

> Heathcot-ites often sound like a nauseous, self-congratulatory group, but if affirmation is genuine it breeds that 'we-feeling' which our reductionist, mechanistic, techne-orientated society will slowly and inevitably destroy if it is not co-operatively challenged. . . . Dorothy Heathcote teaches people to dance with butterflies not fossilise them.[7]
>
> By heroic . . . Dorothy refers to that level of experience wherein a person finds himself at one with the universal elements of existence, seeing himself suddenly not as an individual with private 'worldly' preoccupations, but as part of the mystery and magic of creation.[8]
>
> When the moment of knowing is born, Dorothy weighs and measures it, pronounces it fit, and then, most difficult and important of all, gives it back to the person who made and fought for it.[9]

This last example, which is taken from an extended midwifery metaphor, is particularly revealing, for it combines the image of the plain woman rolling up her sleeves to do the job, with that of the officiating priestess. As we shall see, these archetypal identifications proved to be an attractive synthesis for a discipline which was beginning to see itself as uniquely equipped to lead students from the ordinary to the transcendent, from the 'real world' of the classroom to an 'awesome awareness of universal truths'.[10] With the subsequent need both to substantiate and advertise its metaphysic, the canonisation of a practitioner seemingly so specially able to conjure such transfigurations was then but a small step; other concerns – doubts about the sexual politics of such conflations, for example – could be swept aside.[11] In an epidemic of hagiography, casual utterance becomes inscribed as text, texts become sacred, and dissent is reducible to heresy.

> Wherever Heathcote goes, she generates excitement and even adulation. She emanates power. Her power is like that of a medium, bringing into the present the distant in time or space, making it come alive in our consciousness through imagined group experience. . . . A spell has to be cast; rituals must be followed; conditions

17

have to be right; the universal inherent in this moment must be realised, and she's witchlike in her control leading to this effect.[12]

EAGLE AND MOLE – KEEPING IT IN THE FAMILY

A former school teacher and drama adviser, Gavin Bolton had become a teacher trainer in the great expansion of the 1960s.[13] Established only fifteen miles away from Newcastle at the University of Durham and already an energetic exponent of drama-in-education in his own right, his name and Heathcote's were soon being linked. An admirer of growing dedication, Bolton took up the cause of drama as pedagogy with enthusiasm (thirty years later he was still convinced of 'the revolutionary implications' of Heathcote's methods[14]), setting himself the difficult task of giving his colleague's highly intuitive methodology respectable intellectual form.

In this collaboration we again see Heathcote constructed in conventionally feminine terms ('the midwife of creative knowing'), while Bolton ('the cool evaluator') is allowed to fulfil the expectations of masculinity. If for no other reason than that they will be remembered for having 'mothered and fathered' the pedagogy upon which the reputation of school drama was once staked, in the archives of drama-in-education the names of Heathcote and Bolton – or 'Dorothy and Gavin' as they were affectionately referred to by their followers – will remain difficult to separate. Here is Heathcote delivering a paean to 'Gavin' in 1983.

> We [Gavin and I] were discussing how we realise our own knowledge, and I said that I felt that I 'burrowed along like a mole in the dark', occasionally coming up to look around for a brief spell, whereas I felt Gavin flew over the terrain like an eagle seeing a large landscape and the patterns of it.[15]

This extract was subsequently much used to differentiate between what were seen as the complementary attributes of the two progenitors. Its cosy, *Wind in the Willows* style delivered a reassuring message to a family of devotees who needed little persuasion to respond in like manner to any disparagement – 'please, Eagle and Mole, don't apologise, don't feel threatened'.[16] In the manner of families, Dorothy and Gavin deflected external criticism and quickly closed ranks against attack.

> There is another less happy theme in Gavin's talk which is concerned with ideological conflicts between Gavin, Malcolm Ross and John Fines. My own feeling is that this conflict (made ugly by the fulminatory attacks on Gavin from Ross) arises from the nature of the academic roles shared by all three.[17]

Here, the disapprobatory use of Malcolm Ross's surname heightens the sense of exclusion while at the same time reinforcing the collective solidarity of the family itself. As for John Fines, it would seem that his loyalties are quite clear:

> Now when you have had your hand slapped by someone as good and wise and noble as Gavin the best course of action is to stuff it into your armpit and grimace a little, but quietly in a corner. . . . Surely we should all reverence what he has done and wait calmly but eagerly for the next episode?[18]

The complete unself-consciousness of this unctuous familiarity is well illustrated in the collaboration already cited in which 'Dorothy and Gavin' talk approvingly to each other about Heathcote's 'mantle of the expert' technique.[19] The trouble is that it obscures the vital distinction we must always make between utterance and utterer if we are to attempt a constructive evaluation of what is being said. Here, the employment of first names, the avuncular familiarity and the absence of critical judgement, make it almost impossible to prise the text from the personality. Paralysed by self-referentiality, 'Gavin' becomes inseparable from 'Gavin's theories' so that any challenge to the ideas is read as a threat to the person. This fusion possibly reaches its apogee in a biographical project on Gavin Bolton undertaken in the mid-1990s in which the writer claims that her 'post-modernist, feminist' approach offers up a story unhampered by analysis and where the life and work of her champion would finally become inseparable.

> I linger over the picture of Gavin that brings me closest to my own experience as a drama teacher. He is standing with a group of students, encircled by their joy and energy. There is a tangible human connection between them – the bonding of shared experience. . . . This is the Gavin Bolton I recognise.[20]

This tendency to conflate personality and agency is not, of course, confined to the world of school drama, but is a much more general feature of modernity, as many commentators have noted. Richard Sennett, for instance, makes the point that, as we are now prone to accept public exhibitions of authenticity for guarantees of political competence or incorruptibility, a charismatic leader has no need to resort to demagogy to retain power.

> He can be warm, homey, and sweet; he can be sophisticated and debonair. But he will bind and blind people as surely as a demonic figure if he can focus them upon his tastes, what his wife is wearing in public, his love of dogs . . . What has grown out of the politics of

personality begun in the last century is charisma as a force for stabilising ordinary political life.[21]

Thus, the charismatic leader is free to display strategic or intellectual incompetence, or to admit to ignorance in areas which must seriously challenge his or her credentials to be a leader, just so long as the heart is worn on the sleeve. The cult of personality, which is ready to endorse all manner of actions and pronouncements on the grounds that they are 'authentically' felt by the protagonist, infused drama-in-education in the 1980s, and helped to hold its familial structure together. Or, as a critic once accused of delivering an 'unfettered harangue' against a member of the family more bluntly puts it, 'the veneration of a handful of leading practitioners has been endemic in educational drama circles and is yet another way of maintaining a safe, well defined status quo'.[22]

ASSAULTING THE IVORY TOWERS

Ever since drama teachers first moved away the desks and chairs and asked students to 'find a space', drama-in-education has had 'getting up and doing' at the heart of its methodological approach. There has been an assumption that if drama in school achieved nothing else, at least it released students from the conventional structures of teaching and learning for which the traditional classroom layout was such a stark metaphor, and allowed a new physical freedom within which the expression of ideas and feelings might take place. In the early days 'getting up and doing' in this physical sense dominated the drama lesson to the exclusion of anything much else.

> Pupils who enter a drama lesson do not want to spend long periods of time locked in discussion. At first the class should consider suggestions quickly, begin rehearsal and then discuss and rehearse simultaneously, otherwise a conflict of ideas and personalities develops within the groups and nothing is created.[23]

For this teacher, and for others like him in the 1960s and 1970s, so long as students were purposefully engaged in the prescribed activities, the criteria of Child Drama were considered to be satisfactorily fulfilled. While the 1980s brought the legitimation of discussion as a valid constituent of the new pedagogical approach, the 'getting up and doing' culture remained pervasive.

One consequence of this emphasis on physical as opposed to intellectual activity was that drama-in-education came to be identified increasingly with those students least likely to reach high levels of academic attainment. Drama teachers became institutionally as well as temperamentally allied with the lower ability range. This allegiance, in turn, led to a fiercely reductionist view of all forms of what was disparaged as 'academic elitism'. Writers tempted to argue for a more intellectually rigorous approach to the teaching of drama were peremptorily dismissed as reactionaries who 'would lead drama-in-education away from the classroom where it belongs and towards the slowly stagnating swamps of academia'.[24] The defender of 'Eagle and Mole' already quoted exhorts his champions to 'write for the real audience – classroom teachers, not obscure academics with axes to grind',[25] while another supporter sees no reason for Heathcote to change her idiosyncratic style just because it is 'not accessible to the traditional tools of academic criticism'.

> D.H. [Dorothy Heathcote] constantly apologises for not having the
> answers or the right words. She should not have to apologise. . . .
> Art is process. Creative struggle is infinite. Dead lines for dissertations . . . create exactly that: 'dead-lines' . . . Don't let these 'dead
> lines' rot on these pages – resurrect them. Write or speak to me.
> Write or speak to each other. Write and speak to yourself, but above
> all, do it affirmatively and trust your own intuition.[26]

Writing about school drama in the 1980s swung between extremes of obfuscation and honest naïveté, so that a simple statement of innocent incomprehension was held to be a quite legitimate response when the intellectual going got tough. Thus, Bolton was able to admit, without a trace of irony, that he was unable to use one of the most authoritative analyses of the psychological basis of the arts because he could not understand it.[27] Within the family, such candid declarations served only to reinforce the authenticity of its favoured members. Even a striking lack of school experience could be trumpeted as a strength. Heathcote's amanuenses were keen to point out that she 'never trained as a teacher or taught as a full-time member of staff in a school' and accounted for her 'innocence of vision and expression by the lack of early exposure to intellectual and academic models'.[28]

Once again, by demonstrating, however briefly, their homely lack of academic 'pretension', their 'genuineness' as ordinary, common-sense kinds of people, while implying at the same time that their practices could be 'scientifically' validated if necessary, messengers and messages were jointly endorsed in the terms of the conceptual structures they themselves helped to build. In the chumminess of the drama-in-education conference, theoretical discourse was not so much understood as measured by its author's family status. If 'Dorothy' chose to use a language all of her own to describe her practice, that was merely further endorsement of her unique powers and our feeble comprehension.

Changing times were to force some revision of these anti-intellectual attitudes. A growing demand from teachers for post-graduate qualifications together with pressure on higher education lecturers to research and publish meant a rather closer scrutiny of what passed for academic enterprise within drama-in-education. By the mid-1990s, some of those who had been vociferous in their defence of the folksy and intuitive only a decade before found themselves contributing to journals of research and delivering papers at university conferences. For the most ardent drama pedagogues, family loyalty made this transformation difficult, so that rather than facing up to the challenges of the new decade, ways were sought to validate and revitalise the practices that had been handed down. Action research techniques became popular tools in the study of the interaction between students and teachers involved in what became known as 'the drama process'. Meanwhile, the contradictions and paradoxes inherent in the thinking and practice of drama-in-education remained stubbornly in place.

HOW TO SUCCEED IN DRAMA WITHOUT REALLY TRYING

I have already drawn attention to the dilemmas facing pioneers such as Slade and Caldwell Cook when it came to fitting their desire for uninhibited self-expression to the demands of individual self-control and classroom discipline. For them, issues about the relative quality of students' work in drama were of only marginal interest. These dilemmas are highlighted when we consider the efforts that have been made over the years to describe how students might make *progress* in drama-in-education. As Derek Rowntree explains, the truth about any education system is revealed by its assessment procedures.

> How are its purposes and intentions realised? To what extent are the hopes and ideals, aims and objectives professed by the system ever truly perceived, valued and striven for by those who make their way within it? The answers to such questions are to be found in what the system requires children to do in order to survive and prosper. The spirit and style of student assessment defines the *de facto* curriculum.[29]

Under the Child Drama regime, as we have seen, such matters were thought not to be the concern of educational practices dealing with the intangible qualities of natural creativity and self-expression; the teacher's relationship with the work produced was vitally non-critical. But how then was it possible to know to what extent Child Drama's aesthetic and developmental aims were actually being realised? Attempts to square this circle led to students being assessed not on how much they knew or by what skills they had acquired or, indeed by some measure of originality of response, but on their degree of *complicity* with the structure set up by the teacher. Those members of the class who were (or who at least seemed to be) most *sincerely absorbed* in what the teacher had planned for them were, by this token, the most meritorious; those equally absorbed in rival activities, such as chattering or looking out of the window, the least so.

In England and Wales, this dilemma was first manifest in the 1960s in the arguments over the drama syllabuses of the Certificate of Secondary Education (CSE).[30] Those teachers who did not reject the whole idea of assessment in drama out of hand (and many did) tried agonisingly to evolve means of testing 'involvement', or the 'authenticity of response', or even 'development'. The re-birth of drama as pedagogy in the 1980s only confused matters further as teachers and drama advisers struggled to turn a teaching technique into an assessable subject. The assessment criteria of one of the first General Certificate of Secondary Education (GCSE)[31] examinations in drama reveals this dilemma with startling clarity. Setting its face resolutely away from theatrical practice and critical aesthetics and instead inspired by Heathcote's idea of school drama as a 'learning process', the syllabus unilaterally redefined drama as 'a problem solving activity', and aimed, 'to foster confidence in adopting a view to human problems, ideas and attitudes' by developing in candidates 'competencies met within socially interactive processes'.[32]

The evaluative incoherence of this and other attempts to duck the issue of how the strategies of drama-in-education might help students to get better at drama are well exemplified in Bolton's post-mortem on a well-documented workshop at the Riverside Studios in 1978. After nearly four hours of teaching, he is asked what he thought the group of 16 year olds had learned:

> What do I think they had learnt? . . . trust; protecting; negotiating meaning; and containing. I claim that each of these is a worthwhile experience for me and the class to share. But more than that I would be satisfied if I could guarantee that they have learned three vitally important things:
>
> 1 A new sensing of dramatic form and a glimmer of what works in the dramatic process.
>
> 2 At least a tentative grasp that drama is for understanding – this is its purpose.
>
> 3 That this understanding is reached through finding an integrity of feeling.
>
> I would not expect that the children themselves could articulate these points. If indeed I have planted these seeds then that class and I are ready to move forward with leaps and bounds. I may have achieved in three lessons (three long consecutive lessons)

23

what it takes teachers with their one hour a week six months to achieve – and what those confined to thirty-five minutes periods have little chance of achieving.[33]

It is not necessary to pick over the bones of this workshop to have substantial reservations about this evaluation. For one thing, while it might reasonably be said that the students had learnt to trust a specific person, or set of purported facts, it is unclear how 'trust', or for that matter, 'containing' or 'protecting' can ever be acquired in this generalised sense. Have they learned to trust the untrustworthy? Also, the three 'vitally important things' with which Bolton would express satisfaction seem to be excessively modest outcomes, particularly as there is no expectation 'that the children themselves could articulate these points'. An unarticulated, 'tentative grasp that drama is for understanding' must be very difficult indeed to spot. One is left with the impression that if this really is all that can come from such prolonged and concentrated educational drama work, then, as he rightly points out, what hope for the classroom teacher?

If drama teachers in the 1980s were being presented with these scarcely sustainable, minimal claims as a model of evaluation, it is no wonder that their own more formal assessment schemes were often such a muddle. Take, for example, the labyrinthine grading scheme reproduced in Table 2.1, which is taken from a popular drama-in-education text book of the time.[34]

Looking closely, the first section, 'What is to be evaluated', surely reflects Caldwell Cook's concern with 'right conduct', by grading the degree of student compliance with the structures imposed by the teacher – punctuality, tidiness and following instructions. The second section, 'What is to be assessed', incorporates this hidden agenda of acquiescence (a higher score is awarded to the boy who has submitted himself to the activity sufficiently energetically) and attempts, once again, to grapple with drama-in-education's long-standing preoccupation with the expression of 'true feelings'. While the authors are anxious to grade the genuineness of the feelings expressed, however, it is never made clear how this can be reliably ascertained, particularly if a student's high score in 'maintaining role' suggests more than fair competence in the skills of deception. As one critic has observed,

> When feelings are habitually hurt or not heard, we learn concealment through silence or compliance, showing one set of emotions, but feeling another. . . . The only feelings in others we can readily identify are those which are written on the body, on public display, and which in some way we recognise as part of our own experience.[35]

Table 2.1 Teacher's thinking about her evaluation/assessment of Lance and Martyn[36]

What is to be evaluated	Lance	Comments	Martyn	Comments
Attendance: (10)	9	Grudging	10	
Punctuality: (10)	10		7	Late again!
Respect for space and equipment: (5)	2½	Belongings spread around	5	
Rules of the game/following instructions: (5)	4	Chatting	5	
Homework: (5)	2	Messy journal	5	Impeccable
Total marks out of 35:	27½		31 [sic]	
What is to be assessed				
Level of Personal Engagement:	C→B+	Barely engaged to Committing	B+	Committed?
Expression of feeling:	A	A way with words	B+	Real concern
Work as process:	B	Product-oriented	B+	
Maintaining role:	C→A-	From the superficial to the real, even when we are not watching!	B	Likes to feel safe
Energy applied appropriately:	C	When it suits him	A+	
Expressing in another medium:	C	Thin! Does not see this as a way of being 'seen'.	B+	Thoughtful but dull

The problem is that given the theoretical legacy of drama-in-education, it is difficult to see how the jumble of associated but often contradictory aims which informs its practices could ever produce assessment schemes with much more coherence than this. In allocating marks to students' dramatic work, you can grade the level of a student's co-operation with the creative enterprise and you can grade their creative ability and their acting skills. Beyond that you are in the realm of metaphysical speculation. How on earth Bolton evaluates 'containing', for example, is hard to imagine.

None of this should be mistaken as an argument in favour of a curriculum prescribed by the exigencies of formal assessment; it is simply to apply Rowntree's thesis to the educational system being examined here. My point is that drama-in-education has nowhere more completely exposed the weaknesses of its '*de facto* curriculum' than in its efforts to formulate assessment schemes. To 'survive and prosper' under the scheme in Table 2.1, a student would seem to have to do little more than toe the line and appear to be sincere. The student who is good at drama, in other words, is the one who *can successfully take us in*. Paradoxically, we have a programme which has abandoned the cultivation of Rousseau's natural nobility in favour of the encouragement of the street-wise cut-and-thrust of effectiveness and appearance.

THE TWO WITNESSES

We have seen how the new orthodoxy cast in Dorothy Heathcote's Newcastle workshops was absorbed into the thinking of drama-in-education with especial vigour. Throughout the 1980s and beyond, Heathcote and Bolton seemed able to inspire an astonishingly uncritical dedication which invested in them a unique, apparently indisputable, authority. One enthusiast wrote:

> Learning to teach from Dorothy Heathcote is like dancing with a whirlwind. The symphony she hears sweeps you along with a sense of its rhythm; still you have very little understanding of the steps your feet must take when her leadership is gone and you are left to dance alone.[37]

A heady mixture of awe, whimsy and magic reinforced the evangelical thrust of the new orthodoxy, wrapping Heathcote's already charismatic presence in a cloak of spirituality and giving Bolton's loose and increasingly self-regarding pronouncements, legitimacy. Around these two figures a beleaguered discipline now struggling for survival in a frosty and unsympathetic educational climate, felt confident it could rally. Rather like the seventeenth-century Muggletonians, who, after the collapse of the radical programmes of the English Revolution, put their salvation in the hands of John Reeve and Lodowick Muggleton, believing them to be the 'two witnesses' of *The Revelation*,[38] significant numbers of drama teachers in the 1980s seemed happy to forsake the discourse of the wider educational community in favour of the witness of 'Dorothy and Gavin'. For, like Reeve and Muggleton, Heathcote and Bolton offered a wisdom that claimed its origins in a deep spiritual truth and a unifying vision of humanity which absolved their followers from further moral or ideological speculation.

The dangers of the self-approving system which drama-in-education engendered for itself during the 1980s, and of which Heathcote and Bolton were the unchallenged ambassadors, are obvious. The intense personalising of practice, combined with a mistrust of disinterested analysis, meant that it became almost impossible to challenge the premises upon which that practice was built. Meanwhile, without the checks and reassessments that genuine debate brings with it, the elders became more self-assured and less in touch with reality, gathering their disciples around them as a shield against an increasingly unsympathetic educational world. In the manner of the disappointed Muggletonians, and Fifth Monarchists, and Ranters and Diggers of the seventeenth century, 'when the kingdom of Christ failed to arrive, the faithful could retreat into their own communities and enjoy there much of the equality, comradeship and fraternity that the outside world denied them'.[39]

After such optimistic beginnings, the promised kingdom of drama-in-education must have seemed as far off as ever as the 1980s came to an end – paradise indefinitely postponed. In England and Wales, the 1988 Education Act heralded a very different educational environment from that marked by its predecessor in 1944. Unfortunately, a decade of dramatic hagiolatry was to leave many ordinary drama teachers dangerously ill-prepared for the demands it would make upon them.

3

THE SETTING
Events on the public stage

THE 1960s' SETTLEMENT

From about the mid-1970s onwards, the single-minded preoccupation with the development and analysis of classroom strategies was grounded in a belief that if the dramatic pedagogy developed by Heathcote and Bolton could be shown to be effective, then drama-in-education, recast in this way, would be able to justify itself 'as a core experience in the curriculum'.[1] In fact, the emphasis subsequently placed on the gener-alised, as opposed to the subject-specific, outcomes of classroom drama had quite the reverse effect, significantly contributing to the omission of drama from the prescribed list of subjects of the National Curriculum for England and Wales introduced at the end of the 1980s.[2]

The wider origins of this strategic mistake lie in the shifting of the post-war ideological balance of political life in England. Although the retreat from progressivism was well under way by the mid-1970s, those most well placed to influence the direction of the young discipline were content to keep their heads down amongst their methodologies and rarely looked up to consider the implications of this ideological retrench-ment for a subject with still only the most tenuous of holds on the timetable.

The 1960s – the decade which had seen the burgeoning of drama in schools – were years marked by educational consensus. In the country as a whole there was a general agreement over education which the Centre for Contemporary Cultural Studies dubbed, 'the 1960s' settlement'.[3] An alliance of 'leading sections of the Labour Party, the organised teaching profession, and certain key intellectuals in the new education-related academic disciplines'[4] was in tune not only with the pragmatic socialism of Anthony Crosland, but also with the non-conformity of his Conservative opposite number, Edward Boyle. Crosland and Boyle presided over a period of educational expansion fuelled by popular demand. During the 1960s education grew at a greater rate than any national enterprise except gas and electricity with education spending as a proportion of gross national product rising from 3.2 per cent in 1955 to 6 per cent in 1969. Each year successively greater numbers of students gained the General Certificate of Education at ordinary and advanced levels and there was an expansion of further and higher education and a new commitment to the comprehensive school. Ways were sought to reduce barriers to opportunity for working-class children, traditionally inhibited by the exclusivity of the universities and contained within the low expectations of the secondary-modern school. There was a perception by government, endorsed by Newsom[5] and other reports from within the education establishment, that the young of the nation represented a key resource in a new technological age, and that Britain's economic future depended to a large extent upon that growing population's ability to live within and manage that new age. This ability could only be achieved, and later sustained, it was thought, by opening up educational opportunities right across the social spectrum.

This, then, was the tide upon which drama-in-education found a secure anchorage. Concerned more with the processes of delivery than with the politics of provision, the non-politicians in the settlement alliance (the teachers and their allies in the universities), saw the child-centred, developmental premises of the progressive movement – of which school drama stood as such a prominent representative – as ideally placed to serve the new egalitarianism. Among the state agencies too, there was perceived to be a need for children of different social classes to understand each other better, or, as a Schools Council document argued in 1967, a requirement that education should aim 'to help students find within themselves the resources that alone can help them live at ease in the changing world'.[6] The dismantling of these cultural barriers would come, it was assumed, not as a result of political revolution and reconstruction, but through the increase of awareness and understanding brought about by the exercise of the socio-psychological principles of progressive teaching methods. Child-centred models of classroom practice, it was thought, would help this process of adjustment, particularly for that large group of students whom Newsom had identified as having abilities 'artificially depressed by environmental and linguistic handicaps'.[7] Brian Way is thus perfectly in tune with his time when, in the first chapter of *Development through Drama*, he declares that:

> So far as is humanly possible, this book is concerned with the development of people, not with the development of drama. . . .
> Education is concerned with individuals; drama is concerned with the individuality of individuals, with the uniqueness of each human essence . . . drama encourages originality and helps towards some fulfilment of personal aspiration.[8]

In the secondary sector, this emphasis on autonomous fulfilment was given added impetus because of the undoubtedly beneficial effect the new child-centred methods had on the daily guerrilla warfare of the school. By allowing particularly 'difficult' students informal space to express opinions and debate their concerns, teachers often found the task of pedagogic intervention considerably eased.[9] The exceedingly flimsy content boundaries of the drama lesson made drama-in-education a particularly suitable vehicle for this kind of approach. Drama teachers found themselves increasingly called to service courses directed towards the lower end of the ability range, with repertoires of trust exercises, group therapeutics and games.[10]

While for many teachers who can look back on this time it was indeed a kind of 'golden age', the 1960s' settlement and the child-centred ideas which flourished under its protection were actually the result more of a series of fortunate economic and political coincidences than of a sustainable ideological momentum. A period rich with curriculum initiatives and methodological advances, it was also one marked by political compromise and educational pragmatism. Opportunities radically to alter the structure of the education system – by removing the anomaly of a parallel private sector for example, or even by simply legislating away the lingering tripartite system of grammar, technical and secondary-modern schools set up by the 1944 Education Act – were either not taken by the 1964–70 Labour Government (which after 1966 had a ninety-seven seat majority), or only tardily embarked upon. It seems extraordinary now, but the Labour Party in power asked for no report on comprehensive education, for example, and seemed content to leave the problems of the new schools to the experts.

Similar caution characterised the introduction of the new Certificate of Secondary Education (CSE) in 1965. While the new syllabuses gave teachers control over public examinations for the first time, and introduced continuous assessment on a wide basis, the examination system itself, with General Certificate of Education (GCE) ordinary level remaining for the more able, reinforced the old grammar/secondary-modern divisions and gave them an anomalous structural home within the comprehensive system. Many curriculum initiatives perished as they tried to make headway within the tangle of historical compromises and vested interests which for so long had plagued English education, and which no real efforts were made to eradicate.

Meanwhile, the tendency of the teaching profession to overlook the aspirations of parents for their children and governmental reluctance to become involved with what David Eccles once famously called, 'the secret garden of the curriculum', served to distance and even alienate the general public from educational affairs. This alienation was soon to be recognised and exploited, as a loose alliance of the political Right sought to fill the policy vacuum and mobilise public concern.

NEW IDEOLOGUES

Before the decade was over, the first of a series of polemical literary essays, the notorious Black Papers on education, had been published.[11] Viewed by many teachers at the time as little more than an aberrant outburst from the extreme Right, the writers who contributed to these documents nevertheless set out to challenge the premises upon which the 1960s' alliance had founded its strategies for egalitarian reform.

By attempting to appeal, over the heads of the educational establishment and the political consensus which supported it, to the 'common sense' of the man or woman in the street, contributors found that they could exploit widespread popular uncertainties. It was in the overt populism of this project (and the model it was later to provide for the *poujadiste* ascendancy of the 1980s) rather than in the presentation of a coherent alternative programme, that its success lay. Also, it has to be said that the association in the minds of the press and the public of key elements of the 1960s' settlement, such as the comprehensive school, mixed-ability classes, and progressive teaching methods, with an intellectual 'liberal' elite out of touch with the aspirations of ordinary people, was by no means an entirely mistaken one.[12]

The Black Paper writers mustered discontent around three distinct themes: namely, standards, parents, and teaching methods. Cyril Burt, for example, claimed that 'attainment in the basic subjects' had actually declined since the First World War, and that judged by 'tests applied and standardised in 1913–14, the average attainments in reading, spelling, mechanical and problem arithmetic are now appreciably lower than they were 55 years ago'.[13] Burt's later (subsequently discredited) findings relating to inherited intelligence, proved another popular theme among Black Paper contributors, many of whom were convinced that working-class children were innately less intelligent than their middle-class peers. By this account, devices such as comprehensive schools and mixed-ability teaching were an egalitarian illusion, doomed from the start in the face of genetic reality. At the root of Burt's assertions lay a form of social Darwinism similar to the competitive survivalism favoured by right-wing economists. According to this view, it was natural, indeed *desirable*, that the intellectually able should climb on the backs of the weak. This vigorous, healthy process, it was argued, was being blocked by the cranky permissiveness of 'progressive' teaching.

Parents were central to the Black Paper project, and were to be enlisted in support of it once the amorphous sense of concern already identified had been amplified sufficiently into 'the crisis of education'. The 'common sense' of the 'ordinary parent' was contrasted favourably with the 'woolly-thinking progressivism' of the intellectual Left. Here is Rhodes Boyson (then headteacher of Highbury Grove School) arguing that parents wanted nothing more from the secondary modern school than that it should emulate the grammar school with 'an attractive uniform, some exclusiveness of intake, and the creation of tradition':

> parents see schools largely as places which train their sons and daughters for better jobs...secondary modern schools with progressive methods, rural science, much art and music and freedom of development endeared themselves to no-one other than the vaguely idealistic, unworldly and levitating types so well represented and influential amongst education officials and advisors.[14]

Public reservations about the unfamiliar teaching methods of progressivism were easy to exploit. Concrete evidence played only a small part in this attack, which instead leaned heavily on fears about discipline and control. The comprehensive school was deemed to have made a significant contribution to the 'pop and drug' youth culture of the 1960s and 1970s, while attempts on the part of teachers in the same schools to devise new strategies for the delivery of education were ridiculed as absurd and irresponsible. One contributor wrote:

> Just as the Labour Party and the trades union movement have always acted as an umbrella to shelter crypto-communists and fellow-travellers of all kinds, so the comprehensive platform attracts the educational crank, anarchist, permissivist, sentimentalist as well as some really hard-faced politicians.[15]

The frustrated rage of *petit-bourgeois* aspiration surfaces everywhere in the Black Papers, relentlessly pitting itself against the evils of a utopian intellectualism. Resisting the 'anarchy and permissivism' of the comprehensive were the good old solid 'common-sense' values of the grammar school, with its familiar (if only partially accurate) images of discipline, formal teaching, and academic achievement. There was no place here, it was argued, for the vague idealism of the 'hippie' teacher or for 'time-wasting pseudo-subjects' like social studies – or drama. The populist appeal of the grammar school was that, unlike private education, its 'excellence' was available to all.

While the Black Papers and the associated responses were on the whole ignored by teachers, the speech which Prime Minister James Callaghan delivered at Ruskin College in October 1976 at the launch of the Labour Government's 'Great Debate' on education, signalled to many that the 1960s' settlement was already a matter for the history books. In fact, the speech began a process of governmental reassessment and economic contraction which would last for over twenty years and in which the teaching profession, and those academics most associated with it, were to become marginal to the creation and implementation of education policy. Callaghan laid down the parameters of the debate in a series of questions relating to the 'real world' to which he was in no doubt the nation's education service must perforce adapt:

> Let me repeat some of the fields that need study because they cause concern. There are the methods and aims of informal instruction; the strong case for the so-called core curriculum of basic knowledge; next, what is the proper way of monitoring the use of resources in order to maintain a proper national standard of performance; then there is the role of the inspectorate in relation to national standards; and there is a need to improve relations between industry and education.[16]

From the mid-1970s onwards, advocates of progressive education were to find themselves on the defensive in educational policy-making at all levels. The developments in drama-in-education chronicled in the previous chapter, therefore, must be set against a background of a broken consensus and within a political and economic climate fast changing to meet the concerns which had been so effectively articulated by Cox and Dyson and their fellow Black Paper contributors.

> No longer can it be accepted that progressivism and comprehensive schemes are necessarily right, or that the future necessarily lies with them. The Black Paper has encouraged parents, teachers, M.P.s to speak out on the present day abuses in education. There are many signs that the trend is now back to more balanced and tried views.[17]

SELLING ENCYCLOPAEDIAS

These 'balanced and tried views' were much in evidence in the Labour Government's Green Paper, *Education in Schools*, published in July 1977. It contained, for example, the suggestion that there should be national agreement on curriculum content, with a core of essential subjects:

> it is clear that the time has come to try to establish generally accepted principles for the composition of the secondary curriculum for all pupils ... there is a need to investigate the part which might be played by a 'protected' or 'core' element of the curriculum common to all schools.[18]

Education in Schools also urged the Department of Education and Science to be less reticent about intervening in matters traditionally left to the 'professionals': 'It would not be compatible with the duties of the Secretaries of State ... or with their accountability to Parliament, to abdicate from leadership on educational issues which have become a matter of lively public concern'.[19]

There was to be a greater involvement of the commercial sector in policy committees; a core curriculum should be able to 'offer reassurances to employers' as well as to teachers and parents. Above all, schools were to be diverted from the egalitarian pursuit of that legacy of Renaissance humanism, the well-rounded citizen, to 'education for investment, education for efficiency',[20] to the preparation of students for an effective place in the service of the economy. From the mid-1970s, it was against predictions of economic demand that education policy was increasingly measured.

This change of direction necessarily entailed attacks on the institutions within the service most identified with the old progressive ideal. In 1977, for example, the Schools Council was forced to change its constitution to reduce the representation of teachers. Even the Department of Education and Science itself was not considered sufficiently free from the taint of the 1960s' settlement. From its creation in 1974, the Manpower Services Commission (MSC), which was directly answerable to the Secretary of State for Employment, became an agency of growing importance in the implementation of education policy.

For subjects like drama, which had floated into the curriculum on a wave of progressive idealism, the omens were not good; the coloured lights and noisy disorder of the 1960s' drama lesson must have embodied all that the new ideologues most mistrusted and sought to eradicate. Paradoxically, however, it was the influence of the Manpower Services Commission and its associated enterprises which was to present the fledgling discipline with alternative possibilities. The new 'realism' sought not simply to adjust the balance of the post-16 curriculum, but to inculcate young people, particularly working-class young people, with the values, attitudes and disciplines appropriate for a shrinking labour market. Thus, taking a priority over training in specific trades was the acquisition of general social dispositions suitable for members of the new 'flexible' work force, a menu of what came to be known euphemistically as 'life and social skills' – or simply, 'life skills'.

> Life skills mean problem-solving behaviours appropriately and responsibly used in the management of personal affairs. Appropriate use requires an individual to adapt the behaviours to time and place. Responsible use requires maturity, or accountability. And as behaviours used in the management of personal affairs, life skills apply to five areas of life responsibility identified as self, family, leisure, community and job.[21]

For some drama teachers, the presence of words like 'appropriate', 'personal' and 'self' was enough to signify an identification with the values of individual development and awareness to which they could happily subscribe. By then they had at their disposal a set of classroom practices sufficiently intransitive for questions about the *nature* of the individual development and awareness not to arise. As a consequence, the 'life skills' project had not been long in schools before aggrieved drama specialists were protesting that its tutors and organisers were poaching on their territory.

> Anyone *au-fait* with the aims and activities of Educational Drama will of course realise that this 'new' area [life skills] is in fact based on these same aims and objectives e.g. . . . we as drama teachers have been 'teaching' these 'life skills' now for many years. . . . I feel the ordinary drama teacher is now finding that his specialised field is in fact being 'taken over' by various members of the profession, who I presume feel qualified and confident enough to engage in these activities after one or two training weekends.[22]

Other practitioners began to declare themselves ready and able to participate in the 'life skills' movement. In 1983, a curriculum development leader for drama contributing to a series of articles entitled 'Drama and the Lifeskills Trend' (which included a piece by the Director of Understanding British Industry) saw school drama techniques being used to look at 'different strategies for behaviour, coping, surviving or succeeding'.[23] Another drama adviser predicted that, in future, society would 'need an increasingly versatile workforce able to respond to rapidly changing needs', and that drama would have a significant part to play in developing the 'self-reliance and small-scale entrepreneurial skills that will allow young people to *create* work'.[24] The following year, the editor of *London Drama* was worried that more energy might be spent 'defending drama as a subject than in positively examining the aims and objectives of the new courses',[25] while a contributor to the same journal urged teachers to face up to the fact that 'not only youngsters but professional adults also must be prepared to adapt to the demands of the changed market place' and, 'if you want to survive in the new regime you will have to start teaching youngsters the self-presentation skills involved in convincing an employer of their worth, of dealing with irate customers, or even how to sell encyclopaedias'.[26]

Having identified a place as a service agency in the post-Ruskin dispensation, it is clear that there were plenty of drama specialists who saw nothing amiss in taking whatever opportunities arose to market their practices across a whole range of training schemes and vocational initiatives. One lone voice warned against the indiscriminate embrace of 'life skills'. In a fiery article, David Davis castigated the 'deference' which he saw at the centre of life skills courses and which, in his view, characterised the 'hidden curriculum of society at large'.

It aims to socialise young people in an 'acceptable' way, i.e. it programmes them to accept and deal with unemployment under the guise of preparing them for employment ... there is no place for drama on schemes which help prepare youth to survive under capitalism as unemployed individuals, who will not cause trouble ... I think educators should be opposed to all MSC courses, particularly YTS [Youth Training Schemes], and campaign against them through their union organisations and should not be involved with using 'drama' (role-play) for deference.[27]

The conceptual structures of drama-in-education, however, had no means of taking this or any other prognosis based on political or cultural premises, on board. Progressivism itself lacked any political or historical dimension, and, as we have seen, drama teachers schooled in that tradition were too used to limiting their methodological vision to the inner world of sensation and feeling to be able to grasp the implications of these new realities in significant numbers. After all, had not 'Dorothy' herself involved her post-graduate students in industrial management training courses? Opportunism turned a deaf ear to Davis's counsel as an increasingly inward-looking movement sought to sell the high ideals of its founders for a place on a Youth Training Scheme.

FIGHTING FOR THE ARTS

By the end of the 1980s, a succession of Conservative governments had succeeded in turning the dogmatic populism of the Black Paper writers into policy. Throughout this period of reaction, while arts teachers struggled to counter accusations that the arts in schools were nothing more than unregulated self-expression, enthusiasts for drama-in-education, who had never shown much interest in the arts as a whole, found a solution in simply abandoning drama's aesthetic function for a more politically expedient instrumentalism. Visual art, music and dance in education, on the other hand, fought to lay the ghosts of the 1960s by arguing forcefully that the arts were a fundamental part of our cultural life and that by not giving young people a balanced aesthetic experience, schools would be failing to educate them as intelligent, rational and feeling individuals.

It was in the context of this offensive that the Gulbenkian Foundation, in a language marked by its clarity, accessibility and absence of jargon, published a comprehensive and carefully argued case for the arts which openly confronted the scepticism of their detractors.[28] Providing a useful reference point both for arts workers concerned with education and for teachers involved in the arts, *The Arts in Schools* based its arguments on the conceptual unity underlying *all* arts provision. Its authors were in no doubt that the arts should not be regarded as a means to some utilitarian end but 'are absolutely worthwhile spending time on for the sake of satisfactions that are intrinsic to them'.[29]

> Art in all its forms has been since time immemorial the means by which humans keep up their collective spirits and make sense of each other and their world. A human and intelligently conceived arts education, shading off in a medley of other directions while retaining its own inalienable character, is something whose value only the bigoted or the very stupid could deny.[30]

And it is true that for all the fear of being cast adrift from the school curriculum, few post-war official curriculum policies failed in some measure to take account of the aesthetic field. Only a year after Prime Minister Callaghan's appeal for industrial relevance, Her Majesty's Inspectors of schools were recommending that 'the aesthetic and creative' should be considered as one of eight 'essential areas' of a student's experience.[31] The same commitment was illustrated by the Inner London Education Authority in its endorsement of the Hargreaves Committee report, *Improving Secondary Schools*. Hargreaves proposed six core areas of study for 14 and 15 year olds, of which the 'aesthetic' was one.

> the creative arts should be grouped together, either as a constrained option from which every pupil must select at least one aesthetic subject, or as a combined/integrated course which contains at least two subjects ... this creative, aesthetic potential cannot be allowed to go untapped.[32]

The Conservative Government's 1985 White Paper, *Better Schools*, recommended that the primary curriculum should 'introduce pupils to a range of activities in the arts' while in secondary schools students should study 'music, art and drama on a worthwhile scale'.[33] Even as the 1988 Education Act was being prepared, the Minister of State for Education and Science was repeating this commitment to aesthetic education:

> Education in the Arts is a fundamental part of our educational proposals for the curriculum. Without it we would be allowing our children to have missed a huge area of enrichment during their years in school, and an essential preparation for all that lies before them in their adult life.[34]

With popular educational wisdom by now so clearly favouring the technological and the vocational over the expressive and developmental, these signs should have been encouraging. In schools, music, dance, visual art – and drama – all continued to flourish, but there was an acute consciousness among arts teachers that they were living and working in a climate which was unsympathetic to the kinds of sensitivities they were concerned to foster and sustain. Ten years of free market evangelism had allowed the economic Darwinism of the Black Papers to spread like a virus into whole areas of public and private life; for many it was difficult to see how any activity not readily calculable in terms of financial profit and loss could survive for long.

All these fears seemed to be confirmed by the Conservative Government's 1988 Education Reform Act. Although only four of the Act's 284 pages were devoted to curriculum arrangements – the bulk of the legislation involved financial and management mechanisms designed to promote market values in education – those four pages signalled changes of far-reaching significance. For the first time, there was to be a compulsory national curriculum for all state schools. Rather than taking up the imaginative recommendations of their inspectors,[35] however, the government instead preferred to reassert 'the basic grammar school curriculum devised at the beginning of the twentieth century'.[36] 'Technology' replaced 'Manual Work' (for boys) and 'Housewifery' (for girls), 'Drawing' became 'art' and, after extensive behind-the-scenes lobbying, 'music' was tacked on to the list; otherwise, the Conservative's 'reforming' curriculum was in every way identical to that prescribed for the new state secondary schools in 1904. Teachers only learned later that dance would be covered by physical education and drama and media studies were to be absorbed into English.[37] The arts education community, assuming that this apparently arbitrary selection was the result of a mixture of carelessness and ignorance, lobbied hard, but unsuccessfully, to have the words 'art and music' replaced simply with 'the arts'.[38]

If the failure of the 1988 National Curriculum to enshrine in legislation the recommendations of *Better Schools* with respect to the arts was a serious blow to the future development of a coherent aesthetic curriculum for schools, drama-in-education's reluctance to identify unambiguously with the arts curriculum not only weakened the arts campaign as a whole but also contributed to drama's exclusion from the government's list of prescribed subjects. We have seen how in its formative years, drama in schools was almost defined in opposition to drama elsewhere, most obviously in theatres. In the educational boom years following the war, this paradox certainly did not inhibit, and may even have helped, the growth of drama-in-education. When times became hard, however, self-imposed isolation from the mainstream made it difficult for those who might reasonably be assumed to be school drama's natural friends to come to its aid. Thus, when it was announced in 1987 that drama was not to be a foundation subject, luminaries like Sir Peter Hall, Dorothy Tutin, Richard Eyre, and Dame Peggy Ashcroft who, had they been made aware, would surely have added their influential voices to the struggle for recognition, remained silent.

This strategic *naïveté* is in marked contrast to the way professional dancers and musicians were alerted in the face of a threat to dance and music in schools. When the government proposed to dilute the dance provisions of the National Curriculum, leading ballet dancers rushed very publicly to the support of dance education, while attempts to force a Eurocentric music programme on schools were fiercely opposed by an alliance of conductors and other leading musicians.

> Simon Rattle, Sir Colin Davis, Sir Charles Groves and others are this week writing to John Major. . . . Mr Rattle, director of Birmingham Symphony Orchestra, raises the issue before every concert and urges parents to write to MPs. Mark Elder, musical director of English National Opera, has signed the letter to Mr Major and also written privately to Mr Clarke.[39]

Drama-in-education, however, made no attempt to mobilise a wider constituency. The National Curriculum Council for England and Wales received 1,600 responses to the music proposals referred to above. During the consultation period on the National Curriculum in 1987, in which the very future of drama as a subject was in question, the number of letters of protest from the drama-in-education community scarcely reached double figures.

For those whose faith in the Witnesses remained unshaken, of course, relationships with the theatre industry were superfluous. Instead, they resorted to ever more humiliating demonstrations of drama-in-education's place as a low-status servicing agency for the new curriculum. In 1984, one drama advisory teacher went so far as to argue that drama was not actually a curriculum subject at all but 'a *classroom resource* that should be available to every learner and teacher to make use of the same way as art and craft materials are available'.[40] Two Canadian enthusiasts tried to link drama directly with free-market individualism, bizarrely claiming that drama was 'in the vanguard of the new thinking' because 'the idea of putting one's money into something one can own, is looking more and more attractive'.[41] And even as the Education Reform Act became law, another drama adviser was still pleading for recognition on the basis of drama's general utility.

> It [role-play] is used extensively in Industrial Management Training; it features regularly in counselling situations for professional care workers; it is recognised as an effective tool for people to explore their personal problems, and it serves a whole host of uses when used to simulate real-life situations and experiences. All of

which seems to indicate that Drama should be a central part of the present Government's plans.[42]

The 1980s witnessed a quiet disengagement from many of the proud, dissenting values of progressivism and a corresponding shift towards forms of effectiveness unlikely to be troubled by principle or position. Far from establishing it as a core experience in the curriculum, the internal logic of the practices developed by Heathcote and Bolton and disseminated by their followers conspired with history to exclude drama-in-education from the very curriculum it once sought to colonise. The failure of its most public advocates to appreciate the implications of political change was paralleled by an opportunism on the part of many practitioners who preferred to embrace whatever new initiative seemed to offer the chance of short-term survival, rather than to face up to the challenge of uncomfortable but long overdue re-evaluations. As the 1980s passed into history, the narrow sectarianism of its methodologies together with a lack of curiosity concerning the intellectual or artistic world beyond its own very limited bibliography, looked as if they would lead educational drama blindly yet remorselessly forward out of the subject-based curriculum and into the wilderness.

4

THE DENOUEMENT
Rehearsing the phantom revolution

The situation of our time
Surrounds us like a baffling crime.

(W.H. Auden 1940)[1]

DIGGING UP THE SECRET GARDEN

The relegation of the teaching profession to the margins of policy-making during the long Conservative ascendancy of the 1980s and 1990s was a further manifestation of the pressure to integrate education with the management of the economy. Never again would politicians regard the curriculum as a 'secret garden' best left to the professionals. School teachers, all too easily associated in the popular press with permissive, vaguely leftist thinking and indiscipline, were easy scapegoats when the single-minded imposition of a new enterprise culture began to reveal the country's industrial and commercial shortcomings. The perception that the teaching profession itself bore some of the blame for these shortcomings and that it had as a consequence disinherited itself from the processes of educational policy-making, seemed to bear out the arguments of the Black Paper contributors, and led to more and more governmental intervention in educational affairs.

In its eighteen years in office, the Conservative administration sought to impose on teachers an unprecedented number of new and highly demanding initiatives. In 1984, the Secretary of State for Education, Sir Keith Joseph, announced the introduction of a single system of examinations at 16-plus, the General Certificate of Secondary Education (GCSE), to take effect from 1988. Despite a boycott by teachers of preparation for the new examinations, the government pressed ahead. In the same year, the White Paper, *Training for Jobs*, announced that one-quarter of the government's funding of non-advanced further education (NAFE) would in future be reallocated to the Manpower Services Commission (MSC).[2] Meanwhile, the expanding Technical and Vocational Education Initiative (TVEI), funded with over £1 billion from the MSC, further reflected the government's emphasis on skills training and its mistrust of local education authorities.[3] The proliferation of new curricula for the 14 to 18 age range led to segmentation, duplication and confusion so that it became impossible to raise questions about the aims of education for the age-group as a whole as 'these sub-groups continued to follow distinctive curricula representing competing rather than complementary versions of what education should be about'.[4]

The 1988 Education Act, with its hastily cobbled together National Curriculum and proposals for national testing, simply compounded these problems and seemed set to make still further demands of teachers in terms of time and co-operation.[5] The Assistant Masters and Mistresses Association claimed at this time that staff were being pushed to breaking point by government initiatives which were being introduced only at tremendous cost to individual teachers,[6] while a report in June 1988 from the High Stress Occupations Working Party of the Health Education Authority disclosed that teachers were not only 'vulnerable to major shifts in philosophy and policy introduced by successive governments' but that they were 'sometimes accused of failing to do something in one circumstance and then attacked for doing the same thing in another'.[7] At the same time, cuts in expenditure on education, mostly effected through centrally imposed restrictions on local government spending, served further to demoralise the teaching force.

By the end of the 1980s, many teachers, particularly in the inner cities, were facing larger classes and could rely upon far less help from outside. The delegation of funds under arrangements for the local management of schools led to the rapid contraction of local education authority support services so that by 1995 local support for the arts in schools had been cut by half and only a handful of drama advisers remained in post. The privatisation of school inspection in 1992 and the creation of the Office for Standards in Education (OFSTED) crudely separated inspection from advice, further weakening local education authorities and breaking up invaluable national subject networks. Responsibility for the funding of teacher training – deemed to be a nursery for the 'progressive' ideas castigated by the Black Paper writers – was taken away from the Higher Education Funding Council in 1994 and given to a new quango – the Teacher Training Agency. Meanwhile, what had evolved into a massively prescriptive National Curriculum was proving unworkable – as the profession had predicted – with impossible strains on primary teachers struggling to teach the ten specialist subjects each with its complex grid of requirements.

Effective teacher response to all this proved extremely difficult to organise. That lingering nostalgia for 'those good old days' of the popular imagination, when 'teachers really were teachers, well-loved, well-hated, stern, gentle, telling you what, not asking what you want, sticking to the 3Rs, and not getting mixed up in all this difficult stuff where there's no right answer',[8] made it almost impossible for teachers' organisations to mount a successful public defence of practices evolved in the 1960s and 1970s. Fears about reading standards were stoked up again and the government sought popularity before the 1997 general election by promising to use privatised inspectors to expose and weed out 'failing teachers'. In the early 1980s, teachers had been politically ambivalent as a group with some unions taking selective strike action in support of better pay and conditions while others had campaigned for the retention of corporal punishment; in the general election of 1983, nearly half the teaching force had voted Conservative.[9] As morale slumped to new levels, the proportion declaring they would vote Tory in 1997 was tiny. By this time, teachers in Britain were twenty times more likely to take days off work because of stress than teachers in France.[10]

This, then, is the background against which the battle for drama in England and Wales would be fought. Denied the protection of National Curriculum subject status yet constrained by the same growing emphasis on achievement and accountability, it would be in a demoralised and crumbling school system, amidst the daily skirmishes of classroom, rather than through the rarefied practice of the Witnesses that drama would have to prove its value.

BACK IN THE CLASSROOM

While thousands of young people across the country continued to look forward to their drama lessons throughout the 1980s and clearly found them stimulating and enjoyable, it has to be acknowledged that teaching in an institution is often wearisome and repetitive, that children can be fractious and unpleasant, and that the creative stimulation which they have continuously to inject into the successful drama lesson makes quite unique demands on drama teachers' imagination and energies (see, once more, the 'Air Disaster' lesson in Appendix 1). Some commentators recognised that teachers often found it impossible 'to reconcile abstract ideals with the practical restrictions of time, space and the school curriculum',[11] and many must have wondered how they were supposed to reproduce 'Dorothy's' much-vaunted 'moments of awe' to the accompanying clatter of the school kitchen behind the partition. No teacher would doubt that there are times when Peter Slade's confident assertion that school drama is 'a virile and exciting experience, in which the teacher's task is that of a loving ally',[12] offers us a less than adequate account of the realities of the drama classroom.

In 1975, a teacher trainer described giving a demonstration lesson in front of some of his students which did not go entirely as intended.

Halfway through the second week's lesson, in which there had been further chaos and in which every group improvisation had degenerated into brawling between groups, I brought the class together and said a few quiet words about discipline. . . . On the bus back to college, one student was worried. 'With all respect,' he asked, 'aren't you afraid you might have repressed their natural spontaneity?'[13]

Twelve years later, a young drama teacher wrote this about his experiences as a probationer in an East London comprehensive school:

Truancy was high (teachers as well as pupils) and the nervous breakdowns among staff were many. On my first day I was pelted with stones, told to 'fuck off' and the nicest thing that was said to me was, 'You must be the new fucking poofter drama teacher'.[14]

The pastoral idyll of progressivism can sometimes seem a long way off from the battered corridors of the inner-city secondary school where students are by no means always willing to suspend their disbelief. Part of the trouble is, that while dislike of most other subjects is generally accompanied by a grudging acceptance by students of their legitimacy, those who fail to get enjoyment from the drama lesson really do not see the point of it. Unlike colleagues in science or history, the drama teacher has been divested of any affirming body of 'important' knowledge to justify his or her presence in the timetable, and reference to the subject's expansive pedagogic claims can sound pompous and hollow amid the hubbub of the drama class. After all, a student might not unreasonably reply, if drama really is 'the best possible form of education',[15] why isn't it on the National Curriculum? In the face of this apparently intractable antipathy, some secondary drama classes became general discussion sessions under the validating influence of the Newcastle doctrine; in others, teachers fell back upon old but popular menus of games and exercises in order to keep 'difficult' classes occupied until the life-saving bell. Unfortunately, both strategies simply served to reinforce students' suspicions about drama's legitimacy as a subject, setting up expectations of its practices as indistinguishable, on the one hand, from subjects such as religious or personal and social education or, on the other, from play.

Bolton and Heathcote maintained a significant silence on the rather fundamental matter of how their pedagogical ideas might be accommodated to the weekly 50-minute drama lesson; neither did they advance strategies for the development of GCSE syllabuses or for responding to a developing range of performing arts courses. The paradox here lies not in the omission itself (we all draw up our own agendas) but in the fact that despite of it, as we saw in Chapter 2, letters from the faithful continued to evince an unproblematic equation between the ideas of

'Dorothy and Gavin' and the experience of the 'ordinary teacher'. Instead of addressing these pressing dilemmas, two ideologically opposed camps arose to champion the cause of dramatic pedagogy. One, as we have seen, believed that propagation of its practices would succeed in legitimating drama as a teaching utility within the new vocationalism; the other, by contrast, sought to politicise the same methodologies and press them into the service of revolutionary politics.

WHAT HAVE THE ROMANS EVER DONE FOR US?

Profoundly opposed to any idea of accommodation with the hegemony of the New Right was a loose, often highly factionalised, alliance grouped around concern over issues of class, gender and race. Made up of drama teachers and workers in *theatre*-in-education,[16] this alliance sought to press the dramatic pedagogy of Heathcote and Bolton into the service of social change, believing that its 'revelatory' processes enabled young people to see, understand and challenge what they regarded as the 'objective' structures of political oppression.

In this unlikely appropriation, the 'awesome awareness of universal truths'[17] supposedly nurtured in Heathcote's drama workshops was transformed into 'an expression of confidence in the knowability of the world'.[18] Heathcote was seen to be using drama 'to produce knowledge in young people', that is to say real, unequivocal, objective knowledge of the world as it actually, indisputably, *is*. For at least one theatre-in-education worker, any challenge to this unequivocal objectivism was rejected out of hand as 'the standpoint of one who does not accept the knowability of things'.[19] On closer inspection, this knowledge turns out to be of a rather particular kind, as David Davis, whose passionate repudiation of 'drama for deference' has already been noted, explains.

> For me, the essence of the matter is that we are living in a decadent capitalist culture which is moving to ever higher state control in all walks of life, and which raises the very distinct threat of a nuclear holocaust in a final bid to perpetuate its existence. . . . Drama, on the other hand, working as art, would search out the truth in any particular situation and strengthen those participants in the struggle not to accept life as an object but to take up the challenge to become a subject.[20]

The stridency of this uncompromising appeal for unlimited self-determination stands in marked contrast to the wistful utopianism we have seen up until now. No question here of drama being used in support of government schemes. In 1985, the chair of the National Association for the Teaching of Drama lambasted drama teachers for tolerating 'an ideology which played right into the hands of the present philistine, monetarist government which has brought us to the very edge of extinction'[21] while a political manifesto for drama teachers designed for adoption by the association demanded the 'abolition of examinations' and the 'closure of all universities, polytechnics, colleges of higher and further education and adult education colleges'.[22] Drama teachers were challenged with a series of blunt, rhetorical questions:

> Is the system of which we are part too strong and clever for us? Do the powers that be just let us think we're different while actually absorbing us into their reality? . . . we need to be positive about our achievements. BUT does our work fulfil its potential to challenge the patriarchal, sexist, racist, class-ridden context of the real world? Are we adding to the voices of our young people, are we giving them a way of challenging, a way of saying 'NO!'?[23]

It is doubtful that schools can so easily be dismissed as the unquestioning agents of capitalism, or that their students are the mute recipients of 'patriarchal, sexist, racist, class-ridden' values. To suggest that the battle lines can be so neatly drawn denies both the complex ambiguities of social life as well as the competence and intelligence of individuals; it is altogether too simple-minded a view of the relationship between society and those it sets out to educate. Nevertheless, for all the crankiness of the rhetoric, the writers quoted here display a refreshing consciousness of the ideology behind the free market ascendancy of the 1980s.

Major influences on another, somewhat less dogmatic, section of the left alliance were the de-schooling theory of the Brazilian educationalist Paulo Freire and the dramatic techniques inspired by it of the Latin American director, Augusto Boal.[24] A South American Catholic increasingly drawn to Marxism, Freire rejected the idea of the revolutionary vanguard movement, and instead proposed that intellectuals and peasants should work together to identify, de-mystify and oppose specific forms of oppression. By doing so, he argued, the peasants would own their perceptions in ways which would then enable them to pursue their struggle for liberation with new insight into their historical circumstances. Always considering his Marxism to be an essential part of his Christianity, Freire made a considerable contribution to the development of Latin American liberation theology, along with the famous de-schooler, Ivan Illich.

These close links between Marxism and liberation theology help us to understand the enthusiasm for Freire and Boal expressed by many advocates of drama-in-education. On one level, the association with Illich and the de-schooling movement evoked the anti-establishment progressivism of the 1960s with which drama-in-education was so closely identified; on another, the Latin American context anchored the theory in a most vivid and practical political struggle. In the 1980s, Sandinista resistance to United States imperialism in Nicaragua became a powerful symbol of this conflict. Finally, the Christian ethic implicit both in Freire's and Boal's writings, allowed drama-in-education an anchor in the moral world once again. This unique combination of collective resistance and the self-liberating humanism of practical, non-dogmatic Christianity, filled the ethical vacuum at the centre of the dramatic pedagogy project. As Gustavo Gutiérrez remarks, in his classic text on liberation theology:

> It is not a matter of 'struggling for others', which suggests paternalism and reformist objectives, but rather of becoming aware of oneself as not completely fulfilled and as living in an alienated society. And thus one can identify radically and militantly with those – the people and the social class – who bear the brunt of oppression.[25]

Theatre director Augusto Boal acknowledges his debt to Freire in his influential book, *Theatre of the Oppressed*.[26] For Boal, theatre, like language, is a potential medium of liberation, but for it successfully to serve this purpose the traditional relationship between audience and performer has itself to be 'revolutionised'. In his productions, played out in the poverty-ridden *barrios* of Peru, the actors offered no solutions, but paused to allow the audience to discuss and redirect the story. Here, theatre becomes a forum, a laboratory of social change, where ideas can be tested in action, and where no outcome is preordained.

> the *poetics of the oppressed* focuses on the action itself: the spectator delegates no power to the character (or actor) either to act or to think in his place; on the contrary, he himself assumes the protagonic role, changes the dramatic action, tries out solutions, discusses plans for change – in short, trains himself for real action. In this case, perhaps the theater is not revolutionary in itself, but is surely a rehearsal for the revolution.[27]

The idea of drama as 'a rehearsal for the revolution' had obvious appeal to those seeking ways of confronting government policy in the classroom. Here at last was a process by which students could be led, through drama, to a collaborative understanding of the overt and hidden oppressions of society. Inherent tyrannies of racism, sexism and class would be naturally exposed and condemned, it was thought, not through the imposition of ideas by the teacher, but simply through the questioning, debating, and revising of dramatic pictures made by groups of actors or by the students themselves. 'In the forum theater', says Boal, 'no idea is imposed: the audience, the people, have opportunity to try out all their ideas, to rehearse all the possibilities, and to verify them in practice, that is, in theatrical practice'.[28]

The introduction of Boal's 'forum theatre' techniques to drama-in-education in the 1980s connected neatly with the pedagogic use of drama already fashionable and provided teachers with some interesting new ways of working. To what extent Boal's methods were successful in helping First World students to make sense of the ideological complexities of their advanced consumer-dominated culture is less certain. In the South American context of military coup, torture and exile, deprivation and oppression were easy enough to identify, as both Freire and Boal knew from personal experience.[29] In the densely textured political ethnography of a post-imperial liberal democracy with long-standing theatrical conventions of its own, on the other hand, Boal's techniques could easily lead to over-simplification and to the reinforcement of the stereotypical position-taking of its exponents. One commentator, who worked with Boal in Europe, described the 'oppressions' emerging from his workshops as those of 'hierarchy, sexual discrimination, corruption, systems and noise'.[30] Something less than a comprehensive critique of capitalism. In the context of a school, I have already suggested that there are considerable difficulties in regarding students as the equivalent of an oppressed social order, let alone in knowing what to take their side might mean. The traditional antipathy to education displayed by many white working-class boys, for example, which is held to be a major cause of inner-city truancy in England, would be likely to make them unreliable collaborators in the 'rehearsal for the revolution'.

Nevertheless, the idea of a 'pedagogy of the oppressed' brought about through drama, held many attractions for a loosely constituted group of practitioners who were acutely conscious of the social divisiveness engendered by successive Conservative administrations and who saw the theories of Freire and Boal as a means of clothing the pedagogic techniques of Heathcote and Bolton in the rhetoric of social struggle. The discursive equivocacy of dramatic pedagogy made this project less difficult than might be supposed; the generalisations and ambiguities of the Witnesses could be gleaned to provide intellectual nourishment for all manner of causes. David Davis was keen to point out that 'Gavin' himself had once declared that he wanted to help the student to 'know how and when (and when *not*) to adapt to the world he lives in'.[31] It turned out that 'Dorothy and Gavin' could be as usefully enlisted into the service of the revolution as into the training programmes of the new utilitarianism.

By this time, many of those in the Left alliance believed that the establishment of drama as a learning agent in the service of political change was paramount. Faced with a dominating and apparently intractable ideological system, it was argued, the drama teacher should not seek to 'legitimise the subject by moulding it into an acceptable academic discipline' but should instead use the processes taught by the Witnesses to challenge and subvert the values of that system. 'Radical methodological processes' should be 'matched by a radicalisation of content'. While the consequence of this stand would inevitably be an unfortunate but necessary period on the margins of education, there was no doubt that this course of action was infinitely preferable to taking refuge in 'a straightforward advocacy of theatre arts courses'.[32] 'I think these are the main opposites at the moment. The return to theatre arts on one side and those seeking developments in our work to meet the needs of young people on the other'.[33]

And so we come full circle. The old 'drama' versus 'theatre' argument, springing from Rousseau, endorsed by progressivism, and now ideologically reconstituted in the name of revolutionary politics. Still caught in the loose mesh of moral relativism where 'achieving a change in understanding' has to stand awkwardly for 'seeing the world as we do', advocates of the pedagogy of dissent made claims for the efficacy of their practice no more substantiated than those of their less politically motivated predecessors. It is in this same confident, but un-self-critical, tradition that a later generation of drama practitioners deserted the battlegrounds of radical individualism in order to pitch the tents of improvisation and role-play in the camps of the armies of the revolution. For a minority, still dressed in the uniforms of 1917, the campaign was simply part of the objective struggle of the 'oppressed' classes against world capitalism. For others, a version of the good unconsciously owing much to a residual Christianity, revitalised the dramatic pedagogy project in the service of a shopping list of causes. Drama-in-education in the form of role-play, it was now asserted, was uniquely placed to combat racism and sexism, and to tackle such matters as the problem of unemployment, the Third World, nuclear disarmament and even the National Health Service (see Figure 4.1). For one advisory teacher, the important issue for drama teachers was not drama at all, but rather how they should deal with questions like: 'Why can't I get the job I choose? Why is my dad never going to work again? Why do we let blacks in when there aren't enough jobs for whites? Why has my gran got to wait three years for a hip operation? Why do we spend money on bombs rather than jobs?'[34]

Important questions. And there is little doubt that by asking students to put themselves 'into other people's shoes' in this way, skilful and sensitive teachers may well be able to draw from their students insights into questions of social and individual morality. Yet, uncouple role-play from the distinctive concepts, procedures, knowledge and traditions of the theatre arts and all that is left is a bag of pedagogical tricks likely to be of interest less to radical politicians than to personal and social education teachers, management trainers and therapists.[35] All those who conspired during the 1970s and 1980s to isolate school drama from the

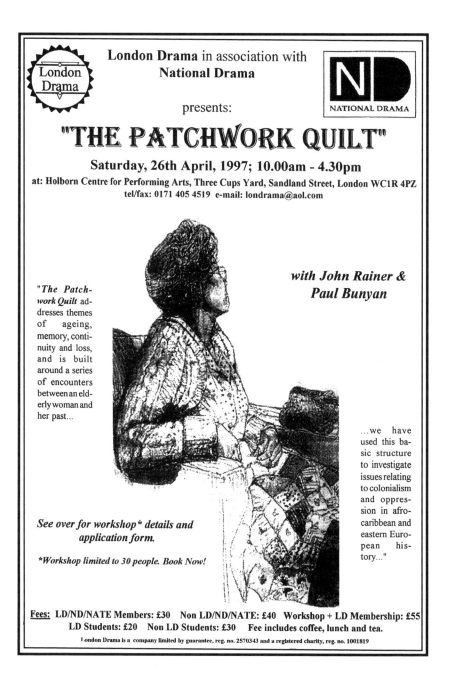

London Drama in association with
National Drama

NATIONAL DRAMA

presents:

"THE PATCHWORK QUILT"

Saturday, 26th April, 1997; 10.00am - 4.30pm

at: Holborn Centre for Performing Arts, Three Cups Yard, Sandland Street, London WC1R 4PZ
tel/fax: 0171 405 4519 e-mail: londrama@aol.com

*with John Rainer &
Paul Bunyan*

"The Patchwork Quilt addresses themes of ageing, memory, continuity and loss, and is built around a series of encounters between an elderly woman and her past...

...we have used this basic structure to investigate issues relating to colonialism and oppression in afro-caribbean and eastern European history..."

See over for workshop* details and application form.

*Workshop limited to 30 people. Book Now!

<u>**Fees:**</u> LD/ND/NATE Members: £30   Non LD/ND/NATE: £40   Workshop + LD Membership: £55
LD Students: £20   Non LD Students: £30   Fee includes coffee, lunch and tea.

London Drama is a company limited by guarantee, reg. no. 2570343 and a registered charity, reg. no. 1001819 arts and to promote it as an educational utility bear a heavy responsibility for this narrow and limiting prescription. For two decades, ears were closed to informed and sympathetic warning voices,[36] and instead the evangelical pursuit of a complex and elusive teaching methodology ignored the reasonable expectations of students, parents and headteachers and resulted in the neglect of the very skills, procedures and insights which give drama its identity.

THE 1990s' SETTLEMENT

In the autumn of 1989, as teachers in England and Wales were wearily setting about implementing their new National Curriculum, on a larger landscape history was on the move. In November, the Berlin Wall was breached, a symbolic act which, probably more than any other, marked the end of over seventy years of Communist rule in Russia and Eastern Europe. Two years later, the Sandinistas were voted out of power in Nicaragua. In Britain the last ever edition of *Marxism Today* was published and Francis Fukuyama triumphantly announced the final victory of capitalism and the end of history.[37] Suddenly, new maps were needed everywhere, not only to chart the fragmenting nationalisms of the post-Soviet era, but also to find a way along the lanes and byways of political and ideological reassessment now the great arterial roads of Marxism had, it seemed, turned out to be cul-de-sacs after all. But while history itself may not have come to an end, the collapse of Soviet power dealt a shattering, if not terminal, blow to confidence in the forward march of the Left on all fronts.

In England, Margaret Thatcher, champion of the Black Paper writers and strident proselytiser of the educational market place, had resigned as prime minister and leader of the Conservative Party in 1990, although the Conservatives managed to stagger on in government and, indeed, to legislate for further fragmentation of the education service. In schools, meanwhile, anger and frustration with the imposition of what was widely seen as a Tory National Curriculum were gradually replaced by weary resignation as experienced teachers grew accustomed to the ten subject format and a new generation emerging from the universities entered the country's classrooms taking the structure and content of the new curriculum for granted. As a result of a review of the new curriculum arrangements, the government was eventually forced to reduce the degree of prescription, so that although for foundation subjects – such as art and music – precise indications of the scope of students' entitlement together with examples of appropriate standards certainly reduced teacher autonomy, once understood and incorporated, most teachers found the framework actually made planning and assessment easier. With the 1997 Labour Government every bit as committed to the raising of basic standards in schools, it became clear that a new consensus of rigour, accountability and high expectations was being consolidated among politicians and educationalists, a '1990s' settlement' around the need, in a fast-changing world, for a versatile and well-educated population.

For drama teachers, watching from the wings as their colleagues struggled with the mutating stage directions of the 1988 Act, this emerging consensus sharpened a sense of isolation. While marginalisation remained the preferred option for a dwindling number of purists (mostly, by now, safely in university departments), drama teachers in secondary schools could see that life on the margins was only one step away from extinction. Many – probably the majority – had anyhow never regarded the 'theatre arts' as an alien presence in their lesson and could see that in a re-invigorated, subject-based curriculum, the survival of drama *as* a subject was dependent upon finding ways of accommodating the principles of progression and achievement which informed the new arrangements.

Early efforts to secure such an accommodation, which began almost before the ink was dry on the legislation, were sometimes little more than attempts to express the familiar mantras of drama-in-education in the new language of criterion-referenced attainment.

> Our attainment targets will be to do with the ability of children to negotiate meaning, to work collaboratively, to select appropriate language and behaviour associated with role, to engage in different types of thinking, to develop an understanding of the medium.[38]

Others tried to incorporate the general pedagogic aims of drama-in-education into thinly disguised programmes of 'theatre arts', where, for example, students were expected to develop 'understanding of the historical use of drama', while still insisting that drama was 'a process which does not aim to deliver a given body of knowledge'.[39] Thus, Gavin Bolton seems to acknowledge the desirability of students learning *about* drama when he suggests that spontaneous make-believe 'only becomes significant as *dramatic art* when attention is given to the art form of theatre', but then goes on to propose that students might somehow acquire this dramatic knowledge and understanding 'without their realising it'.[40]

Probably the most coherent framework for the teaching and assessment of drama within the context of the National Curriculum was produced by the Arts Council of Great Britain in 1992. *Drama in Schools* identified drama as 'an art, a practical activity and an intellectual discipline'.

> It [drama] involves the creation of imagined characters and situations which are enacted within a designated space. A drama education which begins with play may eventually include all the

elements of theatre. Like all the arts, drama helps us to make sense of the world.[41]

The subtle change in phraseology from 'drama-in-education' to 'drama education' was as significant as the document's insistence that drama in schools should offer 'the same synthesis of skills, creativity and knowledge which might be expected of any other arts subject'. *Drama in Schools* proposed a simple framework of 'making, performing and responding' which, its authors argued, applied 'at all levels and to drama in all its many forms'.

> Someone making drama might be a member of a group contributing to an improvisation or an individual writing a play; performing takes place in the infant play corner as well as on the stage of the Royal National Theatre and may involve technicians as well as actors; pupils responding to drama may be found in classrooms as well as in theatres and school halls.[42]

By demonstrating what a student's entitlement to a broad and balanced education in drama might look like, the Arts Council's straightforward and accessible guidance for teachers not only drew drama back into the family of the arts in schools, but also, for the first time, clearly established a continuity between drama in schools and drama in theatres. Unsurprisingly, such ingenuousness was not favoured by those who continued to believe that the pedagogic wizardry of 'Dorothy and Gavin' could inspire an educational revolution. Three years after it became law, the National Association for the Teaching of Drama was still campaigning for the repeal of the 1988 Act and in 1992 Heathcote and Bolton themselves were wheeled in to do their duty by the faithful at a national conference melodramatically entitled 'Education or catastrophe? Which way do we go?'

Developments abroad suggested that this doctrinaire position was breaking down in favour of a more eclectic approach. After a shaky inaugural conference in Portugal (which, despite some careful plotting, a British delegation failed to hijack in the name of the oppressed people of the Philippines and East Timor), the International Drama and Education Association (IDEA) succeeded in opening up debate to a healthy diversity of viewpoint. In similar vein, an international gathering at the University of Exeter in 1995 brought together drama educators from India, Jordan, South Africa, Nigeria, Uganda, Argentina, Brazil, the West Indies, Australia, Canada, the USA and Europe to debate topics as varied as Taoist approaches to Shakespeare's sonnets, researching drama on the Internet, animation theatre and the use of semiotics in drama in Irish schools. Contributions to the journal inspired by this conference – the first serious international journal of drama education research[43] –

completely reflected this eclectic approach, helping to put into perspective the narrow sectarianism which had come to characterise drama-in-education in Britain.

Meanwhile, back in schools, drama continued to thrive. School plays went on much as before, and the numbers taking drama examinations at all ages continued to increase. Away from the hothouse of the drama conference, teachers themselves seemed more healthily sceptical of the sermonising than the pedagogic evangelists liked to think. Although possibly reluctant to agree too publicly with the writer of one popular drama text book that 'drama is fundamentally about how to make, perform and appreciate plays',[44] the vast majority of drama teachers continued to be sensitive to the enthusiasm of their groups for play-making and performance so, that in this respect at least, the basic elements of drama – those which link it conceptually to all the other arts – remained stubbornly in place. For all the curricular setbacks of the 1980s, and the bizarre but sustained campaign *against* subject status conducted from within the field itself, it is a tribute to these teachers that commitment to the subject of drama remained undiminished. As a result, by 1996, research amongst a small group of secondary drama teachers in the south-west of England was clearly indicating 'a shift away from traditional child-centred theory represented by Heathcote and Bolton' and towards the teaching of drama as 'an end in itself'.[45]

For those evangelicals still hoping to find salvation in the words of the Witnesses, however, the 1990s were a period of growing detachment from the practical business of teaching drama in schools. Some turned their backs on the changing world and retreated into the self-absorbing laboratory of action research. In England, away from the spotlight of the National Curriculum, enthusiasts in universities were able to advertise their beliefs to a diminishing number of followers with little fear of challenge from those engaged in more pressing front-line matters, such as the raising of standards of numeracy and literacy in schools. Others channelled their energies into new areas, such as police training, banking, medical and psychiatric care and counselling, as drama-in-education reverted to what is probably its natural home amongst the trainers and therapists.[46] In a volume of research papers published in 1994, it is significant that out of well over one hundred cited authors, only six are theatre practitioners; among the remainder, writers from the fields of psychology, ethnography and mental health figure prominently.[47]

In the 1980s, it became clear to me that an undogmatic, broadly based account of drama education, historically contextualised and anchored firmly in the real curriculum, might help teachers liberate themselves from the narrow prospectus offered by role-play and improvisation and at last connect drama *in* schools to the rich diversity of drama *outside* them. Then, as now, I had no doubt that an account of this kind would have to be built upon secure theoretical foundations which drew their strength from a range of diverse intellectual sources; I knew mine would not be a family affair. Before re-embarking on this task in the 1990s, I want first, as before, to use these sources to throw light upon the theories enshrouded by the familiar shibboleths of drama-in-education – some of which have already been visited in this brief history – to see how well those theories look once the enveloping fog of cant and adulation has been dispelled.

PART II

DRAMA-IN-EDUCATION

INTERPRETING THE TEXT

It seems to me that the first principle of the study of any belief system is that its ideas and terms must be stated in terms other than its own; that they must be projected on to some screen other than one which they themselves provide. . . . Only in this way may we hope to lay bare the devices they employ to make their impact.

(Ernest Gellner 1985)[1]

5

THE OMNIPOTENT SELF

KEAN – 'And sometimes I ask myself if real feelings are not quite simply bad acting.'

(Jean Paul Sartre 1954)[2]

AUTHENTICITY AND THE SELF

In Chapter one, we saw how the ideas which gave birth to drama-in-education had themselves evolved from a peculiarly English manifestation of Romanticism. The Arcadian individualism of Rousseau's 'uncorrupted conscience' found a home in England, not as it had in his own country in the revolutionary agency of *sans-culotte* and *communard*, but in the imaginations of those who sought to oppose the less tangible tyrannies of industrialisation by cultivating the inner world of creative sensitivity and self-expression.

The modern distinction between the artist and the artisan, which invests in the former intellectual and imaginative purposes absent from the craftsman or skilled worker, dates from this time. It was well into the seventeenth century before the word 'art' itself became confined to what we now call the aesthetic field (the nomination previously having applied to all manner of human skills, including medicine, astronomy and angling) and until the late eighteenth century makers of most of what we now think of as art laboured within a framework of secular and religious patronage to which they were bound in greater or lesser degrees of servitude.[3] These 'artists', that is the painters, musicians, writers and actors who served society, expressed the unities and the riddles of the cultures in which they lived in forms which required no public reference to their own individual psychologies. The personality of pre-nineteenth-century poets or performers was not generally considered to be of any particular interest; they were judged simply by their ability to echo and reflect the common experience.

Under the influence of nineteenth-century Romanticism, the work of art came to be considered not so much as the product of a particular form of skilled labour, but rather as a manifestation of the producer's *sensibility*. The artist (predominantly male) was thought to be peculiarly equipped to give expression to this sensibility and was thus able to relinquish his role as craftsman or servant and adopt instead that of the extraordinary individual. Romanticism internalised art, shifting the emphasis away from the skilled exercise of a craft, from production, towards the expression of the psychological processes of the producer. The artist of the Romantic period created from the depths of his being, impelled by the energy of his creative inclinations: he became, for the first time, a *creative personality*.

> the one thing that matters is the artist, so that he feels none of the blissfulness of life except in his art . . . As for the gaping public, and whether when it has finished gaping it can justify why it has gaped, what difference does that make?[4]

Pierre Bourdieu describes how this internalisation of artistic endeavour, exemplified here by the young Goethe, served to remove the work of art from the field of public judgement. If the audience has no say in the matter, then it follows that art's only critical reference point is the authenticity of the artist's intention.

> The declaration of the autonomy of the creative intention leads to a morality of conviction which tends to judge works of art by the purity of the artist's intention and which can end in a kind of terrorism of taste when the artist, in the name of his conviction, demands unconditional recognition of his work.[5]

The implications of this 'privatisation' of artistic endeavour were felt throughout nineteenth-century society. The spiritual elevation of the artist came about against the background of an increasingly insensible, mechanistic social world, where, in the face of a new materialism, powerful historic communalities of shared belief and moral purpose were rapidly dissolving. For many members of the prosperous middle class, increasingly confident of their independence from ancient secular and religious hierarchies while at the same time anxiously searching for forms of authentication to replace them, Romanticism provided a source of spirituality which reflected their own individualistic predilections.

While the influence of this new thinking on the poetry, visual art and music of nineteenth-century Europe was wide-ranging and complex, it was not without its contradictions, not least because technological advances in printing and lithography were beginning to turn the reproduction and dissemination of art into an industry itself. The creative artist, mythologised as a Byronic revolutionary and free spirit, was in fact no less dependent upon the material structures of society than anyone else. Writers and poets found themselves relying increasingly on a market of publishing houses, typesetters, printers and engravers, not to mention whole sections of that hidden army of unskilled wage labour whose aesthetic and economic deprivation stood in such stark contradistinction to the poetic ideal. In the very process of taking a stand against materialism, art had itself become a market commodity.

Most twentieth-century arts educationalists shared the heritage of this Romantic mythology, continuing to champion the cause of individual identity and uniqueness against what they saw as the pervasive and inhibiting influence of materialism but failing to recognise the cultural and economic circumstances within which this much-prized individuality was expressed.[6] Psychological theory gave credence to the idea that we all have within us a 'creative faculty' which (and the horticultural metaphors are irresistible) requires careful cultivation if it is to blossom and flourish. Here is pioneer therapist Carl Rogers:

> From the very nature of the inner conditions of creativity it is clear that they cannot be forced, but must be permitted to emerge. The farmer cannot make the germ develop and sprout from seed; he can only supply the nurturing conditions which will permit the seed to develop its own potentialities. So it is with creativity.[7]

With a sleight of etymology, accounts of this kind decisively separate the created object from the process of creation, so that the agent's creativity is displaced from the critical public domain and secured instead in the mysterious and untouchable recesses of the unconscious. At the same time, it loses its former exclusivity. Creativity, in this sense, like imagination, becomes a function of ordinary human intelligence, no longer the preserve of the special individual but a faculty common to everyone. Twentieth-century psychology succeeded in investing us all with the artist's mystical powers of authentication.

It is in terms like these that the post-war argument for arts education was framed. Students can best exercise and develop their creativity (it was claimed) in an environment free from the pressures of criticism and correction, where they can discover their own authenticity through the autonomous creative processes in which they are encouraged to engage. The quality of their work is seen as a measure of the authenticity of their relationship with it, of their spontaneity and sincerity. The teacher can support and encourage but should never interfere. One of the most articulate exponents of this theory, Robert Witkin, writing about the arts in education from within this nexus of Romantic poetics and psychology, assumes *a priori* that the arts can be best understood as a function of the private, internalised world of the self, or more simply, as the creative expression of subjective feeling.

If the price of finding oneself in the world is that of losing the world in oneself, then the price is more than anyone can afford. . . . In the case of the psychological system, it is the integrity of the world within the individual that is the source of his motivation, his enthusiasm, his feeling response to life.[8]

By re-casting the arts in the role of expressive agent for the creative faculty, the discrepancies of categorisation and assessment which mark public distinctions of artistic value are neatly circumvented. But, as Bourdieu warns us, by adopting this simple expressionist position, with its assumptions about value circumscribed by theories of mental health, we are in danger of slipping into random self-regard. Also, while it is central to Witkin's argument that the exercise of the individual's creative faculty is psychologically desirable, as he denies himself any external evaluative reference points, it is difficult to see upon what grounds this assertion is made. Plainly he recognises the need to establish *some* criteria of worth; that it cannot be socially acceptable to endorse any kind of expressive act, by making no distinction, for example, between the considered arranging of colours by a student in the art lesson and the casual wall-daubing of a teenager's aerosol. However, in his self-imposed isolation from the aesthetic and ideological experience of public culture, Witkin denies himself access to the standards of worth by which society is accustomed to value its art. He thus is driven to manufacture a critical system which has no reference beyond the authenticity of the individual's response and in which teachers are urged not to think of 'the implications and consequences of the behaviour in some social frame of reference' but to 'differentiate between behaviours in terms of their intrinsic character as action and knowing'.[9] In Witkin's confident epistemology, affirmative 'subject-reflexive' behaviour would adequately describe the child artist above, while the teenager's random spray painting would be condemned as 'subject-reactive'.

We have seen how drama-in-education was shaped by this therapeutic theory of the arts; for Gavin Bolton, drama was not so much a cultural form as 'a mental state'.[10] Attempts to bring a political and social dimension to drama in the classroom, therefore, easily led to confusion and incoherence as ideological commitment grounded heavily on the intractable reefs of psychological self-reference. Re-engagement in ideology raises other problems too. By attempting to give the arts a history by relocating them in a social context, teachers not only pose a threat to the liberated, intuitionist self but also lay themselves open to accusations of partisanship and bias. As we shall see, our therapeutic culture uses psychology as a powerful form of protection against such challenges.

THE PSYCHOLOGICAL IMPERATIVE

The idea that the source of our views and preferences can be located in the depths of our psyches and that psychology gives us an account of human agency which transcends politics and morality, was given added respectability in the post-war years by the no-nonsense positivism of Hans Eysenck. Eysenck, who always insisted on the strictest adherence to scientific rigour in psychological experiments, succeeded in popularising a particular brand of objective reductionism, which, in an attempt to establish psychology as the bedrock of the human sciences, set about systematically to redefine ideology in psychological terms. Put simply, Eysenck claimed that ideas, particularly political ideas, were nothing more than the rationalisations of emotions, outward manifestations of our unconscious 'inner world' of suppressed feelings.

> All other social sciences deal with variables which affect political behaviour indirectly. . . . The psychologist has no need of such intermediaries; he is in direct contact with the central link in the chain of causation between antecedent condition and resultant action.[11]

By means of psychological experiment and the analysis of statistical evidence (both subsequently much disputed), Eysenck set about demonstrating the temperamental instability of political 'extremists' of both left and right, in relation to a moderate 'centre' or psychological 'norm'. A simple-minded equation categorised Fascists and assorted totalitarians along with Communists and other left-wing radicals, and set their inherent 'tough-mindedness' against the 'tender-mindedness' of conservatives and liberals. The wide currency of this crude scientism, which has a superficial attractiveness in that it can render harmless the strongly held views of others by reducing them to psychoneurotic symptoms, has all too often allowed supporters of dominant political groupings to discredit radical opposition on grounds of mental instability. For the less than scrupulous British popular press, the word 'loony', with its connotations of abnormality and even madness, is thus more than a useful alliterative prefix to 'left' in the face of serious challenges to the political establishment.

Influential well beyond the experimental school of English psychology, Eysenck's extreme but widely disseminated theories worked on a public consciousness that was warmly disposed to take the claims of psychology seriously. The psychoanalytic movement, for all Eysenck's reservations about its insufficiently rigorous 'scientific' approach, had already laid the ground for a model of the human agent possessed by an unpredictable inner life, a secular devil, which could be exorcised by submission to the psychiatrist's couch.

The unconscious world within the individual, the 'true self' so much loved and sought after by today's psychotherapists, is now widely accepted as a determining concept in our understanding of human agency. Although superficially we may consider ourselves in control of our thoughts and actions, in reality, so the familiar argument goes, deeper and less accessible forces are at work. This picture offers us a particular kind of internal reality to which we can gain access by self-knowledge. By 'knowing ourselves' we can recognise our real feelings, identify our real needs, and understand what things really mean (to us). In this way, morality, and truth itself, have been transformed by a Nietzschean scheme in which it has become acceptable to argue that a particular course of moral action is right for me, or even that a certain proposition, however widely disputed, is nevertheless true for me.

Epistemologically, of course, this deceptively attractive and widely held set of beliefs is infinitely regressive, as Ernest Gellner has amply demonstrated:

> The problem this approach faces, or ought to face (and which in practice it only evades) is this: how on earth is that 'true self' identified? Is it given by God, by nature, or self-chosen? The last of these alternatives is most in keeping with current background beliefs. . . . It involves the absurdity of assuming that the self must somehow choose or invent itself before it exists, and presupposes a curious and in practice arbitrary capacity to distinguish between ephemeral, capricious acts of choice or commitment, and those that are for real.[12]

Christopher Lasch's critique of the effect of this debilitating philosophy on the culture of the United States reveals an emotivist world where 'psychological man' struggles 'to maintain psychic equilibrium in a society that demands submission to the rules of social intercourse but refuses to ground those rules in a code of moral conduct'. Presiding over this profound cultural dislocation are the high priests of psychology, the therapists, the psychiatric masseurs of a national neurosis. They administer to the 'anxiety, depression, vague discontents', the 'sense of inner emptiness' of modern society, but give 'no thought to anything beyond its immediate needs'.

> It hardly occurs to them – nor is there any reason why it should, given the nature of the therapeutic enterprise – to encourage the subject to subordinate his needs and interests to those of others, to someone or some cause or tradition outside himself. 'Love' as self-sacrifice or self-abasement, 'meaning' as submission to a higher loyalty – these sublimations strike the therapeutic sensibility as intolerably oppressive, offensive to common sense and injurious to personal health and well-being.[13]

Thus, in the laboratory of the feelings the encounter-group narcissist searches for a deep cleansing of the self from the destructive, polluting structures of all social institutions. This is pursued in the name of a perfect purity of free aspiration, and realised in a series of personal intimacies unfettered by dead conventions and traditions.

Politically, as recent North American history vividly demonstrates, this over-powering narcissism leads to disengagement and impotence. As long as the criteria for moral action are determined by reference only to the integrity of the self and are judged by the authenticity of the feelings associated with them, then the subordination of those so-called 'needs' in corporate, public action for a collective purpose, becomes increasingly difficult. Narcissism shapes a powerful form of political acquiescence; the individual is responsible for him or herself and for his or her own self-knowledge, and for the preservation of the community, whatever its holistic moral character, only because he or she is aware that it is composed of other individuals with the same kinds of problems in achieving self-authentication. In a narcissistic society, 'awareness' becomes the vapid substitute for moral agency; the pursuit of self as a legitimate end can only make meaningful ethical judgements impossible. With no yardstick beyond self-authentication, no actions can be regarded as reprehensible if they are sincere, or indeed if they *appear to be sincerely expressed*, because their sincere expression is their ultimate justification. Thus, as an individual I look not for good or bad actions but for sincere people, and because I have no means of knowing with what degree of sincerity another person carries out an action, I can only assess how sincere they seem. Or conversely, if I can convince others of my self-authenticity and of the sincerity in which I act, then I can reasonably demand to be judged well. We are in the world of appearances, where what counts is the effectiveness with which an agent adopts the appropriate role in a society made up of improvised encounters. In the words of critic Lionel Trilling,

> Society requires of us that we present ourselves as being sincere, and the most efficacious way of satisfying this demand is to see to it that we really are sincere, that we actually are what we want our community to know we are. In short, we play the role of being ourselves, we sincerely act the part of the sincere person.[14]

The self-justifying and self-referential *naïveté* of this scheme of things has made it the ideological home of much charlatanry, as well as of the simple-minded and insecure. The encounter groups and psycho-dramas, happenings and love-ins of the 1960s were all manifestations of a form of psychological escapism which had as its simple premise the deeply implausible notion that the more individuals exposed their 'real' feelings to each other the better the world would be.

It has to be said that the extraction of the moral dimension from the truly therapeutic processes of mental health care can release some patients from unbearable personal pressure. For those who have suffered severe psychological distress through unreasonable feelings of guilt, such release may represent the first step towards recovery. However, for those of us fortunate enough not to have to inhabit the closed world of psychotherapy, the primacy of self-authentication over disinterested intellection can all too easily lead to the manipulation and exploitation of our perceptions. Richard Nixon's famous 'Checkers' speech on American television in 1952, for example, where, with tears in his eyes, he convinced the American voting public that he was a man who loved dogs, and therefore that they should forget about the election slush fund in which he was implicated, taught that wily politician a lesson which served him well for nearly twenty-five years: voters can be deflected from scrutiny of a politician's inept or corrupt actions so long as he or she appears to display sincere feelings in public.[15]

PHENOMENOLOGY, UNIVERSALS AND THE FALLACY OF INDIVIDUALISM

It is within the discursive framework sketched here that drama-in-education built its conceptual home, ignoring, or unaware of, the paradox that this home was shared by powerful forces within Western culture which also sought to de-politicise contemporary consciousness, but in the name of a naturalism owing more to Hobbes and Adam Smith than to Rousseau and Blake and dedicated not to the fostering of the poetic spirit but to the unfettered exchange and accumulation of goods. The subsequent embrace of phenomenology by prominent practitioners such as Gavin Bolton[16] may be seen as an unconscious attempt to deflect criticism that their elaborately contrived practices could be associated with a view of the world to which most of its proponents were ideologically opposed. Whatever the reason, plentiful reference in the literature of the 1980s to 'personal meaning' and 'universals' suggests how the neo-Platonic apriorism of Edmund Husserl,[17] with his search for the Absolute, for an 'essence' beyond all criticism, upon which all knowledge can rest, could appeal to a discipline adrift in psychological theories of motivation.

Husserl saw it as the task of phenomenologists to identify and describe the essences which he thought made up our experience. Drawing extensively from psychology, he believed that close attention to our mental processes would reveal certain *a priori* truths intuited by the mind which could be isolated from any particular historical or cultural circumstances. In doing so, he set out to relocate our intuitions within an epistemology of timeless imperatives which would be immune from speculation about cause or consequence and of which we simply become aware; under a transcendental phenomenological system of this kind it becomes possible to argue that simply 'knowing oneself' is the key to seeing the world as it actually is. To know oneself is to reveal the essential structures, the 'universals', through which all knowing becomes possible; for Husserl, 'being' and 'meaning' are two sides of the same coin, taking things as they 'appear to the consciousness' is to know their reality.

The idea of phenomenological absolutes or universals fitted neatly with the individualistic premises of drama-in-education, and was widely, if implicitly, accepted. 'True gut-level drama', asserted one of Dorothy Heathcote's amanuenses, 'has to do with what you at your deepest level want to know about what it is to be human.'[18] Bolton went so far as to list the Husserlian essences he believed were revealed by drama and it is no surprise that his 'universals' – 'protecting one's family, journeying home, facing death, recording for posterity, passing on wisdom, making tools, etc.' – turn out to be those of Rousseau's noble savage, the wise paternalist we met in Chapter 1.[19] Not only are these 'universals' quaintly rustic – who *makes tools* these days? – but, as feminist critics have pointed out, in the choice of vehicles for these revelations, 'knowing what it is to be human' often looks very much like knowing what it is to be stereotypically male:

> pioneering brave adventures into the heart of darkness to visit tribes or the wild west, a concern with colonisation, dominance and acts of aggression. At times, there is an embarrassed reference to the position of girls, who are encouraged to take male roles, such as miners, or explorers or footballers, presumably because in the context of the drama they appear more interesting.[20]

Towards the end of her career, Heathcote turned increasingly to primitivism in what seemed to be a quest for forms of phenomenological absolute or 'universal truth'. Her students became accustomed to playing out the inter-cultural dilemmas of tribal communities and to inventing their own 'rituals' for a wide range of simple activities such as choosing a leader or agreeing on laws (see again, the 'Tomb Drama' in Appendix 1). Underlying this imperial view of so-called 'primitive' societies are the phenomenological assumptions already indicated; notably, that there are certain realities, or essences, which form the common features of all human consciousness. Describing a bizarre drama session at an exclusive English boarding school, for example, in which Heathcote had asked a group of boys in swimming trunks to 'assume roles of a primitive tribe', one observer was convinced that by 'identifying and creating' the boys had been able to 'capture the essence of the primitive'.[21]

Psychology and phenomenology can be seen as complementary

responses to twentieth-century secularism which seek to mystify the self and to create a morality of introspection in which political and social questions, such as those surrounding gender, for example, are happily dissolved. Neither could provide a way out of the reductionist and self-regarding conceptual trap which drama-in-education dug for itself, however, for neither system moves beyond the confines of the individual consciousness. Both represent views of the world which can only leave us ethically helpless in the face of the social, cultural and political dilemmas confronting us, for, unlike pre-modern, traditional societies, we have lost the congruence of value through which a culture of membership confers identity and social meaning on the individual. We are faced instead with a curious kind of disembodied identity, self-contained and entirely self-referential, a specifically modern emotivist self, which, according to the philosopher Alasdair MacIntyre,

> cannot be simply or unconditionally identified with any particular moral attitude or point of view just because of the fact that its judgements are in the end criterionless . . . [It] has no necessary social content and no necessary identity can then be anything, can assume any role or take any point of view, because it is in and for itself nothing.[22]

Without doubt this is the vacuum at the centre of drama-in-education, the existential, narcissistic wilderness around which students circle in search of truth, value and meaning, but in which all the so-called social learning of the drama class, however conscientiously engineered, must in the end be condemned to wander aimlessly. In its desolate landscape the only deontological imperative is the absolute relativity of moral values; your actions need no other criterion to command my respect than that you should sincerely believe they are right for you. The moral attitude of an individual has value by *virtue of that individual's individuality*. The transparent circularity of this argument has failed to dislodge it from its influential position in contemporary education. But as John Dunn makes clear in his bleak account of modern liberalism, 'individuals might be all that, humanly speaking, was there; but this consideration alone would scarcely give one grounds for treating them as a commanding focus of value, or for acknowledging a duty to tolerate their idiosyncratic tastes and opinions'.[23]

Nevertheless, individualism stands as the custodian of freedom in our society; challenge it in any terms but its own, so says convention, and that freedom is threatened. Thus, the traditional foes of the educational idealist – state examinations, assessment, externally imposed curricula, vocationalism, and so on – are demonised not for ideological reasons but precisely and solely because they are held to limit the free and arbitrary choices of individuals.

Denied ideology in a society already inclined to reduce the strongly held ideas and beliefs of others to symptoms of psychoneurosis if they are unpalatable or inconvenient, all the radical teacher can hope to achieve under such a limited scheme of things is that by demystifying the processes and contradictions of society in the classroom, significant numbers of individuals re-examining 'their own views and values' may eventually feel inclined to oppose them. It is what David Hargreaves has called the *fallacy of individualism*, or 'the belief that if only schools can successfully educate every individual pupil in self-confidence, independence and autonomy, then society can with confidence be left to take care of itself'.[24] As a programme for the institution of egalitarian change it leaves much to be desired.

6

HAPPENING ON THE AESTHETIC

THE ART OF SCHOOL DRAMA

In the previous chapter, I showed how a combination of nineteenth-century Romanticism and twentieth-century developmental psychology shaped post-war thinking about arts education, turning teachers away from seeing art as a matter of making and interrogating socially valued products and towards the idea of art as a therapeutic engagement with the inner world of individuals. By this account, the so-called 'art process' originates in a kind of psychological drive perpetually striving to 'make sense of the life of feeling'.

> In music, painting, and drama and the other arts, we develop languages, symbolic forms through which we may understand this universe of personal response.... They are the product of a compulsion to make sense of, express and communicate from, the inner world of subjective understanding.[1]

For Malcolm Ross, writing here in the tradition of a line of twentieth-century expressive aestheticians like Marjorie Hourd, Louis Arnaud Reid and Susanne Langer, the extravagant emotivism of the Romantic spirit is simultaneously awakened and tamed by the orderly exercise of creativity; education through art is 'education for emotional maturity'.

> The arts teacher helps children's emotional development by showing them how to express their feelings creatively and responsibly.... Our work differs from that of our non-arts colleagues in that we give pride of place to the formulation of feeling-ideas, to the creation and response to forms that must (and need only) in the final instance, satisfy strictly personal and subjective criteria.[2]

Although Peter Slade had little doubt that Child Drama was art of exactly this kind, the subsequent promotion of drama as a cross-curricular learning utility meant some subordination of this aesthetic imperative. Art now ceased to be an end in itself and became instead 'art form', a vehicle for more generalised learning outcomes. Gavin Bolton was confident, however, that by participating sufficiently enthusiastically, students would still be able to 'feel in their bones'[3] that phenomenological essence, that 'aesthetic meaning', which he believed was there to be 'awakened in all of us'.[4] For him, 'focus, symbolism, tension, resonance, ambiguity, contradiction, ritual, simplicity, contrast, anticipation, resolution, completeness and incompleteness, humour, magic, ambiguity and metaxis, etc.' were 'the inner forms of theatre that children of all ages can sense as significant'.[5]

Unfortunately, the random quality of Bolton's list serves only to obscure the hypothesis which it patently seeks to declare; that is, that art, and drama in particular, seems to have a special ability to engage with our apparent sense of *presence*, to illuminate for us that momentary consciousness of existential insight which, for Husserl's pupil, Martin Heidegger, was the key to understanding the complex relationship we have with our experience in its immediate aftermath.

> Wherever a present being encounters another present being or even only lingers near it – but also where, as with Hegel, one being mirrors itself in another speculatively – there openness already rules, the free region is in play. Only this openness grants the movement of speculative thinking the passage through what it thinks.[6]

While Ross rightly took Bolton to task for the expansive pedagogic claims made on behalf of drama-in-education,[7] neither doubted the essential seaworthiness of the conceptual vessel upon which they both turned out to be embarked. When Ross expressed his dissatisfaction with the 'non-arts outcomes' of drama teaching, he did so in the context of his 'exclusive commitment' to an aesthetic with which Bolton would have had no trouble in identifying. For both, the dramatic 'art form' was there to be discovered, its essential 'rightness' declaring itself through a process of developing aesthetic awareness. Once again, we are persuaded to see the making and appreciation of art as a personal, subjective, and psychologically self-validating process, measurable only against the 'integrity of the individual's feeling life'.[8] A drama teacher sums it up perfectly: 'The aesthetic dimension in Drama is to reveal deeper meanings so that children perceive universal applications personally.'[9]

Ross was sure, though, that drama-in-education's difficulties with art originated in the old 'wrangle between theatre and drama'. 'Drama-in-education,' he once said, 'is a doomed mutant unless it can draw life from the theatre.'[10] As we have already seen, the origins of this wrangle go very deep. In its inaugural statement of objectives, National Drama, an association formed in 1991 to 'represent the common interests' of all British drama educators, managed to avoid making any mention whatsoever of actors, theatres or plays and the authors of a 1995 primary drama handbook must have disappointed and mystified many hard-working primary teachers with this strict reminder : 'Drama is NOT learning lines and performing in front of parents. Drama is NOT getting the children to make up plays in groups while the teacher stands back, out of the story, and watches.'[11]

Despite the jaunty suggestion of two Canadian teachers in the late 1980s that the bridge between 'Dramatown and Theatretown' should be rebuilt,[12] such efforts as were made by drama-in-education enthusiasts to reconnect their private, dispositional outcomes to the demonstrably public ones of the theatre simply advocated the use of 'theatre form' in the drama lesson.[13] Any real progress on this front continued to be inhibited by traditional suspicions of public performance and an unwillingness to disengage from that overriding commitment to personal feeling response charted here. In 1986, Bolton had issued a dire warning against any descent into the training of students 'in theatre skills and textual study'[14] and while by the 1990s he seemed prepared to acknowledge the place of 'theatre' in his work, this was limited to a number of suitably authentic 'theatre experiences'; he remained adamant that what he called 'the basic components of theatre form – focus, tension, ritual, temporary chaos' should never be confused with 'theatre conventions or genres'.[15]

THE TRADITION OF ENGLISH

Drama-in-education was not alone in the post-war period, either in its dedication to personal feeling and experience or in its pursuit of the 'timeless truths' of the human condition. In a long educational association with English there grew up a striking affinity of purpose between the two fields. In the 1960s, writers like David Holbrook evangelised a new kind of English lesson designed particularly to draw into the English experience those young people traditionally alienated by the formal curriculum, those for whom 'creative drama', free as it was from the demands of the written text, seemed an ideal medium. Like the pioneers of Child Drama, Holbrook too drew extensively on psychological theories of art and creativity, inspiring a generation of English teachers with the same kind of progressive idealism that we have already seen in the writings of Peter Slade and Brian Way.

It is hard to see how drama could have gained even a tenuous foothold on the curriculum without the wide acceptance of the centrality of English. Conceptually and ideologically the tradition of which Holbrook was such an articulate advocate provided much needed off-the-peg credibility for the emerging practices of drama in schools. That tradition, most commonly associated with the teaching and writing of

F. R. Leavis and his fellow Scrutineers,[16] had such a pervasive influence that it is difficult to imagine that the study of English has not always had its dominant position in educational thinking. But in 1920, as Terry Eagleton reminds us, English was still considered the province of a tiny coterie of 'patrician dilettantes' on the fringes of academia. Within the space of ten years, however, these Cambridge radicals had so revolutionised the status of English, that, by the outbreak of the Second World War, the subject could with justification claim to be the secular heir of classics and theology, the very yardstick by which what it meant to be educated could be measured.

> English was not only a subject worth studying, but the supremely civilising pursuit, the spiritual essence of the social formation. . . . English was an arena in which the most fundamental questions of human existence – what it means to be a person, to engage in significant relationship with others, to live from the vital centre of the most essential values – were thrown into vivid relief and made the object of the most intensive scrutiny.[17]

The tradition so influentially constructed by the Scrutineers was based on a belief in the existence of a transcendent humanism, an intense, Kantian morality that could be authentically felt through the experience of literature. We may see drama-in-education as having stowed away on this same humanising mission, happy to share the apodictic belief that beyond the messy uncertainties of history lie cosmic values, the eternal verities of liberal civilisation. The so-called 'universals' of the drama lesson, the phenomenological essences that students could feel in their bones, are no more nor less than the moral assumptions of Leavisite humanism, truths which can be as satisfactorily soaked up in the suspended disbelief of the drama class as contemplated and absorbed through 'close reading'. In opting always for 'a level of greater generality or universality',[18] the Witnesses and their followers were unconsciously guiding their classes not towards the trans-cultural commonalities of their imaginations, but in fact to something very like the ideologically prescribed goals of the Scrutineers. Thus it is that for all the professed commitment to the 'lived through experience' of the individual student, the choice of 'universals' and the approval or disapproval of their outcomes were rarely in doubt. When Heathcote used a drama about a refuse collectors' strike as 'an effective tool for gaining insight into the patterns and tensions of community life', complex political and moral statements became muffled in the simple humanising message of tolerance and reconciliation.[19] In other cases, good and evil were so starkly arraigned that the participants would have had to be very dim indeed not to see the point. These are one teenager's comments after a day of intensive role-playing in an imaginary Nazi concentration camp: 'I knew it was bad but not that bad. How many were killed in one day because they were weak, old, tired of . . . for just *no* reason'. [20] Quite so. But has this student really made deeply felt 'social meaning' about the Holocaust, as his teacher would have us believe? In drama-in-education, feelings like these of moral revulsion become reconstituted as 'aesthetic awareness', their intuitive 'rightness' endorsing the methodology. Detached from history, and with no canon of accredited literature against which to measure this 'rightness', there is no way of distinguishing between the feelings of aesthetic and non-aesthetic meaning or between those meanings which are deeply felt and those which are not but the eidetic intuitionism already described.

The transcendence of this version of the aesthetic, existing in a sphere beyond the mere intellectual and utilitarian concerns of society, accessible only through the imagination, insulates it perfectly from those inclined to locate artistic experience in our more earthly preoccupations. If the sub-text of the drama-in-education class reflects the authoritarian idealism of New Criticism, then its text is a masquerade of moral and aesthetic sensibility where experience and feeling too often stand in the place of reason, and where ultimately, in Eagleton's vivid and disturbing example, 'the truth or falsity of beliefs such as that blacks are inferior to whites is less important than what it feels like to experience them'.[21]

The important difference between drama-in-education and the tradition of English lies in the latter's emphasis on *judgement*. However idiosyncratic and contested their conclusions, the Scrutineers were unambiguous about the need for aesthetic discernment, for the allocation of *value* in the arts. Their patrician acceptance that only a minority would be capable of the 'genuine personal response' necessary for the appreciation of their canon had at least the virtue of honesty, and they really did believe that in return for the gift of insight, the few had a profound responsibility for the education of the many. Leavis declared:

> Upon them depend the implicit standards that order the finer living of an age, the sense that this is worth more than that, this rather than that is the direction in which to go, that the centre is here rather than there.[22]

Even as Holbrook was popularising the tradition of English in schools its tenets were themselves coming under scrutiny; the demystifying influence of literary structuralism was waiting in the wings, ready to make itself felt. Structuralist thinkers challenged the transcendentalism of English by refusing to accept that meanings were universally shared and could be revealed through appeals to aesthetic intuition. Instead, they argued that meaning was simply the product of commonly shared systems of *signification*. Literature – just one system of signification among many – was a linguistic construct possessed only of an aesthetic

function by virtue of its place in time and its relationship with those evaluating it. The heavy emphasis on linguistics which characterised
structuralism was in turn extended by post-structuralists like Roland
Barthes and Jacques Derrida, who sought to subvert the very notion of
fixed structure by shifting the focus decisively from author to reader.
Under post-structuralism, the signifying text – literary or otherwise –
becomes 'a seamless weave of codes and fragments of codes, through
which the critic may cut his own errant path'.[23]

The methodological effects of this fracturing began to be felt in the
English departments of schools and universities during the 1970s and
1980s as a growing interest in media education,[24] and the idea that media
'texts' were every bit as valid as printed ones, helped to break the grip of
the Scrutineers. Advertisements, newspaper articles and film reviews all
became legitimate objects of 'deconstruction', a multiplicity of different
'literacies'.[25] For teachers persuaded by these ideas, English did not transcend politics; they saw that the aesthetic which legitimated the
supremacy of their subject (and which helped to give drama its passport
into schools) was as much a product of the processes of history as the
alternatives which sought to replace it.

Beyond the use of the new uncertainties to validate some highly
subjective research projects, there is no evidence to suggest these
profound changes in political and educational consciousness touched
drama-in-education in any significant way. While by the mid-1990s,
some voices were suggesting that these important developments might
also have implications for the teaching of drama in schools, the whole
idea of 'readership' was deeply alien to a set of practices which had long
ago abandoned the idea of actors and audiences. Phenomenology was
providing too comfortable a vehicle for the intuitionism of drama-in-
education for it to be easily abandoned for some hard theoretical
reassessments.

Paradoxically, some of this reluctance may have been fuelled by
English teachers so impressed by the pedagogic techniques of Heathcote
and others in the 1970s and 1980s that they left their subject for drama.
Informal research suggests that these converts form a significant proportion of the drama teaching force and, as a consequence, the percentage of
secondary drama specialists without either theatre experience or first
degrees in drama is disturbingly high. The appeal of drama-in-education
to a certain kind of English teacher is not difficult to fathom.
Spontaneous improvisation can bring the issues discussed in English to
life in a vivid and immediate manner and enables students to use
language in a whole variety of imaginary contexts without requiring
them to develop any additional skills. Understood in this way, it is
perhaps not so surprising that drama-in-education should have come to
be regarded as a valuable adjunct of English. Conceptual and practical

links are strong, to the extent that competence in the teaching of English is often held to be quite sufficient qualification for a drama teacher. In reality, however, while former English teachers are probably confident enough in the use of drama to support the humanising mission of Leavis and Holbrook, they may be rather less happy about the challenges presented by the knowledge, understanding and skills of a comprehensive drama curriculum. The dangers for the subject of drama of this enthusiastic but under-qualified cadre are obvious enough.

NATURALISM AND THE THEATRE

If the aesthetic of drama-in-education owes much to F.R. Leavis and the tradition of English, it is also indebted to twentieth-century dramatic naturalism. Students in schools have become accustomed to making up improvised plays with short, televisual scenes or spontaneously taking on roles or characters in the context of imagined realities. This heritage of dramatic naturalism is readily identifiable in the statements of earlier practitioners, so that when Peter Slade assures us that, 'there is no more certain way of understanding Drama than to act sincerely,'[26] it is difficult not to be reminded of Stanislavski's *creative 'if'*, that 'imagined truth which the actor can believe in sincerely and with greater enthusiasms than he believes practical truth, just as the child believes in the existence of its doll and of all the life in it and around it'. Like Slade, Stanislavski believed that the successful actor had 'to develop to the highest degree his imagination, a childlike naïveté and trustfulness, and artistic sensitivity to truth and to the truthful in his soul and body'.[27]

I have shown how the assessment schemes of drama-in-education are similarly concerned with the truthfulness with which students portray reality in their improvisations, a truthfulness measured not by the accuracy of impersonation so much as by the apparent sincerity and commitment of the attempt, the so-called 'authenticity of feeling' associated with it. And it is surely true that given characters with whom they can empathise and situations close at hand, few young people lack the potential spontaneously to enact human encounters with unself-conscious verisimilitude. In the right circumstances a child does share with the actor that ability to transform, in Stanislavski's words, 'a coarse scenic lie into the most delicate truth of his relation to the life imagined'.[28]

It is this unself-conscious commitment to an authentic 'inner truth' combined with a mistrust of the critical or analytic that binds drama-in-education to that same pervasive naturalism which so decisively frames television drama. The reluctance to make the step from describing the world through the eyes of individuals to any interpretation of those descriptions, draws classroom drama irresistibly back to that ideology of non-ideology which, for Eagleton, 'de-historicises reality and accepts society as a natural fact'.

> This draining of direction and meaning from history results in the art we know as naturalism. . . . Meticulously observed detail replaces the portrayal of 'typical' features; the truly 'representative' character yields to a 'cult of the average'; psychology or physiology oust history as the true determinant of individual action.[29]

For all the claims to the contrary, I doubt that much drama in schools resembles the dramatic didacticism of *Lehrstück* and agitprop.[30] The fundamental lack of specificity in its learning objectives, for one thing, makes it difficult to see how dramatic pedagogy can be commensurate with the didacticism of Brecht or Piscator. Also, drama-in-education's traditional commitment to variations of such existentially passive aims as 'awareness', 'symbolisation' and 'significance', suggests that many practitioners would be more at ease with the introspective symbolism of the later Strindberg, 'pre-eminently the dramatist of a dynamic psychology',[31] than with the raucous theatrical polemics of the Weimar Republic. 'Possible learning areas' listed in a 1997 teachers' handbook, for example, include 'promises', 'oppression', and 'the transience of human achievement'.[32]

The low-key emotional approach of Dorothy Heathcote clearly revealed this commitment to naturalism. At first sight, many of her techniques, such as the breaking up of narrative and the limiting of characterisation, seem sympathetic to Brechtian practice. Where she parts company with Brecht is precisely at the point where, in the playwright's own words, 'the means must be asked what the end is'.[33] It is there that she invariably yields to that 'cult of the average', denying both the specificity and the movement of history in her attempts to universalise the dramatic experience. Heathcote claimed that, for her, the end product of the drama is changed students, 'changed in that their areas of reference are widened, their growth as people is furthered, their understanding of humanity is extended'.[34] She believed that it was sufficient to assume that a process of 'internalisation' had taken place, that the students had 'lived through a problem' and had been encouraged to reflect upon it. Fine aims, certainly, and a worthy description of the personal journeys made by the characters in any Chekhov play. But, as we know, neither Ranyevskaya's understanding of humanity nor her reflection upon her problems will save the cherry orchard. These are precisely the limitations of a naturalism which, as Eagleton makes clear, 'can create no significant totality from its materials', where 'the unified epic or dramatic actions launched by realism collapse into a set of purely private interests'.[35]

If naturalism's strength lies in its 'abstract objectivity', its ability to portray the suffering and injustice of the world with startling clarity, its weakness is that it removes these perceptions from the field of human responsibility.[36] According to the critic Ernst Fischer, there comes a moment of decision when naturalism must either break through to forms of interpretation and action or 'founder in fatalism, symbolism, mysticism, religiosity, and reaction'.[37] The so-called 'moment of understanding', the confident achievement of the drama 'process', is also, and crucially, the moment of choice. We are warmed by recognition, like Brecht's audiences for dramatic naturalism, 'Yes, I have felt like that too,' but our new-found awareness can too easily collapse into the self-regarding inertia and pessimism of a Masha or a Vanya without a parallel understanding of the ideological structures which are the key to change. In drama-in-education, the choice which Brecht would wish to place for us at the heart of the dramatic experience is too often usurped by a vicarious submission to the changeless, where, in Fischer's words, 'the specific nature of a historical moment is falsified into a general idea of being'.[38]

The passive, internalised objectives of educational drama, the 'innerstandings', 'awarenesses' and 'making of meanings', are products both of traditional humanism and the naturalistic conventions within which they are invariably acted out. They reflect a commitment to a transcendent view of the aesthetic which is uncritical because it is beyond criticism. It is this peculiar wrapping of the metaphysical in the commonplace that has contributed so profoundly to school drama's problems with evaluation and assessment. Until drama education can relocate its practices in the critical, public world the high expectations raised by a dramatic pedagogy which at one time seemed not only to offer a new grounding for school drama, but also to restore to drama teaching a sense of direction and purpose, a humane seriousness through which the inner and outer worlds of our experience might be reconciled, can only in the end be frustrated as practitioners methodically turn away from the implications of its outcomes.

7

SIGNIFICANT KNOWING

KNOWING WHAT YOU FEEL

From the end of the 1970s, we have seen how theories of creativity and personal development in drama-in-education were gradually displaced by ideas about learning. Believing that its roots in children's play gave drama-in-education a unique hold on the natural processes of cognition, this new undertaking put forward the case for drama as a special way of inducing understanding, or 'making meanings' for students. The arguments that emerged in support of this cognitive project ignored the social and cultural context in which both knowledge is defined and drama made and performed and instead focused once again on the internal processes governing the reception and ordering of our experience. 'Drama for understanding', it was proposed, was a matter of 'personally engaging with knowledge'.[1]

> In play and in drama there is obvious learning potential in terms of skills and objective knowledge, but the deepest kind of change that can take place is at the level of subjective meaning. The learning . . . has to be felt for it to be effective.[2]

In a simple conflation of this 'objective' and 'subjective' duality, it was then concluded that 'true knowing' is no more nor less than *what you know you feel*.

> The teacher tries to put children in touch with what is deeply felt and then proceeds to initiate a slow process of disengagement from those feelings and values, not necessarily with a view to changing them but with a view to knowing what they are.[3]

Because drama-in-education uniquely offers students access to this authentic emotional inner-world (the argument went on), it is especially well placed to help them 'feel their way into knowledge'.[4] But the objects of this knowledge are not to be the superficial facts of the traditional academic curriculum, the so-called 'value-free "detached" knowledge of subject disciplines'[5] (and presumably, therefore, not theatre conventions or genres). Instead, learning through drama involves a 'felt change in value',[6] and it is these felt values 'that contribute to the child's subjective meaning in playing and are a central feature of the activity of drama'.[7] It is not the teacher's place to examine these values in public, nor to mediate between variant moralities within the group. He or she should instead harness the capacity of drama to enable students *simply to realise what their values are.*

> A teacher may from within the drama use her/his role to open up the door of opportunity for such Realisation. The teacher cannot know exactly what each child will learn or how significant the learning will be. That does not matter. Her/his responsibility lies in detecting which door and when to open it.[8]

It seems that the only criterion for the knowledge sought during this kind of experience is that it should be *significant to the learners*; that it should mean something (though not necessarily the same thing) to each individual. 'Meaning' would thus appear to be a goal in itself, circumscribed by its own intransitivity and revealed only in those rare high points of dramatic concentration and focus that Dorothy Heathcote once called 'moments of awe'. And so, although he is sure that 'dramatic activity used for personal knowledge of this kind is educationally significant', Gavin Bolton admits that he cannot always be specific about *what* meanings are made by students in drama but is happy to trust in what he concedes is an 'act of faith'.[9]

Indeed, it is difficult to see how this sanguineness could be said to be much more than an act of faith. Apart from anything else, these apparent 'moments of awe' are extremely difficult to achieve – as every school drama teacher knows. Even in the controlled conditions of their demonstration workshops, Heathcote and Bolton would often take several sessions to build up sufficient tension and commitment; in the pandemonium of the ordinary school day these 'awesome' dramatic occasions must be very rare indeed. It might reasonably be argued that the time and energy expended on such limited objectives could be more profitably spent. If this really is all that can be accomplished, then it is tempting to conclude that for all the new dressing, this ambitious project reveals little genuine advance on the Newsom Report of twenty years earlier, which endorsed school drama as a way of helping young people 'to come to terms with themselves'.[10]

We must not forget, however, that drama-in-education has also sought to link this idea of personal knowing to the wider project of liberal humanism through its claims to facilitate access to the transcendental essences of phenomenology. By this account based on the assumption that only through self-knowledge can we unlock the fundamental structures of the world and see it as it really is, the personal knowledge gained as a result of the drama experience is not as random and solipsistic as first it might seem, for it has as its object these self-same trans-cultural essences; meaning is both personal *and* universal. We have already seen Heathcote's public-school boys in swimming trunks capturing 'the essence of the primitive'; Bolton's hypothetical drama about the 1984–85 British miners' strike aimed to reveal the 'fairly common universal' of 'how people cope under stress'. In Bolton's version of these politically charged historical events, the high drama of confrontation between police and miners is diluted into a story about 'a torn community', because 'drama can normally only engage with a topic or issue obliquely, for drama's contextual meaning is but a vehicle for a level of greater generality or universality'.[11]

Apart from the presumption here – that only the teacher can know what is *really* going on – the moral and political implications of this retreat from the social and political have been noted; the 'obliqueness' in the above example really serves to fudge and obscure an issue rich in its particularity. Generalisations about 'torn communities' seem a poor substitute educationally for the tempestuous history of the actual, lived events in which Margaret Thatcher and her government set about settling old scores.

Back in the classroom, the assumption that life can be reduced to a series of simple, timeless homilies – 'a policeman is a man with a home and a family; Africans are like us in many ways'[12] – can lead all too easily to that kind of drama teaching in which the dense, thrilling language and brilliant thematic organisation of, say, the first scene of *King Lear*, are abandoned in favour of platitudinous improvisations about family squabbles, on the grounds that the play's themes are 'universal'.[13] As in the concentration camp example cited in the previous chapter, drama then becomes a form of reduction to the obvious, its learning objectives triumphantly achieved only because they are so undemanding of students' intelligence and imagination.[14]

PERSONAL KNOWLEDGE

Still, it is plain that something quite unlike the normal scholastic knowledge transaction is going on in the manipulated make-believe of a successful educational drama session. Under the pressure of sustained role-playing students of all ages do indeed, on occasions, display surprising insights, and it certainly seems that by inducing deep emotional commitment to an idea in this way, the skilled drama teacher can stimulate high levels of expressive coherence in individual students. Neither is it difficult to see how this might be interpreted as the manifestation of a special kind of learning, particularly as the circumstances surrounding such scenes tend to be powerfully mesmeric. Many students seem to exhibit an unfamiliar capacity both for perception and commitment under these conditions.

Unfortunately, the reliance of so much of the drama-in-education methodology on transient and unpredictable 'moments' makes its outcomes difficult, if not impossible, to pin down; the process relies too heavily on the intuition of the teacher. Nevertheless, by the mid-1990s these drama happenings were becoming the subject of a profusion of empirical research projects. In most cases, it was taken for granted that the purpose of research was not to question the orthodoxy but rather to illuminate and celebrate the work of the Witnesses and their followers. Inclined by their historical formation to be suspicious of quantitative number crunching, it is no surprise that these field researchers favoured a more subjective interpretation of events, a 'qualitative' way of doing things involving the collection of data from 'participant observation, interviews, self reports, textual analysis, transcripts, photographic and video images and a whole range of other techniques that feed off the experiences of those being studied'.[15] In the subsequent examination of this data, the fragmentations of post-modernism amongst which the researchers discovered themselves ideologically situated seemed conveniently to authorise abandoning ideas of 'truth, validity and falsification' in favour of the 'struggle, ambiguity and contradiction'[16] of their own intuitions.

> Pain and discomfort seem to go with the design as we chase the moon, and pursue a guiding light in arts education... By participating in this struggle, we join and honour all those reflective practitioners who have preceded and who will follow us. We too join hands, clasp ankles, and form a net, a network of folk dedicated to a journey of becoming which will raise the streams of consciousness to which an artistic–aesthetic curriculum aspires.[17]

The objective truth/subjective value distinction has long preoccupied those interested in the use of drama as a learning method. Bolton maintained that drama-in-education's unique contribution to understanding is made through its reference both to the 'objective' world outside the child, and to his or her 'subjective' internal world, the resultant meaning being 'poised dialectically' between the two.[18] Given the field's long love-affair with psychological and phenomenological accounts of reality, however, it is no surprise that qualitative researchers have been more attracted to the claims of subjective experience.

An epistemology well suited to accommodate preferences of this kind is advanced by Michael Polanyi, whose theories of 'tacit understanding' and 'intellectual passion' proved naturally attractive to those who, in the 1980s, were still seeking to place the practices of drama-in-education within an established, epistemological landscape.[19] For Polanyi, Bolton's 'objective world' is the home of *explicit* knowledge – information in libraries, the content of school syllabuses, and so on. *Tacit* knowledge, on the other hand, is that pre-verbal, a-critical awareness which we share with all animals. It is upon the latter, he argues, that our ability to understand what we explicitly know ultimately depends.

> nothing that is said, written or printed, can ever mean anything in itself: for it is only a *person* who utters something – or who listens to it or reads it – who can mean something *by* it. All these semantic functions are the tacit operations of a person.[20]

It is significant that this tacit knowing, or understanding, while it is necessarily a function of the person, is not just another form of subjectivity, not simply a question of the interpretation of 'reality' by an emotive inner world giving us each our 'personal meanings'. Polanyi here makes a crucial distinction between the passive feelings we all experience, such as pain, desire, jealousy, and so on, and the active commitments of what he calls our 'moral and intellectual passions'. For him, it is these commitments which define the personal.

> we may distinguish between the personal in us, which actively enters into our commitments, and our subjective states, in which we merely endure our feelings. This distinction establishes the conception of the *personal*, which is neither subjective nor objective. In so far as the personal submits to requirements acknowledged by itself as independent of itself, it is not subjective; but in so far as it is an action guided by individual passions, it is not objective either. It transcends the disjunction between subjective and objective.[21]

Interestingly, by rejecting both the scientific view that knowledge is simply objectively out there to be discovered and the relativist one that it is nothing more than the arbitrary construction of the knower, Polanyi attempts here to reconcile the individual with his or her cultural membership. While he proposes that the meanings we make for ourselves as individuals must be commensurate with those of the culture to which we belong, however, he is not arguing that we are in any way *made* by that culture, but rather that we are motivated towards such commensurability by our natural intellectual passion to discover correct solutions.

> The sense of a pre-existent task makes the shaping of knowledge a responsible act, free from subjective predilections. And it endows, by the same token, the results of such acts with a claim to universal validity. For when you believe that your discovery reveals a hidden reality, you will expect it to be recognised equally by others.[22]

It is by this movement to an intellectual position of greater satisfaction, according to Polanyi, that 'we eventually come to hold a piece of knowledge to be true',[23] and, 'our adherence to the truth can be seen to imply an adherence to a society which respects the truth, and which we trust to respect it'.[24]

At first sight, Polanyi's theory of personal knowledge seems to offer the knowing-through-drama project a new coherence. It clarifies and diffuses the objective/subjective dichotomy, it draws a distinction between the driving passions of intellect and morality and what are thought to be our simple, felt responses, and it seeks to identify these passions as unfailingly directed towards the satisfactions of universal truth. Thus, Bolton's 'knowing in my bones' and the sense of 'rightness' felt by participants in an improvised drama, could be said to be manifestations of the tacit feeling of satisfaction gained from having successfully advanced from the problematic to a resolution.

Nevertheless, the theory's essentially emotivist premises fail to overcome Hargreaves' fallacy of individualism because, in the manner of Freudian psychology, it attempts to reduce human motivation to the satisfaction of instinctual drives.[25] Thus, although the theory provides us with a workable description of our feelings about the knowledge we possess, or seek to possess, it cannot give an adequate account of the ways in which those feelings are themselves determined by the ways we know the world. Furthermore, its commitment to a paradigmatic liberal society which fosters 'love of truth and of intellectual values in general',[26] and its concomitant suspicion of ideology, lead its author to the same ontological source as Popper and Eysenck. In much the same manner that Eysenck attempted to portray ideological commitment as psychoneurotic disturbance, Polanyi delivers a withering attack on Marxism – 'a fanatical cult of power'[27] – on the grounds that by denying them their natural universality, it represents no more than the propagandistic misappropriation of moral passions.

THE MEANING-MAKERS

A position so endorsing of the established values of society was unlikely to find favour with those unbending objectivists from the Left we met in Chapter 4. For them (at least those prepared to admit Gramsci into their class analysis), 'meaning' was explicitly understood as the primary hegemonic battleground of the class war, with the state, its institutions (including schools) and its governing class, intent on maintaining their dominant position. Drama teachers were urged to use their pedagogy to get students 'to challenge and resist those unacceptable trends they see in the world around them'. The meanings made in the school drama class should be unequivocally ideological: 'if children are learning through drama, then what are they learning? . . . above all, they are learning that drama and theatre provide a potent means of exposing and challenging the dominant ideology and its prevailing modes of intimidation'.[28]

It is difficult to square these strident calls to arms either with Polanyi's emotivism or with Bolton's remorseless search for ever greater levels of generality, although some certainly made the attempt.[29] In practice, the apparent forthrightness of this approach has frequently been a mask for some behind-the-scenes manipulation. As a more sceptical commentator has pointed out, the teacher using drama to call institutions to account is likely to present students with a narrow and carefully selected range of possible 'meanings' in which the power relations within the drama itself remain hidden.

> Students are not asked to observe the relationship between knowledge and power in the drama, or invited to examine the parameters of the drama itself. Whose voices have been facilitated by this particular selection of knowledge for 'exploration'? What other opinions have been silenced by this choice? . . . there is no need to ask whose universe we are referring to here; inevitably it is the teacher's own.[30]

While this kind of manipulation is most apparent, of course, when a teacher is motivated by an overtly ideological agenda, it is implicit in the processes of drama-in-education more generally. The naturalism of Heathcote and Bolton intuitively avoided the central problem of the *nature* of the knowledge acquired in drama lessons, of *what* might be actually learned by students; a universality of moral feeling, elevated above the everyday conflicts of moral choice, had apparently no need to engage in unseemly political debate. As for the students themselves, it seemed simply to be a matter of allowing them 'to reflect, make sense and give meaning to their feeling experience'.[31] But if, as Bolton suggests, the 'essential goal' in drama teaching is a change in subjective meaning, a 'personal shift in value' for the students,[32] it is surely reasonable to ask: what are the values to which they are being 'shifted' by the drama and how are these new values better than the ones they held before?

This dilemma is well illustrated by the way folk stories, and the archetypes they contain, have been used to preserve the illusion of universality in drama-in-education; what could be more 'essential' than a folk tale? It does not require much scratching of the surface of these fantasies, however, to expose a nest of hidden assumptions. A feminist critic, for example, reflecting on her participation in a drama workshop based on the story of the Selkie or Seal Wife of Northern European folk mythology, notes that the ingenuous use of the powerless feminine archetype common to such narratives straight away raises difficult ideological questions about what can be assumed to be 'natural'. In the version of the story chosen for this particular drama, the Seal Wife has no name of her own and is only defined in relation to her partner, Patrick the fisherman. It seems that no attempts were made during the sessions to offer alternatives to the patriarchal structure of the legend – by having the part of Patrick played by a woman, for example – or to challenge the narrative's insistence on the place of women as loyal wives and child-bearers. While the teacher in this instance has insisted that the participants themselves shape the drama, discovering 'values within the dramatic action, instead of responding to values determined in advance',[33] it is quite obvious from the record that it was the teacher herself who determined the context for the so-called 'meaning-making' through her choice of focus and activity. 'Participants were, in effect, actively excluded from interpreting the narrative, with priority and validation of patriarchal culture having been structurally imposed and made to appear natural.'[34] For this participant, the answer to Bolton's question 'What kinds of meanings are there here?'[35] is disturbingly clear: it is that a woman who questions her 'naturally' subservient position is rightly ostracised by society.[36] Which, of course, begs a further question: is this a 'personal shift in value' that we *want* to bring about for young people?

As another advocate of this form of 'process' drama admits, the 'evanescence' of spontaneous improvisation makes its meaning extremely difficult to control.[37] We know that students respond to drama in a multitude of different ways – one class of Bristol schoolchildren, I remember, could recall nothing at all about an intensive two-day workshop with Dorothy Heathcote when they were asked about it a few weeks afterwards – and clearly, other participants in the Seal Wife drama took away different 'meanings' from those expressed here. The hard fact is that meaning-making is a far more slippery business than Bolton and others allow. However carefully the drama teacher plans for those supposedly meaning-making 'moments of significance', meaning, as the post-structuralism of Jacques Derrida tells us, is 'scattered along a whole chain of signifiers: it cannot be easily nailed down, it is never fully present in any one sign alone, but is rather a kind of flickering of presence and absence together'.[38]

Thus, in the drama-in-education session as much as in the theatre, we may be changed – or remain unchanged – by an immense number of contributing experiences. If we do suffer 'a personal shift in value' after a visit to the theatre, it might be as much the result of an interval conversation or an irritation about the mannerisms of a particular actor as of the 'meanings' disclosed by the play. In school, students' attitudes to their teachers will hugely affect what those teachers' classes 'mean', no less in drama than in any other area of the curriculum. And with the teacher such a conspicuous part of the process, there is no lack of opportunity for some teachers 'to hijack the drama for their own glorification', as other commentators have noted.[39] Drama-in-education offers an accommodating platform for large egos which students may have some difficulty disentangling from any other so-called 'meaning-making' that might be going on.

The questions stubbornly remain. Are the values to which it is proposed students should be 'shifted' in drama those of the bourgeois patriarch, that parade of so-called 'universals' to which the drama teacher claims to have privileged access? As we have seen, and as another critic has noted, 'the imposition of a "universal truth" on a situation has the effect of closing off other interpretations, such as those that might be politically or historically informed'.[40] So, do the meaning-makers have in mind the values of the presumably more politically literate Left alliance from Chapter 4, who in their clear, almost purifying, commitment to a picture of a potentially corrupting world of hegemonising institutions, seem to be proposing a new version of Natural Man, founded not on the pragmatics of the bourgeois consciousness, but on radical idealism? Or is it that *any old values* will do? Perhaps so. After all, Bolton suggests that drama teachers should be primarily concerned with the *quality* of meanings sought and found in the drama.[41] But even if we accept the epistemology, how are we supposed to recognise such quality? In the quest for levels of greater generality and universality would a poor quality meaning be one that was insufficiently generalised? On the other hand, would those pitched in the struggle against oppression accept only meanings which corresponded to their liberationist agenda? Or is a poor quality meaning simply one which is considered by the teacher not to have been deeply enough *felt*?

For all the high-minded rhetoric, when we read of drama 'making meanings' for students it is difficult not to conclude that we are confronted, once again, with that same existential vacuum uncovered in Chapter 5. What seems not to be understood by those who advocate an almost infinite brief for drama as a learning agency is that the hoops through which students are required to jump in exercises like those employed to illustrate the story of the Seal Wife serve to confine rather than expand their understanding. 'In ditching content as too restrictive', writes one critic, 'the lingering belief in the universal nature of the human condition has the same closing effect on expression and imagination as reciting the nine times table'.[42] It is a paradox which must be faced if an intelligible grounding for drama education is ever to be established, and I shall return to it later. Meanwhile, the meaning-makers will have to re-examine the fundamental premises upon which they base their theories of knowledge, and try to understand more completely, not only how things come to mean what they do, but also to what extent it makes sense to talk about making or changing meanings for those we teach. So long as there remains in place that decisive rejection of the idea that there might actually be a body of knowledge constituting the subject of drama and that it is towards this knowledge that learning in drama might reasonably be directed, such a task will not be easy.

8

CULTURE AND POWER

RITA: But when I looked round, me mother had stopped singin', an' she was cryin' . . . I said, 'Why are y' cryin', Mother?' She said, 'Because – because we could sing better songs than those.' And that's why I came back. And that's why I'm staying.

(Willy Russell 1981)[1]

REALLY USEFUL KNOWLEDGE AND THE TRADITION OF DISSENT

While identifying in the quietism of drama-in-education a sustained commitment to the Romantic intuitionism of its founders, we should not forget that classroom drama had its origins in radical forms of educational thinking and can still count among its allies those concerned to offer more egalitarian and humane alternatives to the present market-bound codes of the English school curriculum. Moreover, many of the values and principles proclaimed in drama lessons can be seen to derive from a long, dissenting tradition in English education, a tradition deeply opposed to forms of narrow, self-seeking individualism. It is as the modern heirs of this tradition, and not as the standard bearers of the personal and the private, that drama teachers found themselves healthily at odds during the 1980s and 1990s with the forces engaged so energetically in redrawing the map of English education.

Reminding delegates of the Chartists' opposition to the dry irrelevancy of nineteenth-century state education, sociologist Michael Young called upon drama teachers at a conference in 1981 to keep 'the dissenters' struggle going for a curriculum of really useful knowledge'.[2] For Young, it was the battle over who decides what counts as educational knowledge that was the central issue. How does it come about that certain categories of knowledge and skill are guaranteed a place at the core of the curriculum, other kinds are relegated to the perimeter, and still others, most, probably, fail to qualify entirely? However 'natural' they may seem, these choices represent a particular set of emphases and omissions reflecting consciously and unconsciously the history of what has been thought of as education in our culture. This does not mean, of course, that curriculum content is not powerfully contested. If for no other reason, the slow pace of cultural change guarantees a mixture of what Raymond Williams called residual, dominant and emergent elements.

> An educational curriculum, as we have seen again and again in past periods, expresses a compromise between an inherited selection of interests and the emphasis of new interests. At varying points in history, even this compromise may be long delayed, and it will often be muddled. The fact about our present curriculum is that it was essentially created by the nineteenth century, following some eighteenth-century models, and retaining elements of the medieval curriculum near its centre.[3]

When Williams wrote this in the early 1960s, it was possible to believe that in the compromise between the new and the inherited, between the emergent and the dominant and residual, the liberal arts were fast guaranteeing for themselves a central place in the curriculum of the future. Then the traditional methods and academic content of the grammar school curriculum could be easily represented as fusty and reactionary in the face of the new comprehensive ideal, for there was a Whiggish confidence in the slow but inevitable victory of progressive forces. But, as we saw in Chapter 3, by 1990 a new set of interests, more concerned with consumer choice than intellectual autonomy, had successfully completed a programme of systematic educational enclosure. With a distinctly nineteenth-century National Curriculum in force up and down the land, the ideological landscape must have looked bleak to the nurserymen and women of what by then, in an ironic inversion, could only be described as 'traditional' progressivism.

In a bizarre appropriation of the words 'radical' and 'reform', these new interests effectively redefined the spokespeople of the progressive optimism of the 1960s as themselves agents of outdated, inherited interest. Teachers, liberal college lecturers, once-thought-to-be-enlightened local education authorities, were said to stand in the way of progress; by the 1990s the words 'conservative' and 'establishment' were being widely applied to the assumptions, practices and institutions which at one time seemed as if they might change the educational agenda for ever. In the face of such an onslaught, those dissenters for whom the overthrow of the university-dominated school curriculum in favour of one made up of 'really useful knowledge' once seemed within their grasp, found themselves outmanoeuvred and disinherited, struggling indeed to 'conserve' what they could of the 1960s' settlement.

Of course, drama teachers have long been accustomed to working at the boundaries of legislated educational knowledge. Most probably perceive their work as constituting a modest challenge to formal pedagogic practices and to the idea of 'fitting in'. Also, and commendably, they have become accustomed to taking their stand beside the less able and underprivileged in the latter's all too frequent confrontations with an unsympathetic world. Whatever their practical politics, most drama teachers must have been aware that in some sense what they most valued in their work was being threatened by historical forces deaf to the claims of the old humanist consensus.

Unfortunately, given the cultural and historical formation of drama in schools with its suspicion of the intellectual and the analytic and its faith in psychology and personal values, a coherent opposition from within the field in response to this threat failed to materialise. We have seen how the collapse of the old certainties fractured the drama-in-education community, with some practitioners eagerly claiming a stake in the new dispensation while others began, metaphorically speaking, to pile up the chairs in the streets. When it came to it, some apparently did believe that an arrest on the picket line would be more effective than the oblique search for greater generality advocated by Gavin Bolton.

Despite these very real differences, certain common themes can be traced in the writings of those – quietists and Spartists alike – promoting spontaneous improvisation and role-play during the 1980s and 1990s.[4] First, the child-centred premises of drama-in-education led to a closing of ranks around the idea that drama was uniquely equipped to serve the needs of young people. Second, the long tradition of non-interference in drama, together with the cherished illusion that it is the students rather than the teachers who shape projects like the Seal Wife encouraged a belief that students are in some way 'empowered' by participating in educational drama. Finally, embracing it all, was commitment to an encompassing moral relativism.

POWER AND EMPOWERMENT

The English drama-in-education associations' 1992 joint conference, 'Education or Catastrophe?', highlighted what its organisers saw as a fundamental tension between the aims of drama teachers and the policies of an uncompromising government. For these spokespeople of a long tradition of child-centred education it was a simple matter of pitting 'the child's needs' against 'economic needs'. One of the speakers at that conference had already identified what he saw as a threat to the ideals of a child-centred curriculum consisting of 'meaning-making activities and experiences' tailored to respond to 'a child's present and developmental needs' by what he dubbed an Economic Needs Curriculum inherently 'antagonistic towards the development of meaning-making processes, particularly processes such as drama'.[5] While it is doubtful that these two imperatives can be so guilelessly set in opposition – young people do not in reality exist in a world apart from economics – it is to the prolific and unpredicated use of the word 'need' that I wish to draw attention.

Our increasing dependence on the language of need which this example illustrates may be seen as an indication of the extent to which ours is a society which leans ever more heavily upon psychotherapeutic solutions to its problems. In education, students' 'needs' have tended to be identified either in the context of an individual student's psychological or physical capabilities – 'Clare needs to work with a group more sympathetic to her needs' – or of a group's social, gender or ethnic formation – 'Bangladeshi students need to have teaching materials suited to their needs'. The moral urgency implied by the use of the word 'need' in this way (as opposed, for example, to 'aspiration', or 'preference'), the implied presence of the *incontrovertibly necessary*, gives such claims powerful impetus. The ubiquity of the word in education and the caring services may be seen as an honest attempt to escape from the economic rationalism of today's social and economic planners. The needs of individuals or minority groups acquire moral grandeur in the face of the grim utilitarians of profit and loss. Who could reasonably doubt that the needs of those with disabilities or learning difficulties are indeed 'special'?

The problem is, that by invoking such claims upon the absolute, those unquestionably well-intentioned advocates of need are in danger of putting at risk the freedoms which they seek to preserve. If need is to be established simply by assertion – 'Children need to express themselves freely' – then who is to arbitrate, and by what criteria, between rival claims, such as – 'Children need to be disciplined'? Unless conscience can be mobilised over a broad spectrum, as in the formulation of special needs education where disadvantage is unambiguously manifest, 'need' in its intransitive state can be an unreliable ally. Suitably predicated, it may be readmitted to the discourse of value, but it will lose in the process much of its potency. Consider how the examples in this paragraph rapidly become contentious: *'In order to challenge and change society* children need to express themselves freely', and, 'Children need to be disciplined *to fit into the world of work'*. The child-centred premises of progressive education form only one of many ideological wagons to which the notion of 'need' can be harnessed.

A further characteristic of 'need' is that it is commonly ascribed by the privileged to communities of the powerless. 'Disadvantaged' groups tend to have their 'needs' identified not by their own members but by those, however benevolently intentioned, with some control over them. Social workers speak of the 'needs' of children in care, drama teachers of the 'needs' of the students in their groups. It is perhaps a feature of our pride, or sense of solidarity, that while we ourselves are likely from time to time, in a self-regarding way, to refer to our individual 'needs', we are far less inclined to do so when we speak of groups to which we belong. Here we speak of 'demands', of 'rights', of 'equality' and 'justice'; we return, in other words, to an overtly expressed moral curriculum. Consider, for example, how the so-called 'right to manage', much celebrated by the self-same managers of contemporary society, is neatly balanced in their parlance by the 'need' of the workforce to accept low wage settlements. The pervasive employment of the word 'need' tends not only to internalise and contain dissent but also, unless clearly predicated, implicitly perpetuates the powerlessness and underprivilege of those to whom it is applied. In our enthusiastic and doubtless well-meaning attempts to define and satisfy the 'needs' of our students we can all too easily fail to recognise legitimate aspirations which fall outside or even challenge our prospectus.

Yet for drama-in-education, attempts to satisfy what the teacher has decided are the students' needs have for a long time been seen as emancipatory. According to Bolton, the drama teacher's responsibility is to 'empower' students by setting aside the 'regular teacher/student relationship' for that of 'colleague/artists'[6] and the assumption that the processes of drama-in-education are somehow empowering is widespread within the movement. Under the influence, possibly, of the 'forum theatre' techniques of Augusto Boal where the audience is allowed to direct the events of a play, many writers have assumed that moving from old-fashioned didacticism to a form of pedagogy in which students are prompted to make suggestions indicates 'a transfer of power from teacher to children'.[7] At the same time, the unwillingness of teachers to make judgements about students' work – a negation which has characterised drama-in-education ever since Peter Slade proposed that the teacher's job was to 'guide and nurture' – has helped to foster the impression that students in drama have more control over their learning than in other lessons. As one head of department puts it, 'The very idea of judgement presumes differing status and an unequal distribution of power . . . However, if one works in role then it would appear that the judgemental relationship is obliterated and consequently the status associated with it'.[8] Are we 'really interested in giving children power and responsibility', he asks, 'or are we just pretending?'

The answer must surely be, 'just pretending'. As we have seen in the Seal Wife example, the transfer of power is an illusion; relinquishing his or her control over events is *never* part of the teacher-in-role's plan. Thus, while another enthusiastic worker in role reminds teachers that every group 'will have different needs', he is clear that we owe it to our students to 'structure our work artfully'.

we can plan alternative strategies from which we can choose as necessary. In our ongoing assessment we can then determine whether or not we have achieved our aim. If we have, then we can move on to the next phase of the session. If we have not, then we can reassess and either change our aim or use another strategy.[9]

For all its careful planning – and most possibly *because* of it – drama of this kind is an experience that some actually find 'exclusionary and disempowering'.[10] Whose 'aim', after all, is being pursued here? And how is that young people can be 'empowered' by a process which sets out to give them no particular knowledge or skills but simply to allow them perhaps to 'think with more depth about whatever concerns them'?[11] As one critic puts it, what we are actually seeing here is not so much an exercise in democratic collaboration but 'the will-to-power of the practitioner'.

> drama becomes not about empowerment but about power; role-play itself thrives on conflict, and it is ethically problematic if the main aim is not to explore different cultural, artistic or historical practices, but to colonise the wisdom of the practitioner.[12]

IS EATING PEOPLE WRONG?

Drama-in-education has traditionally put much store on the enacted projection into the lives of others. 'Only in enactment', wrote an early practitioner, 'can we explore what it feels like to be someone else'.[13] But how possible really is it to experience the world as others do through the medium of imaginative empathy? Does closing our eyes and walking across the room, for example, *really* allow us to perceive the world as a blind person does?[14] Can we honestly say that the students in the 'Tomb Drama' described in Appendix 1 have *really* 'experienced the classic confrontation of the traditional tribal leader with members of the community'? These are not trivial questions for a set of educational practices which advertises so confidently its ability to facilitate the brief occupancy by students of other people's moral worlds, and sets out to derive a pedagogy from it.

Social anthropologist Clifford Geertz is clear that we can apprehend such worlds 'at least as well as we apprehend anything else', but maintains that 'we can never apprehend another people's or another period's imagination neatly, as if it were our own'.[15] Instead, he insists that we are inevitably and inextricably bound by the imaginative and moral matrices of our own history and culture, which, while they will intersect in complex ways with other consciousnesses, will never allow the latter to be ours in the sense that we can inhabit them. In this respect, the generalities elided from tribal role-playing may turn out, on closer inspection, to be less like universals and more like very selective projections onto an unfamiliar social structure of the cultural matrices of our own. How much, one wonders, is the so-called authenticity of the Tomb Drama informed by the essences of Hollywood?

Nevertheless, as Geertz points out, the idea of the cultural integrity of 'simpler' peoples is one of 'the most thoroughly entrenched tropes of the liberal imagination'.[16] Thus, when students take on the roles of Native Americans in drama, they are likely to be doing so not so much in order to get to the roots of their imaginative world but to highlight two important principles. The first, that whatever their 'superficial' differences in customs, work patterns and social arrangements, there is a universal 'human-ness' which unites the students with the Native Americans: the second, that viewed from inside (a perspective, it is claimed, made possible through the adoption of role) a seemingly alien culture can both be understood and *justified* in terms of its own internal logic and sense of moral order.

In respect of the first of these principles, our attempts to mine fundamental truths from the superficially more accessible opencast workings of 'simpler' societies rather than from the deep pits of our own may prove more complex than we imagined.

> The image of the past (or the primitive, or the classic, or the exotic) as a source of remedial wisdom, a prosthetic corrective for a damaged spiritual life – an image that has governed a good deal of humanist thought and education – is mischievous because it leads us to expect that our uncertainties will be reduced by access to thought-worlds constructed along lines alternative to our own, when in fact they will be multiplied.[17]

Underlying the second principle is a familiar and understandable reluctance on the part of our post-imperial liberal consciousness to denigrate, or be seeming to patronise, unfamiliar cultural forms. But there is a profound dilemma here. What if the cultural practices portrayed turn out to be horrible? To what extent do we 'respect' a culture that is deeply racist, for example? Are tolerance and understanding really sufficient responses to a society which looks approvingly on female circumcision or acquiesces in the systematic extermination of Jews? What is our response to a religious community which expresses a wish for its women to be specifically excluded from equal opportunities legislation? Are our strong feminist and anti-racist convictions simply to be abandoned as we cross national or even local boundaries?

Written accounts suggest that in practice these difficult questions are rarely addressed in the drama class. As we have seen, the primitivism most commonly evoked is of a strictly acceptable kind, 'noble savagery' at its best; students line up solemnly to honour the tribe's dead or to choose a new chief. The tenets of liberalism are rarely challenged.

The Weismullerian tribalism of these formulaic rituals is probably harmless enough, so long as no great moral or anthropological conclusions are drawn from it. Also, to draw attention to the limits of liberal humanism in this context is by no means to deny its values, or its importance as a concept in the educational processes of a humane society. However, we should not forget the moral limitations of its comfortable consensus-seeking, and be clear that tolerance and understanding can be both a justification for oppression, on the one hand, and a recipe for feebleness, on the other. If drama and the other arts are to have a liberating and empowering social function, then we will have to look beyond the simple assertion of the 'self-evident' truths of liberal individualism and examine more closely the complex relationship between culture and power in our society.

SINGING BETTER SONGS

The coupling of 'needs' to the idea of the moral integrity of cultural groups has led to the establishment of a simple but influential formula. This tells us first that we have an obligation to respect *ipso facto* the values, belief systems and cultural expression of any given community or cultural group. Then, by designating the furtherance of these values, beliefs and expressive forms as a 'need' (consequent upon a community simply *having* particular ideas and customs), any attempt to disseminate alternative cultural values among members of this community can be dismissed at best as an irrelevance and at worst as an unjustifiable imposition. Applying this formula, a manifesto published by the National Association for the Teaching of Drama in the 1980s argues for 'a system of education that operates from within the community and is not imposed from outside. It needs to be based upon the needs of the immediate community, concerned with that community's needs and future development'.[18]

This pious, although by no means uncommon, view is not only flawed in its casual and unpredicated use of 'need', but also because it seems not to recognise the community's place in a wider social and cultural context. In a commendable desire to enfranchise groups presently alienated from the formal and informal hierarchies of the state, conclusions of this kind are drawn from a very narrow analysis of group identity and esteem. The limitations of such an approach, which assumes, first, that a 'community' is a consensual entity existing within fixed boundaries, second, that its 'needs' are unambiguous and readily identified, and third, that they can be pursued in isolation from the interests of the dominant culture, are not difficult to see. In the context of a multi-racial society, for example, it is a perspective which 'reflects a white view of black cultures as homogeneous, static, conflict-free, exotic', and 'ignores the power relations between white and black people, both in history and the present'.[19]

While education clearly has an important function in fostering what David Hargreaves has called the 'dignity and solidarity' of communities (of which, incidentally, the school itself is one), to see schools as only, or even primarily, serving this end, is to subscribe to a distinctly cross-eyed view of culture. To propose that different groups in our society (Afro-Caribbean children, Bangladeshi young women, white working-class boys – however one chooses to draw the divide) should be educated solely according to their ascribed cultural 'needs' is at best to enter into an organisational nightmare, and at worst to practise, as Hargreaves points out, a form of 'educational apartheid'.

> an exclusive focus on community regeneration in deprived areas distracts attention away from national regeneration. A community education which loses sight of the nation as a whole as a community is not worthy of its name and can justifiably be condemned as parochial.[20]

In making claims on the 'common-sense curriculum', drama-in-education has deliberately set out to engage with the localised experience of specific groups of students. Lacking any really satisfactory *critical* dimension, however, it has at the same time denied itself access to culturally endowed systems of judgement, and thus to the means whereby this strictly local experience may be held up against other wisdoms. The 'basic needs of the *majority* of young people (who truly have the *greatest* needs)', wrote a drama adviser in the 1980s, 'must be the baseline for curriculum planning'.[21]

We should beware of mistaking this 'common-sense curriculum' for the 'really useful knowledge' of the dissenting tradition. As Gramsci has taught us, the whole idea of 'common sense' is elusive and deceptive, made up as likely of shared prejudice and ignorance as of collective sagacity; for Bertrand Russell, common sense was 'the metaphysics of savages'. The Black Paper assaults on education might be said to have been popular, not because they were presented as a series of carefully argued propositions, but precisely because, with their emphasis on standards, basic skills, freedom of choice, and so on, they appealed to 'common sense'. Who could reasonably oppose these principles? The point about 'really useful knowledge' is that it is jealously guarded, often far from obvious, and rarely displayed in the columns of the *Sun* or the *Daily Mail* or in the popular discourses of Coronation Street or Albert Square. Politics, sociology and philosophy, those disciplines at the intellectual core of moral understanding and social action are significantly absent from the 'common-sense curriculum'.

There is a real danger that in our well-intentioned efforts to respond to the claims of students' sub-culture (their knowledge), we effectively deny them the knowledge through which they can effect change (our knowledge). Under such a scheme, we go to *Hamlet* at the Royal National Theatre while they must be content with role-playing and improvisation, not only because we have decided that these latter activities are more relevant to their needs, but also because professionally we are not prepared to make qualitative judgements between the two experiences. Who are we (the argument goes) to impose our middle-class values on working-class students, when their needs are so patently different? There is more than a hint of hypocrisy in this negation. In reality, of course, few of us are not disposed to pass critical comments on the dramas we see outside the classroom, and I suspect, if asked, most drama teachers would be able to tell you who was 'good' at drama in their classes. The anxiety to protect students' work from judgement is rarely comprehensive.

This reluctance to admit the wider culture as a frame of critical reference has led some in the direction of a rejection of traditional forms altogether. While it could be argued that this represents a recognition of the class-based, male-orientated domination of certain well-defined cultural forms, mounting a challenge to them will require active engagement with the values of that hegemony and its vehicles rather than a simple denial of the iconography. Furthermore, it is not clear that the art of the past and its present-day derivatives, however superficially 'elitist', can so simply be dismissed on ideological grounds. To do so assumes the existence and recognition of an emergent alternative which is able in superior ways to engage with our sense of presence. Marxist critic Georg Lukács surely has a point when he argues that a social class only thinking 'thoughts imputable to it' will be 'doomed to play a subordinate role' unless it can strike at the heart of 'the totality of existing society'.[22] Or, as poet and educationalist Peter Abbs puts it, we need access

> to both piety before ancestors (so that we are ready to learn from them) and that subverting spirit which seeks to challenge, to retell, to ask again. For it is in this endless dialectic that education, both aesthetic and critical, takes place; and it is our task as teachers to keep it alive.[23]

If, as teachers, we really want to enfranchise all our students, whatever their race, gender or social identity, then we surely have a responsibility to equip them with the means to interpret and appropriate the world in which they live *in the widest possible context*. The exclusivity of certain cultural forms will only be perpetuated and reinforced so long as we continue to assert, in a patronising kind of way, that there are special kinds of cultural experience and knowledge which we have pronounced appropriate for young people, and which they can somehow come 'authentically to know' through a set of intuitive, improvisatory processes with no reference to the lexicon of the wider culture. To deny young people critical access to tradition in the name of a specious identification of 'need' and the phantasm of 'empowerment' is to remove them even further from meaningful access to the hierarchies of control.

For drama teachers, establishing such a context will involve opening up classes to dramatic representations of all kinds – to dramas from the theatre and the street, to the popular narratives of the television screen. It will mean, in other words, locating drama education for the first time within a coherent, discipline-based epistemology.

A new framework for what teachers actually do in their lessons which at the same time opens doors in this way to the possibility of a multiplicity of different practices, must make sense not only to teachers, both of drama and the other arts, but also to headteachers and curriculum managers who will want to be reassured that precious teaching time is being wisely spent. As for the students themselves, if they are to be freed to develop as independent learners, the culture of dependency fostered by dramatic pedagogy – in which only the teacher knows the secret of where the class is being led and students are supposed to learn 'without realising it' – must be broken and replaced with openly shared programmes of study within which students are encouraged to take genuine responsibility for their progress.

In the remaining four chapters, I shall attempt to sketch out such a framework. Although doubtless a heretical project for some, my modest hope is that for the majority, all those fine teachers that is, who work day in and day out to keep the flame of drama burning and yet who have been persuaded to measure what they do against the ordinance of a self-appointed ministry and have, by specious comparison, been found wanting, a theory of dramatic art will help them a little in their continuing efforts to maintain and develop the presence of drama in schools.

PART III

TOWARDS DRAMATIC ART

9

PRACTICAL AESTHETICS AND DRAMATIC ART

> Who benefits from levelling attacks on the canon? Certainly not the disad-
> vantaged person or class, whose history, if you bother to read it, is full of
> evidence that popular resistance to injustice has always derived immense
> benefits from literature and culture in general, and very few from invidious
> distinctions made between ruling-class and subservient cultures.
>
> (Edward Said, on the culture wars in the United States, 1993)[1]

ART AND IDEOLOGY

Surely the most obvious case for the inclusion of drama in the school
curriculum rests on the publicly shared understanding that dramatic art
is, *ipso facto*, a member of the arts community. It would be hard, in other
words, to argue for a balanced arts curriculum in which drama did not
figure. I shall argue in this final section that this membership brings with
it a quite distinct contribution to the education of young people, not
because drama is especially therapeutic or utilitarian, but because it has
manifestly a central place in our social consciousness.

If the case for drama in our schools is to be made in this way, we shall
require an aesthetic theory freed from the psychology of individuals
which is capable of giving us an account both of dramatic art's critical
place in culture and history and of the ways in which drama can reflect
and articulate the ever-changing paradoxes of our common experience.

Previous chapters have proffered many examples of the way in which
the idea of the 'aesthetic' has gained its affirmative power in the modern
world by contrasting itself with the 'de-humanising' materialism of a
prevailing technocracy. Ever since Matthew Arnold gallantly wrote about
culture as 'Sweetness and Light',[2] the imaginative world of the spirit, the
'aesthetic domain', has been a cross of sensibility held out before the
bloodthirsty jaws of mass production and consumption. This resistance
has meant that art and thinking about art have been separated by ever
more absolute abstraction from the social processes within which they are
contained. For Raymond Williams, aesthetic theory has been 'the main

instrument of this evasion', giving us a picture of art-as-medicine in a sick and alienating social world.[3] Hence the emphasis placed by arts educators on 'creativity' as an idealised form of production dislocated from any idea of aim or social function, and 'aesthetic awareness' as unconscious and de-contextualised consumption. These ideas, as we have seen, were the essential props of the post-war arts education project.

If we are to put together a serviceable aesthetic which acknowledges the centrality of history and culture, then regarding art as opposed and somehow superior to the vulgar uncertainties of contemporary experience is not a good way to start. Not only does such a view misrepresent the diverse relationships we actually have with art (we may, for example, make our living by it) but its posture of detachment does not remotely correspond to the reality of artistic production and reception. We can only meaningfully 'create' within the critical parameters of a culture, we can only be 'aware' of what our historical moment and social conditions have on offer. The artist's roots in and engagement with his or her social and historical circumstances are inescapable.

In this respect, we may agree with Karl Marx that it is not 'the consciousness of men that determines their being', but rather 'their social being that determines their consciousness'.[4] Aesthetics, religion, law, politics and ethics all constitute a 'social mentality', or 'ideology', which, according to Marxist theory, is derived from the material relations of production, society's economic base. Ideology in this sense should not be mistaken for those dogmatic prescriptions set up and assaulted by Eysenck, Polanyi and others. It is better understood as that rag-bag of values, metaphors, beliefs and ideas at the centre of our social consciousness, through which we perceive and interpret the world, and which is eventually absorbed into the vernacular of a society as its 'common sense'. Because ideology amounts to nothing less than the way we think about the world and form the grounds for our evaluative judgements, the relationship between art and ideology is a central question.

Antonio Gramsci believed that it is always in the interests of a dominant social class to establish ideological hegemony, that is, to ensure that its own way of thinking about the world is the one most widely held among the population as a whole. The achievement of hegemony would have the effect of limiting the amount of coercion necessary to maintain order by disguising as 'natural' the particular forms of a class's historical advantages and legitimating them as 'common sense'. [5] History offers us many examples of how religious belief has been exploited to maintain hereditary power structures in just this way. By persuading most of the people of Europe for centuries that its representatives had power over their prospects in the eternal afterlife, the Roman Catholic Church must surely have been one of the most effective manipulators of common sense ever. In modern times ideological control has been attempted overtly by propaganda, as in Germany in the 1930s, and more subtly and unobtrusively through the everyday institutions of the state and its dependencies such as education and the media. No-one can surely doubt the extent to which the Conservative government of the 1980s attempted to change the way people in Britain *thought* about such controversial issues as the privatisation of state assets and the re-introduction of selective schools.

Under these forms of ideological acquiescence, according to some Marxist critics, art becomes simply an agent of this hegemony, another 'element in that complex structure of social perception which ensures that the situation in which one class has power over the others is either seen by most members of the society as "natural", or not seen at all'.[6] The paintings, books and dramas of previous ages are thus reduced to little more than expressions of past class-dominated ideologies, such as those represented by the Court, the Church, the State, the market, and so on. As historical artefacts they may have a place in museums or (suitably contextualised) in history books, but any resonances they may still have for us are dismissed as straightforwardly delusory, indications of our own submission to the same 'false consciousness'.

Such a simple scheme of things, however, is deficient to the extent that it can offer no explanation of art's often subversive role or of the ideological challenge issued to their societies by many painters and writers. Georg Büchner's play, *Woyzeck*, for a not exactly random example, uncompleted at his death in 1837, can hardly be said to embody in its staccato scenes, its wild and disturbing caricatures and its working-class anti-hero, the confident bourgeois consciousness of its time, in either form or content. Contemporary examples of the challenges mounted to the hegemony by theatre artists are plentiful, from Julian Beck's Living Theatre of the 1970s to the fierce and persistent rejection of capitalist values by playwrights like Edward Bond. And we should not forget that even the great religious cycles of the Middle Ages were cast out into the town squares by the priests as soon as their rough but popular secularity began to undermine the dignity of the Church.

At this point, the aesthetic idealists would doubtless assert that this is sufficient to refute the argument altogether. For them, Büchner's class formation and his place in history can simply be discounted as of no significance in discussions about his art. As a playwright in pursuit of 'eternal values', they might say, nineteenth-century society must be blamed for not recognising the expression of these values in his work. Likewise, the medieval bishops were simply blind to the earthy naturalism, the 'universal humanity' of the mysteries; to speak in terms of class-based ideological conspiracies is to fail to see how art transcends the prejudices of the historical moment.

Marxist writers, of course, refuse to accept this, but they are faced with

105

a problem. By maintaining that art is not accurately described in these metaphysical terms, and yet at the same time having to admit that it cannot be considered as straightforwardly the reflection of a dominant ideology, then art's relationship to the way we think and feel about the world has to be more complex. The French theorist Louis Althusser proposes that we can resolve this dilemma by understanding the relationship between art and ideology as intrinsically dialectical. Instead of the former being regarded simply as a reflection of the latter, the two should be seen as dialectically linked. Ideology, that collection of signs representing, 'what it feels like to live in particular conditions, rather than a conceptual analysis of those conditions', has art both in its service *and* as its unerring critic. Or, put another way, while critically reflective of our experience, art 'is held within ideology, but also manages to distance itself from it, to the point where it permits us to "feel" and "perceive" the ideology from which it springs'.[7]

The champions of private experience might again argue that this validates their position. Althusser's 'feeling and perceiving' is no more than that personal awareness of the universal which must, by their account, always be superior to the ideological or material. They have a point. If the fault of psychological accounts of art, with their emphasis on the subjective, the spontaneous and the transcendent, is that they offer no analysis of the social and historical forms within which art is created and invested with meaning, then the weakness of the purely materialist and analytic alternative is that it fails to give an account of 'what is actually being lived' in its attempts to describe 'what is thought is being lived'.[8] As a result of this neglect, materialism unwittingly further encourages the disconnection of the personal from the social that it sets out to refute. Its emphasis on the collective and the historical leaves the field of the individual, private response open to those who would wish to elevate such experiences to a level of superior truth and reality. Children's dramatic play, for example, with its beguiling sincerity and apparent structural anarchy, cries out its appeal to the present and the immediate. Small wonder that drama teachers have been so easily able to persuade themselves that they are dealing with a process with powers of intervention profoundly greater than those of mere intellection, or that they hold in such esteem those of their number whose arguments take the form of appeals to experience, personal knowing and the immediacy of feeling.

These protests against the explicit, the formal and the analytic draw some of their inspiration from the perception that our experience, *while we are actually experiencing it,* cannot be reduced to the 'fixed forms' of class or ideological analysis, but is simply spontaneously 'felt'. Yet as Wittgenstein has taught us, it is difficult to see how experience can even be recognised as experience outside the context of the language which articulates it. Kant, too, famously postulated that there can be no percepts without the concepts to make sense of them, and Sartre pointed out that even the spontaneous experience of fear is dependent on our at some time having perceived the fearsome propensity of some specific object.[9] Despite their very different projects, all three philosophers were clear that the immediate readings which constitute our experiencing – 'the experienced tensions, shifts, and uncertainties, the intricate forms of unevenness and confusion'[10] – cannot simply be abstracted from our social consciousness, and recast in the mystifying language of the unconscious, the subjective, and the symbolic; in an important sense, *we learn to know what to feel*. While they live in the present our sensations may indeed defy the forms and structures through which we familiarly interpret and articulate experience, but as they slip inevitably into the past they gather coherence within subsequently emergent forms which they themselves help to shape. What we have here is rather a form of *practical consciousness*, where within the context of our ordinary lives deeply felt appeals to the moral imagination form a continuing dialectic between received understandings and contemporary experience. 'Practical consciousness is almost always different from official consciousness. . . . It is a kind of feeling and thinking which is indeed social and material, but each in an embryonic phase before it can become fully articulated and defined exchange.'[11]

Raymond Williams has called the sum of this practical consciousness, as it is manifest within a culture, and supremely in its art, at a particular historical moment, a 'structure of feeling'. That is to say, that tension which exists between formal ideology, as represented by the institutions of a society, to which its members will to a greater or lesser extent subscribe, and the meanings and values which constitute their lived experience. Or, in Williams' words, 'the area of interaction between the official consciousness of an epoch, codified in its doctrines and legislation, and the whole process of living its consequences'.[12]

> not feelings against thought, but thought as felt and feeling as thought: practical consciousness of a present kind, in a living and interrelating continuity . . . Yet we are also defining a social experience which is still *in process*, often indeed not yet recognisable as social but taken to be private, idiosyncratic, and even isolating, but which in analysis (though rarely otherwise) has its emergent, connecting, and dominant characteristics, indeed its specific hierarchies. These are often more recognisable at a later stage, when they have been (as often happens) formalised, classified, and in many cases built into institutions and formations. By that time the case is different; a new structure of feeling will usually have begun to form, in the true social present.[13]

By linking the ideological forms of society with the complex nuances of our immediate, lived perceptions in this way, it is possible to reclaim art for history and culture with an account of its unique antagonistic presence within our social consciousness which needs no resort to 'aesthetic meaning', or 'feeling form', or 'subjective knowing', or any other form of speculative introspection. For it is here, in this space between our experience and our ability formally to articulate it, that art engages and challenges us. Here, in this grounded aesthetic,[14] occurs that 'rightness', that 'knowing in my bones', that 'sensing as significant', which writers on drama-in-education have identified as being so important. As I have suggested elsewhere, art engages and moves us because it is rooted in the sensibility of culture and because that sensibility is itself informed by the shadows and traces of residual belief inherited by the very language we speak and through which we make ourselves understood.[15]

The idea of art as commensurate with structures of feeling, engaging simultaneously with the content and form of dominant ideologies and with our practical consciousness, gives us the necessary aesthetic foundation for a theory of dramatic art.

ACTORS, AUDIENCES AND TEXTS

Dramatic art is strictly non-sectarian. It is a commodious enough category to embrace not only the orthodox practices of drama-in-education – the spontaneous improvisations and directed role-playing that we have seen up until now – but all those other manifestations of drama in our schools too. The scorned but ever resilient school play will have a place here as will the theatre visit and the examination class. This eclectic approach will certainly mean burying for ever that damaging misrepresentation of Peter Slade's which sought to distinguish between the drama of the child and the drama of the actor. Dramatic art makes no conceptual distinction between the child acting in the classroom and the actor on the stage of the theatre for each is taking part in a drama, each implicitly presupposes the existence of performer and audience. While for the actor in the theatre that audience (one would hope) will be a very real one, the solitary child's make-believe play is likely to require only imaginary watchers. In the drama class, critical observers and listeners are always present, even if they too are participants. Actors and audiences are key components of dramatic art.

Also, although it is true that both actor and child here are involved in a process, the outcome of that process is itself inescapably a product. In more complex forms of drama making, such as the performance of a play in a theatre, many participants with a wide range of specialist skills may contribute to what we commonly know as the *production process*. But classroom improvisations also involve a production process, even though, of course, there may never be a formal, enacted presentation. Students experiment with a theme, they rehearse, reject some aspects, try again, abandon the idea. The teacher may take on a role and direct the action, the drama moves forward. Like the artist beginning a painting or the writer a novel, the possibility of arrival is implicit in the very act of starting the journey.

We may see the dramatic product, the outcome, however provisional, of the production process, as a form of enacted *text*. Drama teachers are used to employing the word 'text' to denote the script of a play, or to differentiate between improvisation and 'text work'. I use it here, however, in the way that it is employed by teachers in media education – to cover any form of active discourse or performance which can be read and interpreted by watchers; borrowing from Roland Barthes, the dramatic text 'is experienced only in an activity of production'.[16] By this simple device, not only is the centrality of *what* is practically made in drama established but we at last have the means of acknowledging that complex 'weave of signifiers' which constitutes a dramatic performance. Design, background sound, the organisation of characters within the performance space, light and shadow – all these and a multitude of other factors *signify* a performance. The audience for dramatic art is thus not restricted to the hunt for a pre-determined range of 'meanings' in fragments of spontaneous naturalism, but, like Barthes' 'passably empty subject', is open to perceive altogether more subtle and unpredictable disseminations.

> multiple, irreducible, coming from a disconnected, heterogeneous variety of substances and perspectives: lights, colours, vegetation, heat, air, slender explosions of noises, scant cries of birds, children's voices from over on the other side, passages, gestures, clothes of inhabitants near or far away. All these *incidents* are half identifiable: they come from codes which are known but their combination is unique. . . . So the Text.[17]

The idea of the dramatic text as metonymic in this way releases us from the iron grip of spontaneity and makes it possible for students to deconstruct and reconstruct, interpret and clarify, edit and change.

Production, then, is the *making* and *performing* of the dramatic text, by writing, improvising, acting or role-playing. It has a meaningful application well beyond the school, of course, but for our purposes it is recognisably what students do in their drama lessons most of the time. In that context it extends as a category from the construction of make-believe play by infants in the play corner, through the making of more formal improvisations or scripted performances at primary and then secondary level, to devised productions and examination assessment pieces. At its most sophisticated, production may also involve a range of non-acting skills such as lighting, stage-management or administration.

The audience, so neglected by drama-in-education, is fundamental to dramatic art. Watching and listening to the dramatic text in performance and *responding* to it are not secondary activities but ones without which there would be little purpose in most of the world's drama. In the educational context, it is the role of the audience, however informally constituted (it may consist only of the teacher or a handful of students), to subject a dramatic text in performance to interpretation and analysis. This form of critical interpretation will be familiar to teachers who invite discussion after a visit to the theatre; it is extended here to cover all the debate that goes on outside the fiction of dramatic text itself, from the critical comments of infants – 'No, you wear the hat' – to the teasing out of ideas in the aftermath of role-playing, a teacher's comments in response to a student improvisation, and group and individual evaluation at all levels.[18]

CULTURAL NARRATIVES

This model of making, performing and responding gives us a simple framework for understanding dramatic art in education and helps us to look afresh at questions of form and content. Under such a scheme, artistic form is no longer understood as a latent, metaphysical property of our dialogue with content, 'sensed as appropriate', but in terms of its structural and ideological relationship to the readings it bears. Brecht's deliberately antagonistic use of form inappropriately, as in the employment of the sentimental ballad to tell stories of economic exploitation, provides a familiar demonstration of the way these two fundamental aspects of drama can serve to elucidate each other. In the drama lesson, this understanding should inform work in all three areas of the framework, demanding an attention to content in the face of an over-emphasis on form (when empty routines or impersonations dominate the work, for example) and to form where the pursuit of content has reduced the drama to mere debate (if, say, a preoccupation with discussions and meetings 'in-role' is inhibiting the production process).

I have suggested that for art to be truly resonant, then it must both engage us with a sense of recognition and challenge us with the revelation of the new. Thus, simply to put students through their theatrical paces, demonstrating, shall we say, the wonders of Shakespeare or the correct way to move on a rake, may be regarded as little more than the transmission of received opinion and residual form (the stubborn persistence of the elocution lesson and the private drama class bears witness to the continuing allure of this particular brand of social induction). Such approaches actively reinforce existing or past practices. At best, they are reflective in an entirely non-critical sense; at worst, they amount to an attempt to keep alive forms which have long since passed from the living consciousness of the culture.

If it is not the aim of dramatic art to reproduce uncritically dominant and residual dramatic forms, then neither should its province be drama with an overt commitment to social transformation. The idealistic picture we have seen of an alliance of pupils and teachers committed to emancipation-through-drama overthrowing the restricting 'oppressions' of bourgeois society, is the product of wishful thinking based upon a mistaken view of the role of art in social and economic change. If Marx and others are right, then although the art which evokes the most profound meanings for a society must be both reflective and critical of that culture, it cannot ever be historically in advance of the economic circumstances within which it is necessarily contained. Theatre may well, and in unique ways, critically articulate for us previously hidden or incoherent cultural shifts already in progress, stimulating our practical consciousness, but it is ill equipped to be the sole inspiration for insurrection. In the end, the seditious undertones of Beaumarchais's *Le Marriage de Figaro*, suppressed by Parisian censors until 1784, pale retrospectively into puzzling insignificance against the conflagration which followed, and which the play may have presaged but hardly could be said to have caused. By the same token, attempts to resuscitate the tradition of agitprop theatre in the service of a variety of just causes, have failed precisely because its exponents have not grasped that agitation/propaganda is a form of drama dependent upon a widely held revolutionary consciousness, present in post-First World War Europe and in late eighteenth-century Paris, but notably absent from the consciousness of Britain in the 1980s and 1990s.

Also, such a view fails to take account of the way theatrical forms and narratives from the past can, in complex ways, continue to provide us with paradigms against which our lives are sorted, judged and given meaning. To speak of them as irrelevant or elitist is to misunderstand how, in many cases, they have become woven into that mesh of communally held meanings without which we would find it impossible to make sense of our world at all. Shakespeare, for example, in his time afloat on the full flood tide of English nationalism at the conjunction of the economic and ideological revolutions of the Reformation and the Renaissance, was highly successful in critically reflecting the diverse resonances of that tide and that conjunction. In doing so, not only did he capture the imaginations of his contemporaries, but he also succeeded in articulating the experience of subsequent generations in whose histories the sounds of those material and cultural collisions still reverberate. At the same time, the experience of those generations was itself perceived through structures of feeling evoked by a specific historical conscious-ness, a consciousness which Shakespeare, among others, helped to form.

If drama teachers are to be serious egalitarians then they must give their pupils access to the narratives of this historical consciousness, for these stories are the key to understanding, articulating and challenging the circumstances of their material and moral lives. There must be a place within dramatic art, in other words, for the teaching of *dramatic literacy*.[19] Of course, in a culture itself composed of 'multi-cultures' these narratives will themselves reflect and celebrate a diversity of traditions within the context of society as a whole; I shall have more to say about this later.

One consequence of the introduction of the idea of dramatic literacy will be that the 'moment of significance', previously born 'sponta-neously' from hours of workshop preparation, can now simply be turned to in the cultural lexicon where it is likely to be found expressed with infinitely more acuity. The stylistic perfection of love expressed through the sonnet Romeo and Juliet share on their first meeting, or the fumbling silences as Lopakhin takes his leave of Varya in *The Cherry Orchard*, are just random examples of the kind of density of human experience collected within our dramatic history whose range and depth of meaning leave even the most accomplished role-playing far behind. As an early critic of drama-in-education noted, the difference between the death of Caesar in Shakespeare's play and a 'killing' in a classroom improvisation is not that one 'comes from the child' and the other is 'literary'. 'Both use an imposed, inherited language. Both are *re*-created by the child . . . the essential difference lies in the moral universe which the play creates; the balance of praise and blame, guilt and innocence, freedom and fatality.'[20]

In reality, the uncritical exclusivity of certain cultural forms is perpetu-ated and reinforced if drama teachers offer their classes only a restricted diet of self-orientated, intuitive, improvisatory exercises, while reserving for themselves the satisfactions of traditional theatre-going. We should remember the teacher Vesovchikov in Brecht's play, *The Mother*. Well-meaning but hopelessly self-regarding, a prototypical progressivist, Vesovchikov's familiarity with the formal knowledge of his culture traps him into devaluing it, forgetting its crucial importance to the workers he is teaching and who must acquire it for the revolution that is about to come. 'Books are nonsense', he proclaims to his class: 'Men are only made worse by them. A simple peasant is a better human being for that reason alone, that he hasn't been spoiled by civilisation. . . . Knowledge doesn't help, you know. It's kindness that helps.'

The old woman, Vlasova, however, struggling with her chalk and slate, is in no doubt as to the value of the literacy which he has, but which she and her comrades lack. She snaps back at him, 'You give us your knowledge then, if you don't need it.'[21] Here the dramatist manages to gather together in one gestic moment the fragmented meanings of a particular historical struggle. It is truly a 'moment of significance', for it not only offers us that special insight into social and political content that only the metaphors of art can bring, powerfully illustrating, in this case, the argument about knowledge, but it also demonstrates how mistaken a view it is to dismiss our dramatic culture as of only marginal relevance to our students. After all, their struggle is Vlasova's struggle, if only they can realise it.

10

THE DRAMATISED SOCIETY

I think there is no world *without* theatre . . . our society is absolutely saturated with drama.

(Edward Bond 1996)[1]

ON THE STAGE OF LIFE

I have argued that art engages with our practical consciousness and articulates structures of feeling in ways prior to or beyond the reach of other forms of discourse. Drama is a 'learning medium' to the extent that *all* art is edifying in this way. We may therefore regard dramatic art not so much as another way of knowing, but rather as a way of participating in dramatic conversations which can lead to new perceptions, *to us making better sense of things*.

Under the scheme proposed in the last chapter, these perceptions are likely to be gained by students at two levels. First, through the *making* and *performing* of their own dramas, where students shape dramatic texts which express the consciousness of their lived present within the accessible context of familiar (though necessarily developing) cultural forms, and second, through the *performing* of other people's dramas, where existing dramatic texts provide access to past structures of feeling now recognisably incorporated in dominant or emergent ideologies within the culture. Simultaneously, a continuing process of interpretation and appraisal by students *responding* to what they see and hear means that dramatic art has the potential for critical articulations, both of the felt, social present, and of the ideological forms embedded in that present.

The reason that dramatic articulations of this kind are likely to be particularly useful to us in making better sense of things is not because they allow us mysterious access to the essence of things, but because dramatisation has always been a characterising feature of cultural life. Dramatic forms are buried within the assumptions we make about ourselves and frame the way we perceive the world. Four hundred years ago the Elizabethans attended the theatre to explore the possibilities of

114

human action in a divinely ordered universe and saw society as a stage with men and women actors upon it.[2] Today, the pervasive presence of television in modern society has meant that we now have access to drama in ways the Elizabethans would never have dreamed possible. Drama has become built into the rhythms of our everyday lives, so that we have become the consumers of huge numbers of electronically reproduced dramatic fictions, fictions which pervade our consciousness and whose moral narratives shape how we think. Any casual observation of dramatic improvisation in school will quickly reveal the extent to which pupils have absorbed the form and vocabulary of the dramatisations presented to them by television.[3]

I would suggest that such incessant exposure to dramatic representation marks our society out as one which is dramatised in very particular ways. First, it is clear that not only has spectating become habitual but that the relationship of the objects of our spectatorship to our understanding of reality has become increasingly ambiguous. As atomised individuals in a culture where representations of political action are electronically reproduced as a series of diverting images while at the same time the characters in soap operas are flesh and blood to significant numbers of viewers, we live in a world where reality can quickly become indistinguishable from dramatic fiction. This opaqueness is well illustrated by an example from the 1988 United States presidential campaign when American television ran a dramatic mini-series about a fictional contender in which some of the real candidates took part. Distinctions between truth and myth, between fact and value, become blurred to the point of dissolution, as we watch film actors cast themselves as presidents, and prime ministers take on roles in patriotic melodramas.[4]

But the pattern of cultural dramatisation goes even deeper than this. I have proposed that as individuals we are committed to a complex network of social relationships taking place against a background of culture and history. We may describe this network as itself a form of dramatic text, in this case, one which enables us to participate intelligibly in social life and against which our participations may be measured. Although, in this sense, we are still actors on the stage of life, unlike the Elizabethans, because of our extensive exposure to dramatised representations of reality, when we try to make sense of our actions we do so with a consciousness which is *itself* dramatised.

The specific conventions of this particular dramatisation – a country, a society, a period of history, a crisis of civilisation; these conventions are not abstract. They are profoundly worked and reworked in our actual living relationships. They are our ways of seeing and knowing, which every day we put into practice, and

115

while the conventions hold, while the relationships hold, most practice confirms them. [5]

We are, so to speak, grounded in a complex matrix of meanings over which we have only intermittent control, but which are nevertheless embodied in social action which we can recognise and understand, and which will make pressing claims to determine who we think we are and how we think we should act. This matrix – as it is manifest in action requiring the acknowledgement of conventions, the adoption of roles and the recognition of characters – can be seen to be fundamentally dramatic in form, presaging intelligibility as a function of the distance between actor and meaning. As we watch and participate, we ask ourselves, 'What does this mean?', or more precisely, 'What drama am I in here?'

ROLES AND CHARACTERS

These days we are all familiar with the idea that participation in social life may be regarded as a matter of playing different roles and we have seen here how the conception of role as a representation of human action and motivation has sustained theories of drama-in-education for many years. For those concerned to turn this proposition into a science of human behaviour, most notably the American ethnomethodologists, all human encounters can be categorised as real-life performances in which we attempt to be effective within a given social 'scene'. In seeking success within these improvisations our aim is always to adjust our performance so that we remain in control of the situation. Erving Goffman has called this process of social manipulation, 'Impression Management'.[6] In Goffman's role-playing social world, the only measure of value in human actions is apparent appropriateness, and our only obligation is to observe the moral demands customarily associated with a chosen social role. The goal of the role-player is thus simply effectiveness, success nothing but what passes for success.

> Society is organised on the principle that any individual who possesses certain social characteristics has a moral right to expect that others will value and treat him in an appropriate way. Connected with this principle is a second, namely that an individual . . . ought in fact to be what he claims to be. In consequence, when an individual projects a definition of the situation and thereby makes an implicit or explicit claim to be a person of a particular kind, he automatically exerts a moral demand upon the others. . . . The others find, then, that the individual has informed them as to what is and as to what they ought to see as the 'is'.[7]

It is difficult not to recognise in this account the familiar processes of drama-in-education. Goffman's contention gives us perhaps the clearest description yet of how the power structures of certain kinds of drama lesson are worked out. As we saw in the Seal Wife drama, the 'teacher-in-role' projects a 'definition of the situation' in just this way, and as a consequence is able to exert a similar 'moral demand' on the other participants. He or she informs them of 'what they ought to see as the "is"' and their degree of acquiescence in this picture then becomes the measure of their success in drama.

Despite the morally impoverished picture of drama painted by its theories, ethnomethodology was increasingly called upon to validate the role-playing processes of drama-in-education. In 1988, Gavin Bolton, speaking from what he regarded as 'an ethnomethodological perspective', claimed that drama was essentially 'a managed accomplishment'.[8] One reason that Goffman's thesis was so attractive to the Romantic intuitionists of drama-in-education, was because it implicitly assumes the prior existence of an interior self upon which roles are superimposed. Under Goffman, the essential self of drama-in-education becomes an impresario of appearance. But the question raised in Chapter 5 still remains: How is this manipulating self constituted? My argument here is that the self is made by the dramatisations within which it is contained, that the dramas we enact demonstrate us rather than conceal us. We do not look *through* the role-playing to the true self behind it, but rather *at* the performances themselves. The acts which constitute our identity, including our gender characteristics, as feminist critic Judith Butler points out, are *performative*.

> if gender attributes and acts, the various ways in which a body shows or produced its cultural signification, are performative, then there is no pre-existing identity by which an act or attribute might be measured . . . As a consequence, gender cannot be understood as a *role* which either expresses or disguises an interior 'self', whether that 'self' is conceived as sexed or not.[9]

Certainly, if Goffman's thesis is right, and the human agent is accurately represented as little more than a role-player struggling to effect his or her will in a world defined by a continually changing matrix of performances, then it can make no sense to speak of the existence of any categorically sustainable theory of value. Indeed, the most accomplished 'impression manager' in today's society might be said to be the confidence trickster, whose very livelihood is dependent upon being able to project a deceptive image to potential victims, a point vividly, if unwittingly, demonstrated by the assessment scheme illustrated in Chapter 2. In the words of philosopher Alasdair MacIntyre,

Goffman's social world is empty of objective standards of achievement; it is so defined that there is no cultural or social space from which appeal to such standards could be made . . . imputations of merit are themselves part of the contrived social reality whose function is to aid or to contain some striving, role-playing will. Goffman's is a sociology which by intention deflates the pretensions of appearance to be anything more than appearance.[10]

For these reasons, and despite their hold on the popular imagination, Goffman's ethically disconnected role-players give us only a very partial account of our engagement in the dramatised society. The truth is that we do not always simply seek to be effective. We may choose to act on the basis of our convictions, quite possibly to our own immediate material disadvantage. We may do things, quite simply, because we know them to be right. Where do these strongly held beliefs come from? Also, if, as Butler suggests, our identities are performative, then what is the source of these performances? What informs the texts that we make as we move about the world? Role-playing can give us no answer to these important questions. To complete our map we will require a model of social agency which will enable us to regain a sense of active moral life as something more than the competition between the wills and preferences of role-playing individuals.

I propose that the key to that model lies in the idea of *character*, for it is in character that we both anchor ourselves morally and find the scripts for our performative acts. The distinction I want to make between role and character within the dramatised society can be seen most easily when we turn to the theatre to look at the stock characters of pre-naturalistic drama. In the European tradition, the character types of the comedy are conventionally traced back to late Greek and early Roman theatre, and probably reach their most refined form in the *soggetti* of the *commedia dell'arte* in the seventeenth and eighteenth centuries. Their traces still appear in popular pantomime. Stock characters remain the heartbeat of most world drama, usually developing, like the plays they serve, from the confirming rituals of particular societies. Thus we find stock characters alive and well in the classic Noh Theatre of Japan, in African theatre and in Sanskrit drama. The Fool, one of the most enduring characters of world drama, pops up in a multiplicity of subtly differentiated local forms. In Indian folk theatre, although he may be known as Konangi, Komali, Hanumanayaka or Joothan Mian depending on the region, wherever the Fool appears he carries with him characteristics instantly recognisable to his audience.

It is significant that the obsessive naturalism of twentieth-century theatre has made our culture suspicious of 'stock-types' in drama; we have tended to psychologise them into trans-cultural Jungian 'archetypes',[11] such as the Seal Wife, or to belittle them as 'stereotypes', inauthentic representations of the true psychological self. If we examine more closely how stock characters relate to the movement and under-standing of a dramatic piece, however, we see that they play a crucial part in delineating the possibilities of action and plot. Their ingrained characteristics, surviving an infinite number of settings, are unmistakable for those watching and listening within the culture which has nurtured them. These behavioural constraints provide audiences with the key to interpreting what is going on. The actors themselves, meanwhile, inform their performances with the same understanding. This shared process of performance and recognition is, in turn, reflected in the social world, so that knowledge of the character provides an interpretation of the actions of those individuals who have assumed the character. It does so precisely because those individuals have used the very same knowledge to guide and structure what they do.

While stock characters are initially identifiable by their appearance (in the distinctive masks of the *commedia dell'arte*, for example), they are also the vehicles for familiar and quite specific moral indicators, which both performer and audience know will determine their action within the drama. We do not need to travel beyond our sitting-rooms to witness this. The employment in television commercials of actors who have come to be identified with a particular set of moral characteristics is a modern example of this form of dramatic signification. The appearance or sound of a well-known television personality can signal values with the utmost economy. Students in drama, of course, although they may not realise it, also use stock characters as an instantly recognisable shorthand for the expression of particular points of view in their improvisations.

For MacIntyre, characters in this sense 'are a very special type of social role which places a certain kind of moral constraint on the personality of those who inhabit them in a way in which many other social roles do not'. They are 'the masks worn by moral philosophies', merging 'what usually is thought to belong to the individual man or woman and what is usually thought to belong to social roles'.[12] Cultures, then, can be seen as literally character-*ised* by the social roles which have become loaded with moral significance in this way. The characters of a dramatised society act as its moral representatives, allowing the moral premises and discourses of its communities a dramatic realisation in the social world. MacIntyre identifies some of the defining characters of Victorian England as 'the Public School Headmaster, the Explorer and the Engineer', and of Wilhelmine Germany as 'the Prussian Officer, the Professor and the Social Democrat'. In recent years, I would say that the ubiquitous (though morally impoverished) Manager has emerged as a defining character in our own society.

This reformulation, emphasising character over role, allows us to entertain the thought that within the model of the dramatised society we may not be so conclusively condemned to a role-playing social world of competing individuals as Goffman and the ethnomethodologists would have us believe. Characters, both on and off the stage, clearly operate in a very different way to the role-playing chameleons of dramatic pedagogy.

We are now in a position to pull some of the threads of the argument together. Text, role and character, I am suggesting, offer us the conceptual basis for interpreting and evaluating the products made and performed in drama. Far from being a narrow or restricting formulation, the idea of text as a sequence of dramatic actions which can be read by spectators may usefully be applied to dramatised interactions of all kinds, from theatre or classroom performances (implicit or otherwise) to the manifestations of the dramatised society itself. Role, of course, drama teachers will be familiar with, and although it is important to draw attention to its limitations as a device for describing human action, it will continue to have a part to play in the drama curriculum. But, by restoring the idea of character to the dramatic vocabulary, we now have the means whereby values may be honestly enacted, debated and judged within the context of the discourse and popular representations of culture. It is this more generally educative function which I now intend to explore.

11

WHAT SHALL WE DO AND HOW SHALL WE LIVE?

'So you are saying that human agreement decides what is true and what is false?' – It is what human beings say that is true and false; and they agree in the language they use. This is not agreement in opinions but in form of life.

(Ludwig Wittgenstein 1958)[1]

FACTS AND OPINIONS

For all its moral relativism and its very post-modern retreat from judgement, drama in schools has always had at its heart some vision of the good life. At its most effective, audience and participants are moved by the moral resonances of its improvised encounters, and most drama teachers, I suspect, although they may not express it quite like this, have an implicit confidence in the power of what they do to enhance the moral lives of their students.

While it would be disingenuous to suggest that dramatic art, any more than drama-in-education, could ever give us *answers* to the ethical dilemmas which have been troubling moral philosophers since Socrates and before, by showing how a theory of art based upon culture and history rather than private experience gives us a purchase on drama which is both interpretative and critical, I believe it is possible to use the model of the dramatised society to settle the dilemma which has haunted drama-in-education from the beginning – that of reconciling absolute moral commitment (to the weak, the exploited and the oppressed) with a belief in the dominion of individual subjectivity.

Education has not escaped the influence of that familiar distinction we like to make between what we think we can know and what we might happen to feel about it. The belief that we can unproblematically divide our experience of the world into objective and subjective categories in this way has been with us since the Enlightenment. The continuing domination of the curriculum by traditional knowledge-based subjects, such as maths and science, demonstrates the extent to

121

which the 'objective' category has achieved pre-eminence. B.S. Bloom's celebrated taxonomy of the cognitive, affective and locomotor domains has remained the accepted ground for the battle for the arts so that arts educators taking up arms on behalf of an under-valued affective domain have had little option but to collude in this opposition.[2] Drama-in-education's claims on forms of absolute, or 'universal', knowledge accessible through an authenticity of feeling can be seen as an attempt to justify drama in terms both of the cognitive and affective realms. As a society, however, we have generally accepted the epistemology of positivism, which allows only empirical evidence and deductive logic into the sphere of legitimate knowledge.[3] Thus, as both Eysenck and Polanyi saw, to be accepted as properly objective subjects, the behavioural sciences – psychology, sociology, and so on – had to be uncontaminated by people's views and opinions; legitimacy would only come from making the study of human behaviour 'value-free'.

By the 1960s, however, doubts about this simple objective/subjective distinction were being voiced by some social scientists and the very idea of the possibility of objectivity began to be challenged. Ostensibly objective research was shown to be defined by a vocabulary of highly subjective assessment categories such as 'normal', 'deviant', or 'unacceptable', and even such commonly used words as 'role', 'status' and 'group', were shown to be open to a wide range of differing interpretations. For all our claims to disinterested cognition, it was argued, we are constantly stuck by our own evaluative frameworks and the cultures which endorse them. The pursuit of scientific objectivity in the area of human behaviour is not only fruitless but actually an impediment to our understanding of the ways we act. Our much vaunted objectivity is circumscribed by the same distinctions of *worth* which made Goffman's model of competing role-players a deficient description of social interaction.

It follows that values may not be disruptive influences after all but the very means whereby we are able to describe and interpret human behaviour in terms of action. What we are faced with is not so much a gauze of subjective value-judgements and appraisals, temporarily hiding from us univocal scientific explanations which require only to be illuminated by rigorous objective analysis, but rather a truly heterogeneous collection of *ad hoc* evaluative descriptions which can only be understood in the context of their particularity. By this distinctly post-modernist account, human explanations can be judged only in their context; there is no universal law, scientific or normative, to which we may appeal, no transcendent essences to fall back upon.

Explanation, in Wittgenstein's phrase, is a family of cases, joined together only by a common aim, to make something plain or clear.

This suggests that a coherent account of explanation could not be given without attending to the audience to whom the explanation is offered or the source of puzzlement that requires an explanation to be given. There are many audiences, many puzzles, and a variety of paradigmatically clear cases that give rise, by contrast, to puzzles about other cases.[4]

If scientific objectivity in the field of human behaviour turns out to be a chimera (and metaphysics an unreliable substitute), then all we appear to have to put in its place is an infinite number of personal subjectivities. Of course, this Nietzschean picture of society as nothing more than a collection of individual 'wills' governed by their own passions and desires has had a profound influence, not just on drama-in-education, but on contemporary society more generally and the ways in which we speak about it. People think and talk *as if* the proposition were true, no matter what their avowed theoretical standpoint may be.

So, if this picture is so satisfying to the modern imagination, why do we at the same time so tenaciously hold on to the idea of objectivity? I think our obsession with objectivity is partly born out of a desire to find secure foundations to which we might cling, indisputable frameworks beyond which we cannot stray, and partly out of our desire (once having reached tacit agreement about these objective frameworks) to be free to chart our own, self-determined (subjective) ends. The pursuit of objectivity thus represents simultaneously a search for constraint *and* a justification for unrestricted freedom of action. It turns the world into a neutral environment within which we can effect whatever purposes we choose.

THE COMMUNITY OF DISCOURSE

Such a model of the disengaged identity claims that what is out there is simply out there; how we then interpret it is entirely up to us – as individuals. However, a moment's reflection will show that the language we use to make these distinctions cannot be a matter of individual choice in this way. Alice was right to be sceptical about Humpty Dumpty's confident linguistic relativism.[5] The way we speak about the world and attempt to make it intelligible implies communally held agreements over language and meaning. Furthermore, as Wittgenstein was concerned to point out, these communally held agreements do not simply allow us to communicate but hold within them the very 'forms of life' by which meaning is itself made possible.

Taking his cue from Wittgenstein, philosopher Charles Taylor argues that we are inescapably part of what he calls *communities of discourse*, and it is these which structure the ways in which we think and speak.

The speaking agent is in fact enmeshed in two kinds of larger order, which he can never fully oversee, and can only punctually and marginally refashion. For he is only a speaking agent at all as part of a language community ... and the meanings and illocutionary forces activated in any speech act are only what they are against a whole language and way of life.[6]

Taylor proposes, that for practical purposes, we might replace the objective/subjective dichotomy with a model of interpretation and action based upon the idea of systems of *inter-subjectivity*. Within such a model, we would seek to understand human agency not in terms of multiplicities of individual consciousnesses operating freely and independently in the epistemological landscape, but rather on the basis that there are inter-subjective standards of rationality by which we attempt to identify personal bias, or false beliefs, from objective claims, standards which will themselves depend on agreement within communities of discourse. For Taylor, these inter-subjective meanings are not simply an intellectual device, another way of doing behavioural science, but actually constitute the social matrix in which individuals find themselves and act. They are embodied in the common and celebratory forms of cultural interaction, as *meaning-full* on the streets and in the homes of a society, as in its theatres, schools and pageants. They are continuously being played out and reformulated by human agents on the multiplicious stages of the dramatised society.

It is clear, by this account at least, that to speak, as drama-in-educationists are prone to do, of 'inner' or 'personal' meanings as if they could be self-sufficient objects of value is inherently to misunderstand the concept of meaning itself. As Taylor points out, for us to speak intelligibly about meaning, our use of the word must satisfy criteria: it must be meaning for a subject, an individual or a group; it must be meaning *of* something, a situation or an action for instance; it must be meaning in a field, that is, related to the meanings of other things.[7] Mediated of necessity through the accumulated understandings of their percipients, the meaning of particular situations or utterances will, of course, vary in some respects between individuals, but at the same time those individuals can *only* make sense of themselves against a wider culture of meaning: the community of discourse.

Translated into the metaphors of the dramatised society, while I might be the star of my own life narrative, I am equally constituted as a bit-part player in the dramas of others and in the cultural text into which I am written. Whether I like it or not, I am part of a history, the bearer of some tradition. To be a policeman, therefore, is not, as Bolton's simple individualism would want us to believe, simply to be 'a man with a home and a family' who happens to put on a helmet from time to time, but to receive

elements of one's very identity from the meanings of a specific community of tradition and value and the characters who represent it.

So it makes little sense to speak of drama teachers 'making' meanings
for students. Students' understandings are circumscribed not only by
their own histories but by the cultural field against which they are identified. Certainly teachers can demonstrate alternative ideas in an effort to
encourage students to reorganise their understanding, but claims to be
able to intervene strategically in meaning formation are highly tenden-
tious. This is so, not only as I suggested in Chapter 7, because teachers
themselves 'mean' things to the students – they are the objects of interpretation as are all their pedagogic and non-pedagogic messages – but
because ideas perceived to be at odds with the received meanings of peer
group and family will be filtered through that gauze before they can
make a substantial impact on a student's world picture. It is naïve to
imagine that drama teachers, by virtue of a set of superficially engaging
practices, can operate outside this framework. A drama will in reality
have widely variant meanings for teacher and taught so that what
appears to the former as essential revelation might well be more
prosaically inspired, by a desire to please the teacher, for example, or a
fear of getting it wrong, or by a host of considerations about what the
others think.

Thus, while it might well be a legitimate aim of a pedagogy to challenge the fields of meaning by which assumptions are made, the efficacy
of any such project, in terms of its ability to change the way students
think about the world, must be strictly limited, however sophisticated its
methodology. For Taylor,

> Already to be a living agent is to experience one's situation in terms
> of certain meanings; and this in a sense can be thought of as a sort
> of proto-'interpretation'. This is in turn interpreted and shaped by
> the language in which the agent lives these meanings. This whole is
> then at a third level interpreted by the explanation we proffer of his
> actions.[8]

It seems likely that it is only at this third level, the *interpretation of actions*,
that drama-in-education, or any other form of institutionalised pedagogy, can intelligibly claim to make meaningful interventions. It can offer
explanations, it can attempt to make sense of utterances and situations,
but it can only do so within the structures of meaning already embodied
in the self-interpretations of the participants (teacher and taught) and
through the language of the culture by which those interpretations are
both articulated and constituted. The drama teacher is engaged, not in
revealing truths purporting to transcend language and culture, nor in the
reduction of understanding to a matter of subjective preference, but in
what Hans-Georg Gadamer has called a 'conversation' between

researchers and subject matter. 'Understanding should not be thought of so much as an action of one's subjectivity, but as the placing of oneself within a process of tradition, in which past and present are constantly fused.'[9] The outcome of these conversations is not a moment of a-temporal revelation but what we might regard as *an adequate comprehension* of the matter under consideration.

THE TEACHER AS CRITIC

Informed by this theory of interpretation, it becomes easier to see how the model of the dramatised society might offer a serviceable conceptual structure for exploring through drama the fundamental questions of human agency. From the family to the state, through the dramatisation of individual encounters to analysis of the great dramatic rituals of nations, a whole range of formal and informal human institutions now offer themselves up for interpretation. Like classroom improvisations, we can read them too as *dramatic texts*, deconstructing them for the messages they contain and the devices they employ to achieve their effect. For, as Clifford Geertz points out:

> The greatest virtue of the extension of the notion of text beyond things written on paper or carved in stone is that it trains attention on precisely . . . how the inscription of action is brought about, what its vehicles are and how they work. . . . To see social institutions, social customs, social changes as in some sense 'readable' is to alter our whole sense of what such interpretation is.[10]

I am aware that the fact that this theory of interpretation is based, not on the authority of naturalistic realities, but upon the inter-subjectivity of meaning, will lay it open to accusations of conservatism, of complicity with the prevailing hegemony. Simply to interpret society in terms of its own structures of meaning, it will be said, can only perpetuate those structures, and, by implication, the power relations embodied in them. It is at this point, and for these reasons, that the critical teacher intervenes, taking the 'adequate comprehension' of the group and subjecting it to analysis, questioning the motivations and interests implicit in it, exposing their origins, their distortions, their purposes and functions. Like the revolutionary in Brecht's song:

> He asks of property:
> Where d'you come from?
> He asks of factions
> Whom do you serve?[11]

By adopting a critical standpoint of this kind, the teacher attempts to get behind the resultant meanings by submitting them to what the critical sociologists have called, *ideologiekritik*. According to Jürgen Habermas, *ideologiekritik* (literally, 'the critique of ideology') addresses itself to 'what lies behind the consensus presented as fact, that supports the dominant tradition of the time, and does so with a view to the relations of power surreptitiously incorporated in the symbolic structures of the systems of speech and action'.[12]

The teacher of dramatic art engaged in the critical interpretation of meaning has thus two defined but interdependent roles. First, as a participant in the interpretative process, he or she must share and contribute to the understandings delivered by the group. This is not for non-interventionist 'child-centred' reasons of the kind which attribute equal value to the beliefs of individual students simply on the grounds that they are individuals, but because, as I have argued, meanings may not be arbitrarily imposed but are held only against a background of collective understanding. In this respect, the group represents not an aggregate of its individual members' personal knowledge, but a structure of understanding against which meanings are measured and modified. Thus, while it may not make sense to talk of the teacher 'making' meanings for the group, he or she can nevertheless participate, as an influential group member, in the processes whereby interpretations are produced. It is not in any way the object of this interpretative stage to produce unanimity of belief in relation to a subject, but rather, as we have seen, to reach *temporary satisfaction* with a shared understanding of how things are. It is only at this stage, when the group is satisfied by and committed to the coherence of its interpretation, that the teacher steps outside in the role of the critic. *Ideologiekritik* can only be effective in this context if it can engage with perceptions which have already been organised and understood.

It is important to stress again that the teacher's analysis is not offered from the point of view of some kind of previously undisclosed objective truth. The factors he or she brings to bear on the original interpretation are not revelations, 'universal meanings' standing beyond criticism, for they too are only articulated and made sense of against a field of meaning. Any such analysis is itself the potential object of further interpretation, modification and re-expression. On the other hand, neither should the critique be thought of as the arbitrary prejudices of an individual teacher's subjective beliefs, for it is the teacher's responsibility to present a critique formulated within the frames of what are generally understood to be the tests of evidence and deductive thinking. What is offered may well not correspond to a consensus – indeed, its purpose may often be explicitly to challenge consensus – but to dismiss it as biased, or 'purely subjective', is to fall back into the false dichotomy I have exposed here and to succumb to the implied belief that there is something out there sufficiently objective against which such bias might be measured.

To summarise, we cannot make sense of things, including ourselves, outside meaningful structures with which we are familiar; we can only do so through the language by which those meanings are expressed. Our search for meaning is therefore dialectical, not in the simple subjective/objective construction favoured by drama-in-education, but in the sense that it is a continuous movement between preconception, revision and confirmation, Gadamer's conception of the hermeneutic circle. The progression is thus not from 'the particular to the universal' towards ever more diffuse levels of generality, but rather a circle of modification, where participants in, or observers of, the drama, return to reassess, or even reject, their understandings in the light of dramatic explorations which are themselves continually being modified. Teacher and taught unite as researchers, using the dramatic model to interpret human interaction, organisation and meaning, counting success as the achievement of a level of intelligibility in relation to the subject matter sufficient to satisfy the investigation. As human agents we have all sorts of governing beliefs and attitudes; what unites us is that we justify them in the terms that our society *counts* as justification. Thus, the teacher's final critique of these 'adequate comprehensions', while it makes no claims on objectivity, must nevertheless be justifiable in this way.

LEARNING HOW TO ACT

I have shown how the apparently unlimited choices offered by modern individualism have led drama-in-education helplessly into a void where values themselves become 'personal' and where there seems to be no possible recourse to moral imperatives beyond the feelings of individuals. If, as I have suggested, however, despite the remorseless abdications of post-modernism, the ways in which we think and act are in fact anchored in the decisions we make about *grounds* and these evaluations are not individualistically preferential but socially defined, then our judgements about values must take place not in psychological isolation but within the context of standards agreed by communities of discourse.

By such an account, our actual lived politics and morality originate not in the depths of our psyches nor in the semi-mystical essences proposed by the phenomenologists, but reside instead in the multifarious communities of which we are, of necessity, members. Our self-understanding depends not so much on the 'inner' and the 'personal' as on our characterising ourselves as moral agents in our communities of discourse. Morality begins, as Emile Durkheim reminds us, only in so far as we belong to a human group.

> Since, in fact, man is complete only as he belongs to several societies, morality is complete only to the extent that we feel identified

with those different groups in which we are involved – family, union, business, club, political party, country, humanity.[13]

The family, the gang, the school, the nation: these are our moral constituencies, the spaces defined by distinctions of worth, within which, and only within which, we can comprehend the self. In this sense, the community actually tells us who we are – even as we stand out against it. Our 'self-interpretations' are drawn from the interchange carried on by the community which 'provides the language by which we draw our background distinctions', and without which human agency 'would be not just impossible, but inconceivable'.[14]

In this way, not only are the moral dilemmas which accompany us through our lives usefully made sense of in terms of our overlapping membership of many such communities, but our selfhood can also be understood as being worked out against the conflated interchanges of the networks of moral loyalties they imply. The gradual secularisation of Western culture, accompanied historically by the development of increasingly sophisticated forms of communication and by an expanded social mobility, allows individual members of today's national communities to owe allegiance to a vastly more complex and contradictory range of moralities than could have even been imagined in our ghostly versions of the relatively stable, pre-industrial past. The profound dilemma facing many young Asian women seeking partners in contemporary Britain provides an example of the tension that can be generated by conflicts between rival moral memberships. Owing deep cultural loyalty to a tradition of arranged marriage, they may now also be members of a European, inner-city culture committed to the right of free marital choice.

For teachers, many of the day-to-day problems of discipline and commitment are ascribable to conflicting moral loyalties; yet without these complex networks of membership, in which, of course, teachers themselves share, our sense of ourselves would be severely diminished. Hargreaves makes the point that the predominance of the 'fallacy of individualism' in English education has in many cases blinded teachers to a hidden curriculum of collectivism. Drama teachers too, he suggests, 'have unwittingly become victims of the cult of individualism, and in so doing they are in real danger of ignoring the powerful corporate potentials of drama'.[15] Drama-in-education's commitment to 'group work', for instance, is ironically always framed in the individualistic language of co-operation, tolerance and empathy, reflecting the idea of the group as simply an aggregation of individuals relating to each other. Significantly absent from the discourse are the complementary concepts of duty, loyalty and obligation, unintelligible, of course, to the spirit of the disengaged consciousness, but utterly comprehensible and reassuring to

129

students. Moral behaviour of necessity requires submission to a set of rules, to a moral authority, which, as Hargreaves points out, 'must be obeyed not in a spirit of passive resignation but out of enlightened allegiance'.[16]

A conceptual scheme of this kind which postulates moral knowledge as a form of social solidarity allows us to break conclusively with psychologism and its narrow, emotivist premises. As agents, we do not in fact 'discover' our values by dredging our unconscious but, rather, actively mediate between the differing claims of many allegiances. In doing so, we exercise our moral imagination, weighing up consequential considerations against higher, deontological claims, measuring a whole range of 'oughts' against our perceptions of the moral environments in which we are compelled to be agents; we assess the strengths of our loyalties. Our moral feelings are reflections of our relative commitments to membership. Our social class, our gender, our ethnic group, our trades union or our church, are communities of moral discourse to which we belong and which, in crucial ways, tell us not only how we should feel but also what we should do and how we should live.

We can now perhaps see more clearly how the dramatised society is moved by the characters representing its moral communities, those fusions of role and morality which so profoundly characterise its distinctions of worth both on and off the stage. It becomes possible to demonstrate how the 'stock-type' has a vital part to play in the dramatisation and interpretation of our social lives. If our morality turns out to be the result of the contracts we make with communities and the (often conflicting) loyalties they demand from us, then the collisions of these loyalties, sometimes the result of very stark contradistinctions, while disturbing to our moral equanimity, create the tensions which inform the dramatic art of secular society.

Romantic individualism sought legitimacy for our choices through reference to the 'truth' of our emotional experience. We have seen how drama-in-education conceptualised itself simply as a vehicle for the exposure and expression of personal moral feelings or 'subjective knowing'. Employed as a kind of living laboratory, however, where decisions about what moves us morally can be made in the dialectical context of rival commitments after rigorous experiment and analysis of the kind described above, drama education can be released from the confines of psychology to engage with the political and moral structures of contemporary society. Like all art, drama can expose and articulate the deepest and most significant dilemmas of our culture, but like all art it negotiates and articulates in the public domain by which it is both valued and defined.

SUMMING UP: DRAMATIC ART AND THE DRAMATISED SOCIETY

Dramatic art dissolves the old distinction between 'drama' and 'theatre' and proposes a programme of drama education located in the public world. Within it, drama is described as a textual message system crafted specifically to convey meaning to watchers. A tripartite structure of making, performing and responding, makes it possible to formulate the dramatic text as the product of the drama lesson and to make it available for evaluation and revision by the participants.

As a fully paid-up member of the arts community, dramatic art shares with the other arts the potential for engagement with the structures of feeling of our historical moment. At the same time, it is instrumental in the promotion of dramatic literacy, for by seeking as wide an appropriation of dramatic tradition as possible while making no easy or patronising assumptions about cultural relevance, dramatic art is the genuine servant of cultural egalitarianism.

The model of the dramatised society is the backdrop to dramatic art. In it, we are described not simply as role-playing individuals acting out our preferences against a known 'objective' world, but rather as moral agents making sense of ourselves and our actions through our membership of, and potential challenges to, communities of discourse. In this way the institutions of the dramatised society may themselves be regarded as dramatic texts containing representative characters who act as yardsticks for our actions and beliefs.

The reading of these dramatic texts constitutes a way of approaching questions of understanding and meaning which rejects the objective/subjective distinction and replaces it instead with a commitment to interpretation. In the classroom, dramatic strategies enable the teacher both to establish a framework for the collective interpretation of the meanings expressed in the dramas produced and to subject those dramas to criticism.

Above all, dramatic art gives us an aesthetic located in the dramatised inter-subjectivities of our social being and in contact with the moral and political implications of that being. As actors in a dramatised culture, we write and perform our dramatic texts according to the dramatic forms which that culture, its traditions, its conventions, its history, make available to us. However, our cultural membership is diverse and the forms with which we are familiar and which tell us who we are, often contradictory. It is here that the dramatic aesthetic most powerfully engages, for it is able to connect us with history in ways which liberate our understanding, while simultaneously (and necessarily) connecting us to the communities of value and meaning by which we make sense of our lives.

131

12

THE DRAMA CURRICULUM

Take, for one moment, from a cultural and aesthetic point of view, the very term 'educational drama'. Can you not see what a desperate mutant it is? Envisage the whole intricate evolved world of drama . . . with all its connections with mime, with carnival, with commedia dell'arte, as well as its obvious contemporary relationships with video, radio and television, not to mention its characteristic forms in Japan, China, India and other non-western cultures and, then, repeat the term 'educational drama'. . . . What an immense contraction is involved; what a severe blinkering of vision.

(Peter Abbs in an open letter to Gavin Bolton 1992)[1]

WIDER LANDSCAPES

We know that when Peter Slade introduced the concept of 'Child Drama' in the 1950s, he sought to categorise it as an exclusive form of educational activity, quite distinct from what was generally understood as theatre practice. I have traced the debilitating legacy of this distinction and shown how, by restoring the general synonymy of drama and theatre, dramatic art makes no such division. Dramatic art is genuinely inclusive, as happy with the vulgar spectacle of carnival and circus, for example, as it is with the metaphorical complexities of Elizabethan verse or the dramatic play of the infant classroom.

It follows that dramatic art, unlike drama-in-education, has a curriculum of its own which can be practised, developed and taught. It is, in other words, unambiguously a subject discipline. This is not to suggest that the wide variety of issues and concerns which have offered themselves as the subject matter of dramatic pedagogy now vanish from the drama teacher's prospectus. I have already indicated how teachers of dramatic art can engage with the paradoxes and dilemmas thrown up by their work with young people, and the effective teaching of plays – a key element of the drama curriculum – can hardly be expected to avoid contact with the moral and political. Nigel Williams' *Class Enemy*, for example, set in an inner-city classroom of such savage repute that no

132

teacher dare enter, raises profound questions about school and society, while Ena Lamont Stewart's *Men Should Weep* says things about the exploitation of women far beyond the reach of the most earnest anti-sexist role-playing. Even Shakespeare's *King Henry the Fifth* can hardly fail to raise issues of war, history and patriotism. A carefully designed drama curriculum makes these kinds of exploration more rather than less likely; as we have seen, the solipsistic freedoms of drama-in-education have often been an excuse for the inconsequential and banal.

The clear subject identity engendered by placing dramatic art generically within the arts gives educational drama a disciplinary coherence at last. The speculative colonisation of the curriculum suggested by drama-in-education more often than not stood in stark contrast to a limited and limiting practical agenda, where rigid adherence to the complexities of methodology effectively stifled a whole range of alternatives. Dramatic art, on the other hand, simply encompasses all that is the art of drama. Its limits come where that categorisation is least distinct, where drama merges with other forms of human expression, such as in performance art, or music theatre and opera perhaps, or at the edge of certain forms of religious ritual. For most purposes, dramatic art's unequivocal identification with such culturally familiar concepts as actors, theatres and plays, gives it an identity readily accessible to a wide constituency.

In the language of curriculum theory, this shift involves the replacement of the infinitely weak 'classification' of dramatic pedagogy with the far stronger subject identity of dramatic art; this, in turn, allows the 'frames' within which knowledge is transmitted during the drama class to become much weaker. In Basil Bernstein's model of the classification and framing of educational knowledge, classification refers to the degree of boundary maintenance between the contents of curriculum subjects, frame to the range of options available to teacher and taught in the control of what is transmitted and received. 'Strong frames', he says, 'reduce the power of the pupil over what, when and how he receives knowledge, and increases the teacher's power in the pedagogical relationship'.[2] The authoritarian presence of charismatic drama teachers like Dorothy Heathcote sets up strong framing which reduces the real options of the students to control events. *Ad hoc* rules about what was and was not acceptable had to be quickly assimilated by Heathcote's classes as the subject-defining boundaries were effectively non-existent. Dramatic art, on the other hand, presupposes the shared understanding of its parameters by teacher and students, allowing for a relaxation of framing and a consequent expansion of the range of transmittable knowledge. Thus, while the lesson might simultaneously involve a variety of different activities – a group of students researching, another planning some lighting, another improvising a scene – all understand that what they are doing is learning in drama. The relatively strong classification of dramatic art, and the weak framing it allows, give students the freedom to explore and take control of their learning within clear contextual limits.

At its core, the dramatic art curriculum offers opportunities for students at all levels to explore the expressive potential of theatre, as performers possibly, but equally as writers, designers, directors, technicians, animateurs and experimenters. It encourages them not only to share the deep, corporate satisfactions of the dramatic experience, but also to carry forward a developing expertise and appetite for drama into life outside the school. While students in the school drama lesson may well still be confronted from time to time by forms of role-playing and improvisation, with an understanding of the place of these practices within dramatic art they will be able to make sense of them in a wider theatrical context. Their work in the classroom or drama studio, their out-of-school play rehearsals, their parents' involvement with amateur dramatics or the community play, their visits to the theatre, even their articulation of the conventions of *East Enders*; all these will be perceived as legitimate elements of the subject of drama.

The formulation of dramatic art, therefore, represents not a new set of rules and methodologies but, rather, the redirecting of the best of existing practice in the field of drama education towards more eclectic but clearly subject orientated ends. This eclecticism insists that the word 'drama' must be allowed a wide interpretation and cannot be unilaterally confined by a section of the dramatic community and employed exclusively to describe its own idiosyncratic and limiting practices. Or, as John Allen, the first of Her Majesty's Inspectors for schools with responsibility for drama, once remarked, 'contrary to what some enthusiasts believe . . . drama in schools is basically and essentially no different from drama anywhere else'.[3]

PRACTISING DRAMATIC ART

Because dramatic art has no pretensions to be an educative system, it makes no essential claim on the moral or psychological development of young people. That is not to say that individual teachers or institutions may not have strong views about what young people should be taught (nor, indeed, that mine are not reflected in this book). The fact that my classes study the playwright Caryl Churchill rather than Terence Rattigan, or explore the subtle relationship between the Madagascan Hira Gasy players and their audiences and neglect Restoration comedy, however, is a choice I make as a teacher; like all other syllabus choices it will be a product of more diverse perceptions. So long as what I am doing is helping my students to develop their dramatic skills and their knowledge and understanding of drama, then the range of content from which I am able to choose remains as large as the subject of drama itself.

The practical exploration of all aspects of theatre craft, however, *is* central to the study of dramatic art.[4] In drama, as in the other arts, without skills in their chosen medium, even the most creative of students will find it hard to make progress. Much as visual arts teachers help students to develop manipulative skills in a range of media – painting, sculpture, graphics, ceramics – so drama specialists have a responsibility to equip those they teach with the tools of dramatic expression. Students engaged in the production process do not simply 'stumble upon' the appropriate theatrical forms for the expression of their ideas, but must have demonstrated both the structures and the disciplines which can help them. If, for example, they are to appropriate forms of popular dramatic expression, then they have at some time to be taught about documentary, street theatre, pantomime, the well-made play, farce, and so on. While eschewing the prescription of content, dramatic art insists on a rigorous and critical approach to the making of dramatic texts.

Improvisation will probably remain a key tool in the making of dramas. It is a simple and accessible form of dramatic expression requiring few resources. Dramatic art, however, does not regard improvisation as a precious manifestation of the creative spirit requiring protection from the polluting interference of the teacher, but rather as a sturdy and flexible mechanism which gives teachers direct critical access to the production process. Drawing from media education, by treating students' improvisations rather like the rough-cuts of films, the teacher can ask for a drama to be run again, can suggest alterations, can examine 'freeze-frames', can send the group away to 're-cut' their work. Others in the class may participate in this editing process, becoming collaborators in the conversations which lead to the expressions of adequate comprehension we saw in the previous chapter.

Art teachers imbue students' paintings with value by displaying them on the walls of the classroom; music teachers encourage their students to sing and play for others. It is difficult to see why students in drama should be denied similar opportunities. I have argued that communication to an audience is intrinsic to the aims of all aesthetic production and that the intention of a group making a dramatic text is always some real or implied future performance. Even the successful role-player has an eye on how his or her performance is being perceived by others in the developing fiction. Dramatic art entails students learning about the complex relationship between audience and performers and the ways in which *mise-en-scène* draws all the textual signifiers of a drama together. As well as helping them make their own productions more effective, the teacher of dramatic art will want students to understand how the words of the playwright are read and turned into performance by directors, actors and designers, so that they themselves can grow in confidence in these key interpretative roles.[5]

In my account of the dramatised society, I showed how film and television have enabled us to witness dramatised fiction on an unprecedented scale. Few of us make or perform in plays, but millions of us watch them. Although many examination syllabuses acknowledge this and expect students to show a critical aptitude in relation to theatre performance, drama-in-education has had little to say about the way plays are received by audiences. Lacking a suitable critical vocabulary with which to express their thoughts and feelings about what they experience in the theatre, some students may inevitably fall back on forms of criticism which depend upon privileged knowledge of the play as literature. Literary criticism tends not only to favour the more scholastic student but also perpetuates the idea of theatre as 'high art' and turns out to be impotent when faced with the rough and tumble of distinctly non-literary drama such as carnival or circus. Theatre semiotics offer an altogether more subtle means of introducing students to the critical appreciation of performance and systematic guidance in performance analysis must be part of any dramatic art curriculum. The framework reproduced in Appendix 2 is only one example of such a scheme.[6]

With these principles in mind, it is easy to see how the problems with assessment encountered earlier begin to dissolve. If there are certain basic elements which can be said to constitute the subject of dramatic art then proficiency in these is our measure of progression and attainment in drama. Our students get better at handling and comprehending the medium, become more adept at making, performing and understanding dramas of all kinds. Achievement in the different elements should not be regarded as a set of educational hurdles but as markers in educational programmes which aim to develop students' ability to produce and critically interpret dramas. Then, in the same way that visual arts teachers may wish to make judgements of worth between one painting and another, or music teachers between students' compositions, so dramatic art has its criteria of value, eclectic and contested certainly, but shared and understood within the context of culture. It is against these criteria that the quality of students' work in dramatic art is measured.

As dramatic art extends the range of possibilities of drama in schools to embrace all possible forms of theatre, so it also oversteps national and cultural boundaries to open up the curriculum to drama from across the world. Drama-in-education, as we have seen, aimed to iron out cultural difference in a search for commonality in archetype and universal. Its increasing reliance on psychological naturalism made it particularly ill-equipped to embrace non-European forms, while the celebration of universals sometimes turned out to be little more than the tacit acceptance of a distinctly Western view of things. China must surely have one of the most exciting theatrical cultures ever, yet in Heathcote and Bolton's neo-colonial adventure there in 1995, the students remain securely in an imaginary hotel as the travel-worn box of tricks is unpacked again, this time to 'train Chinese staff regarding the expectations of Western tourists'.[7] By contrast, dramatic art would want to turn for inspiration to the culture itself, to a performance of *The White-Haired Girl*, for instance, a classic of Chinese revolutionary theatre with its origins in the rice-planting songs of northern China, or to the Beijing opera. Dramatic art goes out of its way to seek out the unfamiliar and to celebrate difference and diversity.

I argued in Chapter 8 that we can never know the cultural forms of others as if they were our own. Furthermore, if we fail to ask what a piece of drama 'could mean to its own people for whom it exists in the first place', our commitment to multiculturalism may turn out be a cover for another essentialist project – the quest for a universal language of theatre. This point is made forcefully by Indian director and critic, Rustom Bharucha in his critique of Peter Brook's 1980s' production of the *Mahabharata*. 'Nothing could be more disrespectful to theatre', he argues, 'than to reduce its act of celebration to a repository of techniques and theories'.[8] I am sure that Bharucha would agree though that we owe it to students to challenge the parochialism of the episodic, domestic naturalism which pervades the homes and classrooms of the First World. As they gaze upon its staring eyes and bejewelled collar, our students may not feel the resonances of the mask of the Barong like the people of Singapadu, but the challenge the Barong presents to their existing perceptions of drama will open up stimulating new channels of dramatic exploration.

In England and Wales, the multicultural dimension argued for here is no less than that already enshrined in music and art. The National Curriculum expects children from the age of five to be performing and listening to music 'from different times and cultures', and in guidance on equal opportunities in the curriculum, the Runnymede Trust suggests that good practice in art is marked by 'a balance between examples of Western and non-Western art'.

> As pupils become familiar with a variety of cultural traditions and genres, they make imaginative use in their own work of diverse media, methods and approaches ... Concepts such as 'high' and 'low' art, and 'classical', 'primitive', 'ethnic', 'African', 'popular', 'folk', 'tribal', and so on, are considered analytically and critically.[9]

Dramatic art insists that good practice in drama is similarly characterised.[10]

Finally, dramatic art does not neglect the wider curriculum. It offers the drama room as a kind of laboratory in which the content of our lives in the dramatised society can be explored and interpreted.[11] The form in which this process of critical interpretation and adequate comprehension takes place is that of the dramatic narrative. We learn through the stories we and others tell; in a dramatised culture these stories will themselves take the form of dramatisations, so that we are presented with a series of interlocking dramatic narratives which are the substance of our social lives, and in which we are both participant and spectator. In dramatic art we test out our performances against the distinctions of worth which give our actions meaning in the social world; we make sense of the dramas we watch and in which we are participants in the context of the culture and history upon which they are grounded. To render this act of interpretation conscious, and dramatic art makes claims to be able to do this, is to make both understanding and judgement possible.

THE ARTS, THE SCHOOL AND THE COMMUNITY

Some drama educators have adopted a rather superior attitude to the wider arts. Gavin Bolton once claimed that because drama is useful for 'teaching about life', it is justifiably separated from the other arts in a way which 'other educationalists with a vested interest in the arts do not always wish to acknowledge'.[12] Fortunately, support for this self-imposed segregation is not widely shared. Peter Abbs' 1990s' twelve-volume library on aesthetic education is the culmination of a project aimed to demonstrate how collaboration and cross-fertilisation between the arts can enrich students' experience and that by compartmentalising the arts we simply reinforce a peculiarly European view of aesthetics.[13] On the political front, Ken Robinson has been another doughty campaigner for schools to take a 'whole arts' perspective.

> The need should be recognised for a policy for all of the arts in schools and arts teachers in the same school should therefore discuss and co-ordinate policies wherever possible, and especially in relation to the allocation of time and facilities.[14]

Part of the problem is that the drama specialist is often in a rather isolated position in school, having to fight lone battles with caretakers and timetable-planners while holding the drama banner as high as he or she dares; relatively few drama teachers are lucky enough to teach within large drama departments with well-equipped facilities and a team of supportive colleagues. This sense of isolation is exacerbated by the fact that the private world of the drama class is rarely if ever exposed to the wider school community, so that the only opportunities the drama teacher has to demonstrate his or her worth may well be the extra-curricular ones offered by the public performance. But, as we have seen, the whole idea of performance to an audience has been either ignored or actively discouraged by the guardians of drama-in-education. The drama teacher may thus have to live with the demoralising paradox that success in the terms of the subject orthodoxy will neither be seen nor understood by the school community, while the popular, public achievements of the school production are regarded as marginal by the advocates of dramatic pedagogy.

The identification of performance as a key element of dramatic art, however, allows the drama teacher to emerge from the wings and to regard public acknowledgement as entirely consistent with classroom practice, so that the school or class play becomes an element of the dramatic experience to be made available to all students as they pass through the school. A whole range of alternative performance options become possible with students participating in assembly presentations, lunch-time shows, festivals, television and radio dramas, and so on. And this is not a potential confined to secondary education, as the flyer for *Jopco* reproduced in Figure 12.1 amply illustrates. Here, all the 9 and 10 year olds from one class of an inner-London primary school quite literally *made* an opera, first learning something about the form from their teacher, then experimenting amongst themselves with musical ideas and finally taking on all the roles in the production process.

David Hargreaves has described the school play as 'a paradigm for other aspects of the creative arts', 'an exemplar of differentiated team work' remembered by pupils 'longer than almost anything else about school'.

> Yet in most schools the play is part of the extra-curriculum – an optional and occasional (perhaps annual) activity involving a minority of the pupils in their spare time. . . . Most pupils' experience of drama must be confined to 'drama lessons' and the easiest way to conduct such a short lesson is to devote it to improvised drama and movement, with its focus on individual objectives. One of the central functions of drama is thereby distorted.[15]

Traditionally, the nights of the school play have been occasions for the informal gathering of the school community. At their best, these are times when it is possible to have a powerful sense of the school being at the centre of the lives of those it serves. On one particular occasion, I remember, over two hundred students from all parts of a large city comprehensive had researched, written and performed a music drama about their locality and its old mining tradition. Almost all their parents – and many of their grandparents – had been involved in one way or another, as had the school's music and art departments, the latter to the extent of structuring lessons around projects associated with the show. In the hall, on a packed first night, the atmosphere was electric. Anyone

❖Junior Opera Company❖

Rhyl primary
School Rhyl
Street
NW5

Year 5 children from Rhyl primary School
in Kentish Town have formed an Opera
Company called Jopco. We started from
Scratch we've all got different job's in
the company writers, set design, wardrobe,
Stage managers, electricians, performers
and composers, production manager and
Public relations department. We had Six
Weeks todo it now we have two weeks left.
The plot is about Somebody afraid of her
mum and dad Splitting up. And the lie
She tells. The Performances are on
Wednesday 20th and Thursday 21st November
5Pm+7Pm   Tickers cost £1 For Adults
50p for under 16 and are available
from 3.35→4:00pm at the school
gates from monday 11th November.
for more information tel 0171 485 489

Figure 12.1 Junior Opera Company flyer

who has experienced the massive outpouring of energy and enthusiasm harnessed by a successful community play of this kind will know what rich and unforgettable festivals they can be. The flexibility of a well-structured secondary arts faculty should be able to make this kind of learning experience possible as an integral part of the curriculum. Not only would ventures of this kind greatly enrich the work of drama departments, but they would also increase the confidence and self-esteem of individual teachers.

This, then, is the case for dramatic art. At its heart is my contention that drama occupies a place at the very centre of the way in which we make sense of ourselves and order our lives. I have argued that in the theatre and on the street, in televised reproductions and in the school, we have multiple versions of our dramatised society displayed for our interpretation and critical analysis. As we emerge from the reverent and narrowly self-referential introspection of drama-in-education into the altogether brighter light of what is, literally, a whole world of drama, dramatic art allows us to engage with the abundance of cultural form that then presents itself. In schools, by bringing drama out into the open, so that it is no longer regarded by the rest of the institution as freemasonry conducted behind the closed doors of the drama studio, but as an intelligible set of skills and expressive practices frequently made manifest in performance, dramatic art allows drama teachers to shed their role as curricular missionaries and the evangelical defensiveness which grew with it. Dramatic art makes it possible for teachers to share intelligible accounts of what they hope to achieve with colleagues, parents, head-teachers, and above all, with the students themselves.

APPENDIX 1

FOUR DRAMA LESSONS

These four accounts of drama lessons cover a period from 1965 to 1991. Real and imaginary, illustrating the idealism and the reality of over thirty years of drama-in-education, they are set out here as reminders of classroom aspirations.

A PICNIC IN THE COUNTRY (1965)

A drama lesson is just ending. The class lines up quietly and begins to file out into the foyer, joining other children already beginning to move to different classes. The empty hall seems vast and gloomy, full of interesting corners and patches of light. The curtains are closed and spotlights cast irregular pools of shiny light on the floor, emphasising the pattern of polished wood blocks. An intense orange light shines in your eyes. It fades to a full glow, and with a clatter the drama teacher jumps from the stage and begins to sort through some records by the gramophone. With a slight movement he signals to the class next door to come in, and the hall is once more full of children.

They enter excitedly chattering to one another, removing jackets and pullovers as they go, each finding a safe spot to dump satchels, books and the many things that children always seem to carry with them. The teacher takes little apparent notice, but the children are obviously aware of his presence, and he seems to be summing up the mood of the class while experimenting with brief snatches of music on the gramophone. Some of the class are discussing something important in pairs and small groups. Some are leaping and weaving around the others as if they are casting spells. A small boy in one corner is walking stiffly, like a clockwork toy. A few children make straight for the gramophone and, as they ply the teacher with questions, try to read the name on the record label as it revolves. They admire the sleeve – an arresting picture – it is *The Firebird*.

A loud crash from the gramophone speaker, set high on the wall, temporarily halts most of the class. They turn and look, not at the loud-

142

speaker but at the teacher, who takes this opportunity to give a sharp clap, followed by a gesture which obviously says, 'Come and sit down over here'. There is a brief jockeying for places, but very quickly the class is in a semi-circle round the steps on one side of the stage. Some lean on the stage, some sit cross-legged, while others lie with their heads propped in their hands. All seem quite relaxed, especially the teacher. From this distance what he says is barely audible, but soon hands shoot up and the children seem to be offering suggestions. A rucksack... camera... sandwiches... primus stove... thermos flask... At a decisive movement from the teacher the semi-circle disintegrates, and the children are scattered around the hall, some sitting, some lying, some seeking the splashes of light, some preferring the dark corners. A few children perch on the edge of the half-dozen rostrum blocks placed haphazardly about the floor. Stacks of metal chairs line one wall; the occasional child finds a haven near them. The teacher's voice is now quite clear. The whole class is silent as he begins a story: 'It is early on a summer's morning. Outside the sun is shining. We are asleep in bed; very soon the alarm clock will sound...' The children seem asleep – some restlessly, some deeply. The teacher meanwhile has moved imperceptibly over to the stage, and suddenly he rattles a side-drum, and the class reacts – some quite violently. They seem absorbed in the real process of getting out of bed. Some manage it straight away, some roll over and pull bedclothes over their faces, while others are quite obviously finding cold lino under their bare feet. 'Go into the bathroom and have a good wash. Don't forget behind your ears! Clean your teeth and get dressed.'

The children's activities begin to vary. Some obviously wash in their pyjamas, while others get partly dressed first. Some make tap noises as they fill their own wash basins. A general hatred of washing is shown by perfunctory and noisy splashing, but just a few hold their heads under the taps. The narration continues, and the children rush down to breakfast, cut sandwiches and pack things to take for a day in the country.

They set off to catch the bus in a happy mood, whistling, running and skipping. To help them music blares through the loudspeaker: a 'pop' record from the past – Jumping Bean – just the thing to convey the spirit of setting off, and the children respond to it well. They meet friends and begin the bus journey, amid much slapstick comedy with imaginary bus conductors.

The transition from one activity to the next is quite natural. The teacher never says things twice, in fact he hardly interrupts the action: the children seem to hear every word without apparently listening. Most of the time they are completely absorbed in what they are doing, and only occasionally, when they need to sort out some snag, do they become conscious of the hall and their neighbours. The hall is transformed every few moments into a fresh location, sometimes by sounds from the gramophone, sometimes simply by the sincerity and absorption with which the children create their own ideas for the story. Moods vary tremendously, and the class is at one moment noisy and lively, at the next quiet and intent.

The only control over mood is by the teacher suggesting where they are and what they are doing, or by the type of sound they can hear. Now, for instance, they are searching for wild flowers and listening for bird songs. 'Morning', from *Peer Gynt*, sets the quiet atmosphere. They cross a farmyard and feed ducks and dogs, providing their own noises (some of the walkers forsake their walk to become, briefly, a farm dog). They choose a spot, eat their meal, rest and begin to play ball games. An unusual record is used for this – an almost forgotten 'hit' – a clever, twangy, fast guitar piece called *Little Rock Getaway*. After the games, and a short spell of fishing, everyone goes in for a swim. The children swim with lazy strokes to *The Swan of Tuonela*, covering vast areas of the hall. All sorts of interesting experiments are going on: someone in the corner is trying a backstroke, blowing bubbles as she goes.

Soon the excursion comes to an end, the children pack up their things and head for home – a shower of rain causing a mild panic on the way. At last when they are back in bed all is still, once more.

Quietly, and only gently breaking the spell, the teacher calls the class to him. In a very different mood from when they came in, the class is again clustered in a semi-circle round the gramophone at the foot of the steps. The children seem relaxed and satisfied. Quiet discussion is taking place now, and it seems to draw naturally to a close with a few of the class getting up and collecting their things, while the teacher returns to re-sort his records. Ties are replaced, blazers and cardigans put on, as the children drift towards the door into what is obviously the routine of forming quiet lines ready to go. The timing was just right, the bell rings and the teacher sees the class out into the foyer.

This is just one example of a drama lesson, and is the sort of work that a first-year class in a secondary school might be doing.

From R. Pemberton-Billing and J. Clegg (1965) *Teaching Drama*, London, University of London Press, pp.11–15.

TOMB DRAMA (1976)

Frequently Heathcote will deliberately set a drama back in time to a more primitive age when tribal conflicts are acted out face-to-face and issues can be seen more clearly. An example of this occurred in the tomb drama.

... Jerry (a tall black 12 year old), takes over the leadership of the tribe. He has secured the support of the dead bodies (who are by this time sitting on chairs rather than lying in the tomb). When he addresses the community, he can get their attention by using a formal posture, coupled with phrases like 'The spirit of our fathers has spoken'.

. . . when the children come in for this last day of drama, there, along the end of the long hall, are stretched scrolls with the descriptions and interpretations the adults have written on them. The session begins with the reading of this record.

After reading the record, the children drape or tie swatches of black and brown fabric about them and go back into their roles as tribe members. Before long, Jerry is instructing the corpse of the dead man for his role in the ceremony to come. He tells him what to say and directs him to speak in a deep voice.

When he and the man-in-role as the dead man are ready, Jerry calls the group together to listen to the words of the spirits. 'Spirits!' he calls ceremoniously.

'Spirits!' Heathcote repeats.

'Come, Spirits!' Several other tribe members join her in repeating this invocation ritualistically.

Then the voice of the dead resounds in an authoritative, sepulchral tone: 'Let the dead be worshipped. May the words of those who watched be destroyed.'

Jerry turns to his tribe. 'You have heard the Spirit tell us to tear up the reports that they wrote.' With a long spear he points to the back of the large hall. 'Let every tribe member go over to the papers and tear up those papers.' Heathcote is clearing her throat and visibly tense at this point. She values the written word and efforts of the adult students very highly, so she finds Jerry's leadership painful to follow.

A girl, looking up at Heathcote's agonised face, shouts, 'I cannot bring myself to tear them.'

'What the Spirits said, we must do,' warns Jerry. He ceremoniously tears the first sheet, saying, 'In the name of the Spirits.' The tribe hesitates. 'Go ahead, tear!' they join him. After a few moments of frantic tearing, Jerry looks as the shredded bits of paper and says with conviction, 'These are not our words, not our laws. We have our own laws.'

'Then we can never learn from others,' Heathcote says in a soft, regretful tone.

'No, we will not learn from others. I want all the tribe to grab these and put them in a pile over there.'

After they dutifully do that, Heathcote says humbly to her leader, 'The unlaw is now piled beside the true law.'

Jerry points to the pile. 'I have read it, and these Spirits have read it, and they know it's the wrong law. Now we shall learn our own law.' He then leads a procession down to the other end of the large hall and again invokes the Spirit of the dead.

'Spirits! Spirits! We have done what you have asked. What is your wish?' The Spirit doesn't answer. 'Spirits! Spirits!' Jerry calls again. 'The words of our tribe are now the only words.'

'Behold the words of the past,' the Spirit says solemnly. 'Thus have died those words that are not our words. May they never return.'

'Yes, oh Holy One.'

Then the tribe follows Jerry's lead and sits in a circle. They begin to think about what they have just done. One girl in role as a woman of the tribe thoughtfully confronts Jerry, 'You have just torn up what our tribe is about. What are we if we are not that?' 'That we have not wrote. This we have wrote,' he says, pointing to their records. 'That is not our law,' he says, forcefully gesturing with his spear.

'How do we know?' asks the girl.

'The Spirits have spoken. No reporters will come on our land.'

'But I trusted the words of those reporters.'

'Why did you trust them?'

'Because they spoke true about our tribe.'

Another woman says, almost to herself, 'It is against our law to destroy.'

Jerry is hard pressed now; he calls on the Spirit again. 'Why did we tear up the laws of the strangers? this woman asks. Our law says not to destroy.'

The Spirit replies, 'Let those of our tribe behold the words of the past. You are as we were, and thus it shall be done and understood in our tribe. That which is gone is of the eyes of those who are not of us.'

'You hear?' says Jerry, vindicated. 'After this, no one shall come in and visit us.'

When the drama is over, the children discuss what they have done. They have experienced the classic confrontation of the traditional tribal leader with members of the community who are ready to open themselves to new understandings ... The problems on both sides are the heart of anthropological investigation.

B. J. Wagner (1979) *Dorothy Heathcote: Drama as a Learning Medium*, London, Hutchinson, pp.206–8.

AN AIR DISASTER (1981)

The teacher has the use of the hall for 35 minutes, has a class of thirty 10 to 11 year olds of mixed ability and with slightly more boys than girls. The class is used to this pattern of lesson and is always anxious to show its work.

As they enter the hall the class is noisy and untidy, so in order to create a more self-disciplined atmosphere, the teacher decides to try some 'warm-up' exercises. The first one involves running everywhere and 'freezing' when the cymbal is struck. The movement produces quite a few collisions and people giggle during freeze-times. Clearly the children need a more static piece so they are put in pairs to work a mirror exercise. They have to match each other's movement without speaking. There is a great deal of talking and laughter and the imitation is not accurate. There is a feeling that this is a very familiar exercise for the class and one which does not provide much interest any more. The teacher feels valuable time is slipping away and that perhaps it would have been better to have started as he had originally intended. So he stops the class and calls them to sit round him. The proximity of the boys sitting closely in a tangle of children leads to horseplay which the teacher resolves by separating offenders.

His questions quickly produce from the children the focal point he requires. They have much more information than he requires and having appeared to be soliciting their knowledge of the recent disaster he is constrained to allow more random talk than he really wants or time allows. So he cuts through the wealth of information that the raised hands and voices represent, to announce that they are going to make their own disaster. When he dismisses them, he tells them that they must form a group and work out whether they are the crew, the passengers, ground control, etc. The class is already full of planning talk while he is still dealing with a boy who is asking if it is alright if he is the hijacker who makes the plane crash. Although that was not his intention, the teacher allows this as the class is already moving away into noisy bunches. The parted combatants now reunite and immediately begin to wrestle as hijacker and guard. Indeed, an alarming number of the boys seem to have cottoned on to the idea. Where a quieter group are simulating the cabin and the controls they are set upon by another group of lusty hijackers. This is not part of their plan and they protest ultimately to the teacher as they are not as strong or as numerous as their attackers. The teacher stops the class and warns the children that they will not be allowed to make their play if they don't behave. He sorts out the groups and sets them to work once more, making sure that the difficult boys are settled to plan their piece. He has even suggested to them that they are survivors, dazed and injured who have to find help. The boys are excited by the prospect and soon the teacher feels able to leave them to get on by themselves.

The rest of the class is busy, not apparently working to a plan but making it up as they go along. They shout instructions to each other as the noise is intense. They have set out chairs more or less elaborately and these clatter over as the crash occurs in different parts of the hall. The teacher is aware that the noise level is such that it might invite intervention of the headmaster and also the time indicates that only seven minutes are left. He stops the class and asks them to sit down to watch their pieces. Talk immediately resumes and this he quells, stressing that they have to pay attention to the scenes of others to be able to criticise them, especially as they will put the scenes together to make a play. As some semblance of quiet is apparent he invites the naughty boys' group, with which he had planned, to show theirs first. The piece starts as he might expect with the survivors reeling about like drunken men. But soon a dispute about food and water arises and the exhausted men fight with remarkable energy. Already people are walking through the hall and embarrassed by what appears as riot, the teacher stops the piece. As he asks for the next, the bell rings and amid cries of frustrated actors, the chat of the naughty group, the increasing horde invading the hall and the clatter of the dinner ladies, he promises they will see the rest next time.

Nothing has worked as he had planned, he feels exhausted and depressed because the idea was a good one. He dare not evaluate the lesson because the lofty aims remain as an indictment of his ability to produce drama with the class. For the children there is no such heart-searching. In the playground they are doing much the same as they were previously doing in the hall. The lesson was very much as usual with the opportunity for some fun and a break from the more formal task of writing. As usual, one had to make up a story about a given idea, and act it with friends – if there was time. 'Sometimes it gets boring when you have to do the same idea again or when you have to do the same thing, like being mirrors, and that.' To be honest neither class nor teacher could really justify the work to an anxious mother, irate father or sceptical deputy head.

This imaginary incident might seem a cruel exaggeration of an unfamiliar scene; it is not. Its details are fictional, but the experiences they exemplify have been seen again and again.

B. Watkins (1981) *Drama and Education*, London, Batsford, pp.64–6.

DRUGS (1991)

General aims	What you need	Strategies
To develop awareness and knowledge of the dangers associated with drugs and also the exploitation of young people through the drug industry.	Optional – drug information leaflets available from doctors' surgeries and hospitals.	Teacher in role. Group work, pair work, signing, mime, using a model, verbal and non-verbal language work.

Action points

Stimulus

Improvise a scene at the front for the rest of the group to watch. TIR [teacher in role] as the customs' officer. Two volunteers as drug dealers.

Play out the scene. The dealers are bringing drugs in through customs.

Afterwards comment on the effectiveness of the scene, discuss things like tension and suspense. How might they develop this scene?

Replay the scene using suggestions from the group to develop tension and suspense. Also consider how the space is used.

Ask the question, 'As a customs' officer who has done this work for some time what would you be looking for?'

Take their suggestions and if they do not raise it, which is unlikely, discuss body language. These ideas will help the volunteers get the scene 'right'.

This lesson was devised to challenge a group of students who had an idealised idea of drug taking. They were interested in 'playing' junkies but the learning contract made with the class was that at the start they were in role as drug dealers who were not users. This distancing was deliberate, not only to protect the students (some of whom may well know more about drugs than others), but also to enhance the possibilities for the drama.

To ensure that the students are engaged in this activity they must feel that it is a tense moment. The TIR can be very suspicious and almost catch the drug dealers, but lets them pass through.

Group work

In groups they generate their own scenes based on the one observed. Their objective is to create a 'customs' scene with tension in it.

Having watched a scene unfold in this way most students are capable of developing their own work. In our lessons we found that this was an excellent way to practise and develop specific skills. In this case developing the use of tension within a scene and shaping their own work.

Whole group with teacher in role

TIR as police spokesperson giving a press conference. The police have failed to locate the drugs dealer but they must not allow the press to get hold of this information. They are concerned to keep up the appearance of an efficient police force.

Students in role as members of the press. The press strongly suspect that a huge amount of heroin has entered the country and want to get the police to admit their failure.

Teacher role play allows a lot of information to be given which will enhance future work: for example, possible corruption in the police force, responsibility of the press to police and public, etc. Signing will be important here. Similarly setting mode and language register through the example. In this scene we wanted a formal meeting and we worked for this by speaking in role in a heightened way and referring to the normal procedure at a press conference. By careful use of expression and body language the teacher can demonstrate what is said is not the whole truth.

This sequence is followed by a further six action points, culminating in a final 'press conference'.

Reflection

Questioning by the teacher of the group out of role. There is new information now for this confrontation between the police and the press. How does it change the scene?

Having played the press conference scene at the beginning it is interesting to compare the two scenes. Invite the students to say how they think it is different and why this should be. It may have become necessary earlier in the work to refer to leaflets that have been produced about drugs and drug taking. Whether this is the case or not it would be useful here to refer to such materials and to agencies where advice can be sought.

Development

You may care to consider the following:

Make a list of legal and illegal drugs. Why are some legal and others not?

Watch the BBC Scene programme *Too Nice by Half* which focuses on two school boys who become involved with drugs.

Design a warning commercial to campaign against drugs. This could be videoed or recorded.

Find a map which takes you to the producer of the drugs. In fact this is a peasant farmer who gets more for this particular crop than any other but is still very poor. How can you persuade him/her to change the crop he/she grows?

From K. Taylor (ed.) (1981) *Drama Strategies*, London, Heinemann with London Drama, pp.32, 33 and 37.

APPENDIX 2

PERFORMANCE ANALYSIS

This questionnaire was devised by Patrice Pavis to help drama students with no particular knowledge of semiology in the interpretation and analysis of aspects of theatre performance. With some adaptation and simplification, and used selectively, drama teachers might find elements of this questionnaire useful for looking at performance with their pupils.

1 GENERAL DISCUSSION OF PERFORMANCE

(a)   what holds elements of performance together
(b)   relationship between systems of staging
(c)   coherence or incoherence
(d)   aesthetic principles of the production
(e)   what do you find disturbing about the production; strong moments or weak, boring moments.

2 SCENOGRAPHY

(a)   spatial forms: urban, architectural, scenic, gestural, etc.
(b)   relationship between audience space and acting space
(c)   systems of colours and their connotations
(d)   principles of organisation of space – relationship between on-stage and off-stage – links between space utilised and fiction of the staged dramatic text – what is shown and what is implied.

3 LIGHTING SYSTEM

4 STAGE PROPERTIES

type, function, relationship to space and actors' bodies.

5 COSTUMES

how they work; relationship to actors' bodies.

6 ACTORS' PERFORMANCES

(a)   individual or conventional style of acting
(b)   relation between actor and group
(c)   relation between text and body, between actor and role

152

(d)   quality of gestures and mime
(e)   quality of voices
(f)   how dialogues develop.

7 FUNCTION OF MUSIC AND SOUND EFFECTS

8 PACE OF PERFORMANCE

(a)   overall pace
(b)   pace of certain signifying systems (lighting, costumes, gestures, etc.)
(c)   steady or broken pace.

9 INTERPRETATION OF STORY-LINE IN PERFORMANCE

(a)   what story is being told
(b)   what kind of dramaturgical choices have been made
(c)   what are ambiguities in performance and what are points of explanation
(d)   how is plot structured
(e)   how is story constructed by actors and staging
(f)   what is genre of dramatic text.

10 TEXT IN PERFORMANCE

(a)   main features of translation (script to stage)
(b)   what role is given to dramatic text in production
(c)   relationship between (written) text and image.

11 AUDIENCE

(a)   where does performance take place
(b)   what expectations did you have of performance
(c)   how did audience react
(d)   role of spectator in production of meaning.

12 HOW TO NOTATE (PHOTOGRAPH AND FILM) THIS PRODUCTION

(a)   how to notate performance technically
(b)   which images have you retained.

13 WHAT CANNOT BE PUT INTO SIGNS

(a)   what did not make sense in your interpretation of the production
(b)   what was not reducible to signs and meaning (and why).

14

(a)   Are there any special problems that need examining
(b)   Any comments, suggestions for further categories for the questionnaire and the production.

P. Pavis (1985) 'Theatre analysis: some questions and a questionnaire', *New Theatre Quarterly* 1(2), p.209.

NOTES

PREFACE

1 Figures from Arts Council of Great Britain (1992) *Drama in Schools: Arts Council Guidance on Drama Education*, London, Arts Council of Great Britain. For a report on primary drama, see Department of Education and Science (1990) *The Teaching and Learning of Drama*, London, HMSO.

2 Department of Education and Science (1989) *Drama from 5 to 16: Curriculum Matters 17*, London, HMSO.

1 THE PLOT: THE RISE OF DRAMA-IN-EDUCATION

1 G. Bolton (1995) in G. Bolton and D. Heathcote *Drama for Learning: Dorothy Heathcote's Mantle of the Expert Approach to Education*, Portsmouth, New Hampshire USA, Heinemann, p.4.

2 For example, Sarah Kofman argues that in Rousseau's 'nature/culture' duality, 'nature' represents not only the patriarchy of Rousseau himself but a phallocratic discourse which aims to perpetuate a binary divide between the sexes. See S. Kofman (1992) 'Rousseau's phallocratic ends', in F. Fraser and S. L. Bartky (eds) *Revaluing French Feminism; Critical Essays on Difference, Agency and Culture*, Indianapolis, Indiana University Press, pp.46–59.

3 G. Bolton. (1986) 'Teacher in Role and teacher power', in *Positive Images: 1985 Conference Publication*, St Albans, Joint Committee (NATD, NATFHE Drama, NAYT, NADECT, NADA), p.38.

4 J.-J. Rousseau (1960) *Politics and the Arts: The Letter to M' d' Alembert on the Theatre*, trans. A. Bloom, Glencoe, Illinois, Free Press.

5 Ibid., p.126.

6 I wander thro' each chartered street,
Near where the chartered Thames does flow,
And mark in every face I meet
Marks of weakness, marks of woe.
    (William Blake, *Songs of Innocence and Experience*, 1794)

7 H. Finlay-Johnson (1911) *The Dramatic Method of Teaching*, London, James Nisbet, p.19.

8 Ibid., p.27.

9 H. Caldwell Cook (1917) *The Play Way*, London, Heinemann. Caldwell Cook was Head of English at the Perse School, Cambridge.

10 Ibid., p.4.

11 H. Finlay-Johnson, op. cit., p.13.

12 K. Groos (1901) *The Play of Man*, trans. E. L. Baldwin, London, Heinemann.

13 Board of Education (1931) *Report of the Consultative Committee on the Primary School* (The Hadow Report), London, HMSO, p.76.

14 In G C.T. Giles (1946) *The New School Tie*, London, Pilot Press, p.45.

15 Ministry of Education (1951) 'Report of Informal Committee', chaired by A. F. Alington (later HM Staff Inspector of Drama), and then G. Allen (HM Staff Inspector for English), unpublished.

16 P. Slade (1954) *Child Drama*, London, University of London Press.

17 Ibid., p.68.

18 Ibid., p.271.

19 'Child Drama is a part of real life. . . . It is quite different from any conception of theatre, which is a small – though attractive – bubble on the froth of civilisation' (ibid., 337).

20 P. Slade (1958) *An Introduction to Child Drama*, London, Hodder and Stoughton, p.2.

21 Ibid. pp.64–5.

22 Ministry of Education (1963) *Report of the Minister of Education's Central Advisory Council entitled 'Half our Future'* (The Newsom Report), London, HMSO, p.157.

23 Department of Education and Science (1967b) *Report of the Central Advisory Council for Education (England) entitled 'Children and their Primary Schools'* (The Plowden Report), London, HMSO.

24 B. Way (1967) *Development Through Drama*, London, Longman.

25 Ibid., p.2.

26 Some examples are R. Pemberton-Billing and J. Clegg (1965) *Teaching Drama*, London, University of London Press; J. Hodgson and E. Richards (1966) *Improvisation*, London, Eyre Methuen; P. Chilver (1967) *Improvised Drama*, London, Batsford; B. Walker (1970) *Teaching Creative Drama*, London, Batsford; J. Goodridge (1970) *Drama in the Primary School*, London, Heinemann; D. Bowskill (1974) *Drama and the Teacher*, Bath, The Pitman Press.

27 See J. Pick (1967) 'A little food for thought', *English in Education*, 1(3), p.58; J. Pick (1970) 'Skeletons in the prop cupboard', *Higher Education Journal* Summer, 17(5), pp. 23–6; J. Pick (1973) 'Five fallacies in drama', *Young Drama* 1(1), pp. 10–11; J. Clegg (1973) 'The dilemma of drama-in-education', *Theatre Quarterly* 9, pp.31–42.

28 D. Heathcote (1973) *Theatre Quarterly* 10, pp.63–4.

29 D. Heathcote (1972) 'Drama as challenge', in J. Hodgson (ed.) *The Uses of Drama*, London, Eyre Methuen, p.159.

30 J. Fines and R. Verrier (1976) 'The work of Dorothy Heathcote', *Young Drama* 4(1), p.3.

31 B.J. Wagner (1979) *Dorothy Heathcote: Drama as a Learning Medium*, London, Hutchinson.

32 Good examples from this period are A. Lambert *et al.* (1976) *Drama Guidelines*, London, Heinemann; A. Lambert and C. O'Neill (1982) *Drama Structures*, London, Hutchinson; N. Morgan and J. Saxton (1987) *Teaching Drama: 'A mind of many wonders . . . '*, London, Hutchinson. See also books aimed primarily at English teachers such as K. Byron (1986) *Drama in the English Classroom*, London, Methuen; J. Neelands (1984) *Making Sense of Drama*, London, Heinemann; J. Neelands (1992) *Learning through Imagined Experience*, London, Hodder and Stoughton.

2 THE PLAYERS: WITNESS AND REVELATION

1 P. Slade (1954) *Child Drama*, London,University of London Press, p.52.
2 D. Bowskill (1967) 'Drama in secondary education', *English in Education* 1(3), p.13.
3 D. Heathcote (1967) 'Improvisation', *English in Education* 1(3), p.27.
4 'Dorothy Heathcote in interview with David Davis' (1985) *2D: Journal of Drama and Dance* 4(3), p.75. Earlier in the interview, Heathcote speaks of how she has been 'building the possibility of thickness'. The point is, nowhere is this idea of 'thick description' explained. We may only surmise that she has been reading Gilbert Ryle, who introduces 'thick description' as a way of doing ethnography in G. Ryle (1971) *Collected Papers, Vol. 2: Collected Essays 1929–1968*, London, Hutchinson.
5 G. Bolton and D. Heathcote (1995) *Drama for Learning: Dorothy Heathcote's Mantle of the Expert Approach to Education*, Portsmouth, New Hampshire, Heinemann, p.195.
6 E. Gellner (1985) *The Psychoanalytic Movement*, London, Paladin Books, p.154.
7 R. Lee (1984) 'Two mules waiting', *Drama Broadsheet* 3(1), p.9.
8 J. Kelly (1985) '652 Theatre Project; a season with Dorothy Heathcote at Earls House Hospital', *Drama Broadsheet* 3(2), p.4.
9 L. Johnson and C. O'Neill (eds) (1984) *Dorothy Heathcote: Collected Writings*, London, Hutchinson, p.13.
10 J. Kelly (1985), op. cit., p.4.
11 As a feminist critic pointed out at the time, 'there was a time, after all, when "witch" and "midwife" referred to the same person'. A. Seeley (1987) 'A woman that attempts the pen: a look at the work of Dorothy Heathcote', *2D: Journal of Drama and Dance* 6(2), p.7.
12 B.-J. Wagner (1979) *Dorothy Heathcote: Drama as a Learning Medium*, London, Hutchinson, pp.14–15.
13 In 1964, at the Institute of Education, University of Durham.
14 G. Bolton and D. Heathcote (1995) op. cit., p.5.
15 D. Heathcote (1983) in W. Dobson (ed.) *Bolton at the Barbican*, London, National Association for the Teaching of Drama (NATD), Longman, p.20. The epigram for this piece is the chorus from Yeats' poem, 'The Only Jealousy of Emer':

... How many centuries spent
The sedentary soul
In toils of measurement
Beyond eagle or mole ...

16 J. Neelands (1983) 'Whose art is it?', *Drama Broadsheet* 2(1), p.21.
17 Ibid.
18 J. Fines (1983) 'The edges of the matter', *London Drama* 6(8), p.4.
19 G. Bolton and D. Heathcote (1995) op. cit.
20 L. Jardine (1995) 'Biography as research for education: reading Gavin Bolton', *The NADIE Journal* (Australia) 19(2), p.45.
21 R. Sennett (1977) *The Fall of Public Man*, Cambridge, Cambridge University Press, p.270.
22 H. Fletcher (1995) 'Retrieving the mother/other from the myths and margins of O'Neill's "Seal Wife" drama', *The NADIE Journal* (Australia) 19(2), p.36. For the outraged response to her carefully argued feminist

critique, see *The NADIE Journal* (Australia) 20(1), pp.4–8. For further examples of the family's response to criticism, see G. Bolton (1992) 'Have a heart!', *Drama* 1(1), pp.7–8 and G. Bolton (1993) 'Piss on his face', in C. Lawrence (ed.), *Voices for Change*, London, National Drama Publications, pp.22–5.

23 G. Fairclough (1972) *The Play is NOT the Thing*, Oxford, Basil Blackwell, p.8.

24 S. Welton (1985) 'Towards the swamps?', *Drama Broadsheet* 3(2), p.13.

25 J. Neelands (1983), op. cit.

26 R. Lee (1984) op. cit.

27 G. Bolton (1981), 'Drama in the curriculum', *2D: Journal of Drama and Dance* 1(1), pp.13. Reprinted in D. Davis and C. Lawrence (eds) (1986) *Gavin Bolton: Selected Writings*, London, Longman, p.227. He is referring to R. W. Witkin (1974) *The Intelligence of Feeling*, London, Heinemann.

28 L. Johnson and C. O'Neill (1984), op. cit., pp.9–10.

29 D. Rowntree (1977) *Assessing Students: How Shall We Know Them?*, New York, Harper and Row, p.1.

30 The Certificate of Secondary Education (CSE) was introduced in 1965 for those 16 year olds not among the top 20 per cent of the ability range already taking the General Certificate of Education (GCE) at Ordinary Level.

31 The General Certificate of Secondary Education (GCSE), introduced in 1986, combined CSE and GCE in a single system of national examinations at 16-plus.

32 Midland Examining Group (1986) *GCSE Leicestershire Mode III Drama*, Cambridge, pp.2–3. See also D. Cross (1990) 'Leicestershire GCSE Drama: a syllabus with a clear direction', *2D: Journal of Drama and Dance* 9(2), pp.18–24. 'The Leicester GCSE . . . was devised to encourage teaching for understanding. The pedagogy was not being invented, it had been developing for some twenty years, with its leading national figures in the drama sphere being Dorothy Heathcote and Gavin Bolton.'

33 G. Bolton (1980) 'Theatre form in drama teaching', in K. Robinson (ed.) *Exploring Theatre and Education*, London, Heinemann, p.86, reprinted in D. Davis and C. Lawrence (eds) (1986), op. cit., pp.178-9. For a full account of this workshop, see G. Bolton (1979) *Towards a Theory of Drama in Education*, London, Longman, Chapter 8.

34 N. Morgan and J. Saxton (1987) *Teaching Drama: 'A mind of many wonders . . .'*, London, Hutchinson.

35 H. Nicholson (1995) 'Drama education, gender and identity', *Forum of Education* (Australia) 50(2), p.34.

36 N. Morgan and J. Saxton (1987) op. cit., p.206.

37 B.-J. Wagner (1979), op. cit., p.231.

38 See C. Hill (1983) in C. Hill et al. (eds) *The World of the Muggletonians*, London, Temple Smith.

39 Ibid., p.12.

3 THE SETTING: EVENTS ON THE PUBLIC STAGE

1 G. Bolton (1981), 'Drama in the curriculum', *2D: Journal of Drama and Dance* 1(1), p.15, reprinted in D. Davis and C. Lawrence (eds) (1986) *Gavin Bolton: Selected Writings*, London, Longman, p.229.

2 As part of the *Education Reform Act 1988*, London, HMSO.

3 Centre for Contemporary Cultural Studies (1981) *Unpopular Education*, London, Hutchinson.

4 Ibid., p.65.

5 Ministry of Education (1963) *Report of the Minister of Education's Central Advisory Council entitled 'Half our Future'* (The Newsom Report), London, HMSO.

6 B. Morris (1967) *The New Curriculum*, London, HMSO, p.6.

7 Ministry of Education (1963) op. cit., p.xvi.

8 B. Way (1967) *Development through Drama*, London, Longman, pp.2–4.

9 For example, see L. Stenhouse (1969) *Schools Council Humanities Curriculum Project*, London, Longman.

10 And particularly, I remember, after the school-leaving age was raised to 16 in 1972 (ROSLA).

11 In the first instance, two issues in 1969 of the *Critical Survey*, a periodical associated with the literary *Critical Quarterly*. Edited by C. B. Cox and A. E. Dyson, they appeared under the titles, 'Fight for Education' and 'The Crisis in Education'. Over the following five years, further 'Black Papers' appeared echoing the right-wing sentiments of the original contributors.

12 For all too familiar examples from the newspapers of the time, see Centre for Contemporary Cultural Studies (1981), op. cit., Chapter 10.

13 C. Burt (1969) in B. Cox and A. Dyson (eds) *Black Paper 2. The Crisis in Education*, Critical Quarterly Society, p.23.

14 Ibid., p.57.

15 R. Pedley (1969) in B. Cox and A. Dyson (eds), op. cit., p.85.

16 From Prime Minister James Callaghan's Ruskin College speech of 18 October 1976, *Education* 148(17), p.333.

17 B. Cox and A. Dyson (eds) (1969), op. cit., p.15.

18 Department of Education and Science (1977a) *Education in Schools*, London, HMSO, pp.8–13.

19 Ibid.

20 See M. Kogan (ed.) (1971) *The Politics of Education: Edward Boyle and Anthony Crosland in Conversation with Maurice Kogan*, Harmondsworth, Penguin Books.

21 J. Ellis (1983) *Life Skills Training Manual*, London, Community Service Volunteers, p.3.

22 'Letter from a drama teacher' (1983) *2D: Journal of Drama and Dance* 3(1), p.2.

23 K. Joyce (1983) 'Drama in personal and social education', *2D: Journal of Drama and Dance* 3(1), p.13.

24 D. Morton (1983) 'Drama for capability', *2D: Journal of Drama and Dance* 2(3), p.6.

25 L. Johnson (1984) Editorial, *London Drama* 6(9), p.3.

26 E. Fennel (1984) 'Teacher or trainer? – the dilemma of YTS', *London Drama* 6(9), p.19.

27 D. Davis (1983) 'Drama for deference or drama for defiance?', *2D: Journal of Drama and Dance* 3(1), p.35.

28 *The Arts in Schools* (1982) London, Calouste Gulbenkian Foundation.

29 Ibid.

30 Editorial, *The Times Educational Supplement* (6 February 1981) quoted in *The Arts in Schools* (1982), op. cit., p.28.

31 Department of Education and Science (1977b) *Curriculum 11–16* (The Red Book), London, HMSO, p.6. The eight areas were: the aesthetic and the creative, the ethical, the linguistic, the mathematical, the physical, the scientific, the social and political, and the spiritual.

32 Inner London Education Authority (1984) *Improving Secondary Schools* (The Hargreaves Report), London, Inner London Education Authority, p.59.

33 Department of Education and Science (1985) *Better Schools*, London, HMSO, pp.20, 22.

34 A. Rumbold in Department of Education and Science (1987b) *Speech by the Minister of State at the Annual Conference of the National Association for Education in the Arts, 28 October 1987*, London, HMSO, para.42.

35 Department of Education and Science (1977b), op. cit.

36 R. Aldrich (1988) in D. Lawton and C. Chitty. (eds) *The National Curriculum*, London, Institute of Education, University of London, p.23.

37 It is worth noting that this archaic structure did not apply to Scotland or Northern Ireland, both of which had more flexible arrangements in which drama appeared alongside the other arts.

38 In the same way that 'Science' stood for physics, biology, chemistry and so on. See *Education Reform Act 1988*, London, HMSO, p.2. For a synopsis of the proposals, see Department of Education and Science (1987a) *The National Curriculum 5–16: A Consultation Document*, London, HMSO.

39 *The Guardian*, 27 January 1992.

40 J. Neelands (1984) *Making Sense of Drama*, London, Heinemann, pp 6, 7.

41 J. Saxton and P. Verriour (1988) 'A sense of ownership', *The NADIE Journal* (Australia), 12(2), p.9.

42 G. Readman (1988) 'Drama in the Market Place?', *2D: Journal of Drama and Dance* 7(2), p.11.

4 THE DENOUEMENT: REHEARSING THE PHANTOM REVOLUTION

1 W. H. Auden (1940) 'New year letter, January 1940' , in E. Mendelsone (ed.) (1976) *W.H. Auden Collected Poems*, London, Faber & Faber, p.205.

2 Department of Education and Science (1984) *Training for Jobs* (White Paper), London, HMSO, p.14.

3 First piloted in 1983, the Technical and Vocational Education Initiative aimed to make students better equipped to enter 'the world of work'. Courses emphasised initiative, motivation and enterprise, as well as problem-solving skills and other aspects of personal development. The TVEI came to an end in 1996.

4 B. Reid and M. Holt (1986) 'Structure and ideology in upper secondary education', in A. Hartnett and M. Naish (eds) *Education and Society Today*, London, The Falmer Press, p.92.

5 The proposals for testing were contained in Department of Education and Science (1988) *National Curriculum: Task Group on Assessment and Testing Report* (The Black Report), London, HMSO.

6 T. McElligott *et al.* (1988) *Report on TVEI*, Assistant Masters and Mistresses Association.

7 Health Education Authority (1988) *High Stress Occupations Working Party Report*, reported in *The Times Educational Supplement*, 3 June 1988.

8 This ironic assessment appears in F. Inglis (1985) *The Management of Ignorance*, Oxford, Basil Blackwell, p.17.

9 In the 1983 general election, a MORI poll showed the Tories commanding 44 per cent of support among teachers in England and Wales with Labour on 26 per cent. By 1987, Tory support had dropped to 24 per cent, *The Times*

Educational Supplement, 29 May 1987.

10 See research carried out for *The Times Educational Supplement* by Research Services Ltd in 1996. Reported in *The Times Educational Supplement*, 10 January 1997.

11 M. Wootton (ed.) (1982) *New Directions in Drama Teaching*, London, Heinemann, p.4.

12 P. Slade (1958) *An Introduction to Child Drama*, London, Hodder and Stoughton, p.2.

13 D. Self (1975) *A Practical Guide to Drama in the Secondary School*, London, Ward Lock Educational, p.7.

14 D. Dorne (1987), 'What future for British political community theatre?', unpublished essay, University of Bristol.

15 G. Bolton (1995) in G. Bolton and D. Heathcote *Drama for Learning: Dorothy Heathcote's Mantle of the Expert Approach to Education*, Portsmouth, New Hampshire USA, Heinemann, p.4.

16 Theatre-in-education (TIE) involves actors engaging students in issues with a mixture of performance and role-play. Formed in 1975, The Standing Conference of Young People's Theatre (SCYPT) was for years the strident voice of theatre-in-education in Britain. Characterised by the schismatic nature of its Marxist political affiliations, for a long period until the split in that movement, it was dominated by the Workers' Revolutionary Party. Throughout the 1980s, its conferences and debates were marked by the internecine feuds between factions of the radical Left. A much reduced force by the 1990s, SCYPT maintained a vociferous presence at international drama-in-education conferences.

17 See D. Heathcote (1980) 'From the particular to the universal', in K. Robinson (ed.) *Exploring Theatre and Education*, London, Heinemann, Chapter 1. This quotation comes from J. Kelly (1985) '652 Theatre Project: a season with Dorothy Heathcote at Earls House Hospital', *Drama Broadsheet* 3(2), p.4.

18 G. Gillham *et al.* (1985) Editorial, *The SCYPT Journal*, 14, p.6. For a reverential example of this bizarre appropriation, see also G. Gillham (1989) 'What life is for: an analysis of Dorothy Heathcote's "Levels of explanation"' *2D: Journal of Drama and Dance* 8(2), pp.31–8.

19 Ibid., p.6.

20 D. Davis (1983) 'Drama for deference or drama for defiance?', *2D: Journal of Drama and Dance* 3(1), p.35.

21 W. Dobson (1985) 'Professors who live in glasshouses', *Drama Broadsheet* 4(1), p.7.

22 J. Clark and J. Spindler (1986) *Education for Change in our Society*, National Association for the Teaching of Drama, p.21.

23 J. Clark (1986) 'An introduction to conference 1986' , *Drama Broadsheet* 4(2), p.3.

24 P. Freire (1972) *Pedagogy of the Oppressed*, trans. M. Bergman Ramos, Harmondsworth, Penguin Books. Freire's account of the ways in which language can contribute to the revolutionary struggles of underprivileged groups was influential in a whole range of Third World literacy projects.

25 G. Gutiérrez (1974) *A Theology of Liberation: History, Politics and Salvation*, trans/eds I. Caridad and J. Eagleson, London, SCM Press, p.146. See also D. McLellan (1987) *Marxism and Religion*, London, Macmillan.

26 A. Boal (1979) *Theatre of the Oppressed*, trans. C. and M. O. Leal McBride, London, Pluto Press.

27 Ibid., p.122.

28 Ibid., p.141.

29 Freire's work devising literacy programmes in Brazil was cut short by the military coup of 1964. Exiled, he carried on his work in Chile. Boal was imprisoned, tortured and exiled after the military coup in Brazil in 1971.

30 D. Griffin (1983) 'Augusto Boal's "Theater of the Oppressed" ', *2D: Journal of Drama and Dance* 2(2), p.7.

31 D. Davis (1983), op. cit., p.34.

32 Ibid., pp.372–3.

33 D. Davis (1987) 'Drama as a weapon', unpublished address to the conference of the National Association of Drama Advisers.

34 See J. Neelands (1985) 'Issues or contexts?', *Drama Broadsheet* 4(1), pp.10–13.

35 Thirty-four so-called 'drama conventions' were tabulated and advertised as 'the basic building blocks of effective drama'. They included techniques such as 'role on the wall', 'still photographs' and 'meetings'. See J. Carey (1995) 'Resources Pull-out', *Drama* 4(1), pp.29–32. Also J. Neelands and T. Goode (1990) *Structuring Drama Work – A Handbook of Available Forms*, Cambridge, Cambridge University Press.

36 Not least from Her Majesty's Inspectors. See Department of Education and Science (1989) *Drama from 5 to 16: Curriculum Matters 17*, London, HMSO.

37 F. Fukuyama (1992) *The End of History and the Last Man*, New York, The Free Press.

38 S. Hubbert (1989) 'Box and Cox' *London Drama* July, p.17.

39 D. Morton (1989) *Assessment in Drama* (discussion and working document), Leeds, City of Leeds Education Department, pp.12, 15.

40 G. Bolton (1992) *New Perspectives on Classroom Drama*, Hemel Hempstead, Simon and Schuster Education, p.19.

41 Arts Council of Great Britain (1992) *Drama in Schools: Arts Council Guidance on Drama Education*, London, Arts Council of Great Britain, p.1. I was privileged to be a member of the working group for this project. *Drama in Schools* was distributed by the Arts Council to every school in the country.

42 Ibid., p.10.

43 *Research in Drama Education*, Abingdon, Carfax Publishing.

44 A. Kempe (1990), *GCSE Drama Coursebook*, Oxford, Basil Blackwell, p.iii.

45 S. Cockett (1996) 'Aims and values in the practice of drama specialists in secondary schools', in J. Somers (ed.) *Drama and Theatre in Education: Contemporary Research*, Ontario, Captus University Publications, p.214.

46 For examples, see John O'Toole's work with the police, in J. O'Toole (1989) 'Police Academy' in *The NADIE Journal* (Australia) 14(1), pp.24–26; Heather Smigiel and workplace training programmes, in H. Smigiel (1995) in `Drama in workplace training', *The NADIE Journal* (Australia), 19(1), p.3–14; Jim Mienczakowski in psychiatric settings and drug and alcohol detoxification units, in J. Mienczakowski (1995) 'An ethnographic theatre' , *Drama* 3(3), pp.8–12.

47 See D. Hornbrook (1995) 'Mr Gargery's challenge: reflections on the NADIE Journal International Research Issue', *The NADIE Journal* (Australia), 19(1), p.83.

5 THE OMNIPOTENT SELF

1 E. Gellner (1985) *The Psychoanalytic Movement*, London, Paladin Books, p.5.

2 J.-P. Sartre (1972) *Kean*, trans. F. Hauser, London, Davis-Poynter, Act 1, Scene 1.

3 Alongside this there existed, notably in the theatre, systems of commercial production of which Shakespeare's early joint stock company at The Globe and Blackfriars theatres is a famous example, although this too required noble patronage to protect its members from vagaboudage.

4 J. Goethe, *Samtliche Werke*, XXXIII, pp. 17–18. Quoted in M.H. Abrams (1953) *The Mirror and the Lamp*, Oxford, Oxford University Press, p.90.

5 P. Bourdieu (1971) 'Intellectual field and creative project', in M. Young (ed.), *Knowledge and Control*, London, Collier-Macmillan.

6 Most famously, of course, Herbert Read. For his classic argument for art as 'the basis of education', see H. Read (1943) *Education through Art*, London, Faber and Faber. Later in the century, Malcolm Ross took up the cause of the 'education of sensibility'. See M. Ross (1978) *The Creative Arts*, London, Heinemann.

7 C. Rogers (1970) 'Towards a theory of creativity' in P. E. Vernon (ed.) *Creativity*, Harmondsworth, Penguin Books. It is worth noting that only when eighteenth-century humanism had established the centrality of human agency in the ordering of the world was the idea that acts of creation could be dispositional possible; before that, creation was understood as the prerogative of gods and monarchs. Attempts to prefix with 'creative', in its modern sense, a universe-creating Jehovah or even a royal decree, reveals the word's redundancy in a pre-Enlightenment context. For a stimulating discussion of modern ideas of creativity, see S. Bailin (1994) *Achieving Extraordinary Ends: An Essay on Creativity*: Norwood, New Jersey, Ablex Publishing. See also S. Bailin (1998) 'Creativity in context', in D. Hornbrook (ed.) *On the Subject of Drama*, London, Routledge, Chapter 3.

8 R. W. Witkin (1974) *The Intelligence of Feeling*, London, Heinemann, pp. 1, 2.

9 Ibid. p.33.

10 G. Bolton (1985) 'Changes in thinking about drama in education', *Theory into Practice* 24(3), p.155.

11 H. J. Eysenck (1954) *The Psychology of Politics*, London, Eyre Methuen, pp.9–10.

12 E. Gellner (1985), op. cit., pp.89–-90.

13 C. Lasch (1980) *The Culture of Narcissism: American Life in an Age of Diminishing Expectations*, London, Sphere Books, pp.12–13.

14 L. Trilling (1971) *Sincerity and Authenticity*, Cambridge, Mass, Harvard University Press, pp.10–11.

15 See R. Sennett (1977) *The Fall of Public Man*, Cambridge, Cambridge University Press, p.263. In their assessment scheme quoted in Chapter 2, Morgan and Saxton would surely have been pushed not to give Nixon an 'A' for 'maintaining role'. A serious (and worrying) point.

16 D. Davis and C. Lawrence in D. Davis and C. Lawrence (eds) (1986) *Gavin Bolton: Selected Writings*, London, Longman, p.194.

17 See E. Husserl (1960) *Cartesian Meditations: An Introduction to Phenomenology*, trans. D. Cairns, The Hague, Martinus Nijhoff.

18 B.-J. Wagner (1979) *Dorothy Heathcote: Drama as a Learning Medium*, London, Hutchinson, p.76.

19 D. Davis and C. Lawrence (eds) (1986) op. cit., p.226.

20 H. Nicholson (1995) 'Performative acts: drama, education and gender', *The NADIE Journal* (Australia), 19(1).

21 B.-J. Wagner (1979) op. cit., pp.220–1.

22 A. MacIntyre (1981) *After Virtue: A Study in Moral Theory*, London, Duckworth, p.30.
23 J. Dunn (1979) *Western Political Theory in the Face of the Future*, Cambridge, Cambridge University Press, p.43.
24 D. Hargreaves (1982) *The Challenge for the Comprehensive School*, London, Routledge and Kegan Paul, p.93.

6 HAPPENING ON THE AESTHETIC

1   L. McGregor *et al.*(1977) *Learning through Drama*, London, Heinemann, p.16.
2   M. Ross (1978) *The Creative Arts*, London, Heinemann, pp.63–4.
3   G. Bolton (1982) 'Drama as learning, as art and as aesthetic experience', in M. Ross (ed.) *The Development of Aesthetic Experience*, Oxford, Pergamon Press, p.146, reprinted in D. Davis and C. Lawrence (eds) (1986) *Gavin Bolton: Selected Writings*, London, Longman, p.162.
4   G. Bolton (1984) *Drama As Education*, London, Longman, p.146.
5   G. Bolton (1986) 'Weaving theories is not enough', *New Theatre Quarterly* 2(8), p.370.
6   M. Heidegger (1978) *Basic Writings*, ed. D. Krell, London, Routledge and Kegan Paul, p.383.
7   In M. Ross (ed.) (1982) op. cit., pp.148–52. For those interested in the archaeology of this quarrel, see also Bolton's touchy response to Ross in G. Bolton (1983) 'Drama in education: learning medium or arts process?', in W. Dobson (ed.), *Bolton at the Barbican*, London, National Association for the Teaching of Drama/Longman, 1983 and in G. Bolton (1984) op. cit., Chapter 7.
8   M. Ross (1978)op. cit., p.50. See also Ross's project on students' self-assessment in the arts through 'feelingful talk' in M. Ross *et al.* (1993) *Assessing Achievement in the Arts*, Milton Keynes, Open University Press.
9   M. Bell (1986) 'In search of a middle ground or drama as a learning arts process', *2D: Journal of Drama and Dance* 6(1), p.30.
10 M. Ross (ed.) (1982) op. cit., p.152.
11 N. Kitson and I. Spiby (1995) *Primary Drama Handbook*, London, Watts Books, p.2.
12 N. Morgan and J. Saxton (1988) 'Who's tripping over my bridge?', *The NADIE Journal* (Australia) 13(1), p.6.
13 To any disinterested observer, a curiously pleonastic notion. Would using 'musical form' in the music lesson be such a radical idea? See G. Bolton (1980) 'Theatre form in drama teaching', in K. Robinson (ed.) (1980) *Exploring Theatre and Education*, London, Heinemann, Chapter 3, reprinted in D. Davis and C. Lawrence (eds) (1986) *Gavin Bolton: Selected Writings*, London, Longman, pp.164–80.
14 G. Bolton (1986) op. cit., p.370.
15 G. Bolton (1992) *New Perspectives on Classroom Drama*, Hemel Hempstead, Simon and Schuster Education, p.114. For more internal wrangling about the supposed differences between 'theatre' and 'drama', see G. Bolton (1981) 'Drama in education – a reappraisal' in N. McCaslin (ed.) *Children and Drama*, 2nd edn, New York, Longman, reprinted in D. Davis and C. Lawrence (eds) (1986), op. cit., pp.254–69. Also, N. Morgan and J. Saxton (1987) 'The relationship between theatre and drama' , in *Teaching Drama: A mind of many wonders . . .*, London, Hutchinson, Chapter 1.

16 *Scrutiny* was the influential journal of the Cambridge School founded by F. R. Leavis and Q. D. Roth in the 1920s.

17 T. Eagleton (1983) *Literary Theory*, Oxford, Basil Blackwell, p.31.

18 G. Bolton (1986) 'Teacher-in-role and teacher power', in *Positive Images: 1985 Conference Publication*, St Albans, Joint Committee (NATD, NATFHE Drama, NAYT, NADECT, NADA), p.39.

19 B.-J. Wagner (1979) *Dorothy Heathcote: Drama as a Learning Medium*, London, Hutchinson, pp.203–6.

20 B. Edmiston and J. Wilhelm (1996) 'Playing in different keys: research notes for action researchers and reflective drama practitioners', in P. Taylor (ed.) *Researching Drama and Arts Education: Paradigms and Possibilities*, London, Falmer Press, pp.93–4.

21 T. Eagleton (1983), op. cit., pp.26–7. The language of feeling pervades teachers' verbal evaluations of students' work. How often, I wonder, are they asked what they *thought*?

22 F. R. Leavis (1930) *Mass Civilisation and Minority Culture*, Cambridge, Cambridge University Press, pp.4–5.

23 T. Eagleton (1983), op. cit., p.138.

24 Research by the National Foundation for Educational Research and the British Film Institute in 1988 suggested that about 35 per cent of British secondary schools were undertaking media education. See J. Bowker (ed.) (1991) *Secondary Media Education: A Curriculum Statement*, London, British Film Institute, p.2.

25 The journal of the National Association for the Teaching of English (NATE) has been a locus for many of the debates within English on these matters. See also *The English Magazine*, London, English and Media Centre.

26 P. Slade (1954) *Child Drama*, London, University of London Press, p.108.

27 C. Stanislavski (1980) *My Life in Art*, trans. J.J. Robbins, London, Eyre Methuen, p.466.

28 Ibid., pp.466–7.

29 T. Eagleton (1976) Marxism and Literary Criticism, London, Eyre Methuen, pp.30–1.

30 *Lehrstück* ('didactic play') was used to describe a form of radical music theatre in the 1920s designed to instruct the performers rather than entertain an audience. Bertolt Brecht was the most famous exponent of these plays, which are sometimes seen as the precursors of theatre-in-education. *Agitprop* (agitation–propaganda) was a form of theatre used to extol revolutionary change. The Department of Agitation and Propaganda was set up in 1920 by the Central Committee of the Soviet Communist Party to supervise the propaganda campaign in the media.

31 R. Williams (1979) *Modern Tragedy*, London, Verso, pp.111–12.

32 A. Owens and K. Barber (1997) *Dramaworks*, Carlisle, Carel Press, pp.34, 66, 109,

33 B. Brecht (1978b) *Brecht on Theatre: The Development of an Aesthetic*, ed. J. Willett, London, Eyre Methuen, p.110.

34 D. Heathcote (1980) *Drama as Context*, National Association for the Teaching of English, Aberdeen, Aberdeen University Press, p.48.

35 T. Eagleton (1976), op. cit., p.31.

36 R. Williams (1979), op. cit., p.69.

37 E. Fischer (1963) *The Necessity of Art*, trans. A. Bostock, Harmondsworth, Penguin Books, p.78. Drama-in-education has succumbed easily to forms of symbolism. For example, see G. Bolton (1978) 'The process of symbolisation

in improvised drama', *Young Drama* 6(1), pp.10–13, reprinted in D. Davis and C. Lawrence (eds) (1986) op. cit., pp.145–8.

38 E. Fischer (1963) op. cit., pp.95–6.

7 SIGNIFICANT KNOWING

1 G. Bolton (1982) 'A statement outlining the contemporary view held of drama in education in Britain', in M. Goethals (ed.) *Opvoedkundigdrama*, S-Gravenhage, The Netherlands, University of Leiden Press, reprinted in D. Davis and C. Lawrence (eds) (1986) *Gavin Bolton: Selected Writings*, London, Longman, p.15.

2 G. Bolton (1979) *Towards a Theory of Drama in Education*, London, Longman, p.31.

3 G. Bolton (1986), 'Teacher-in-role and teacher power', *Positive Images: 1985 Conference Publication*, Joint Committee (NATD, NATFHE Drama, NAYT, NADECT, NADA), p.38.

4 G. Bolton (1979) op. cit., p.87.

5 G. Bolton (1982) 'Freedom and imagination', unpublished paper, reprinted in D. Davis and C. Lawrence (eds) (1986), op. cit., p.20.

6 G. Bolton (1979) 'An evaluation of the Schools Council drama teaching project (10–16)', *Speech and Drama* 28(3), reprinted in D. Davis and C. Lawrence (eds) (1986), op. cit., p.215.

7 G. Bolton (1983) 'The activity of dramatic playing', in C. Day and J. Norman (eds) *Issues in Educational Drama*, London, The Falmer Press, p.55, reprinted in D. Davis and C. Lawrence (eds) (1986), op. cit., p.59.

8 G. Bolton (1986), op. cit., pp.38–9.

9 G. Bolton (1982) 'Drama as learning, as art and as aesthetic experience', M. Ross (ed.) *The Development of Aesthetic Experience*, Oxford, Pergamon Press, p.141, reprinted in D. Davis and C. Lawrence (eds) (1986), op. cit., pp.158–9.

10 Ministry of Education (1963) *Half our Future* (The Newsom Report), London, HMSO, p.157. See also Chapter 1.

11 G. Bolton (1986) op. cit., p.39.

12 G. Bolton (1979) *Towards a Theory of Drama in Education* London, Longman, pp.41–2.

13 See D. Hornbrook (1988) 'Go play, boy, play: Shakespeare and educational drama', in G. Holderness (ed.) *The Shakespeare Myth*, Manchester University Press, p.149.

14 B. Edmiston and J. Wilhelm (1996) 'Playing in different keys: research notes for action researchers and reflective drama practitioners', in P. Taylor (ed.) *Researching Drama and Arts Education: Paradigms and Possibilities*, London, The Falmer Press, pp.93–4.

15 J, Somers (1996) 'Approaches to drama research', *Research in Drama Education* 1(2), p.170.

16 P. Taylor (1996) 'Doing reflective practitioner research in arts education', in P. Taylor (ed.) op. cit., p.44.

17 Ibid., p.55.

18 G. Bolton (1985) 'Gavin Bolton interviewed by David Davis', *2D: Journal of Drama and Dance* 4(2), p.14.

19 For examples, see G. Bolton (1984) *Drama As Education*, London, Longman, pp.155–6; G. Bolton (1982) 'Drama and meaning', unpublished paper

reprinted in D. Davis and C. Lawrence (eds) (1986), op. cit., pp.252–3; M. Flemming (1984) 'A sense of context', *Drama Broadsheet* 2(3), p.3.

20 M. Polanyi (1959) *The Study of Man*, London, Routledge and Kegan Paul, p.22.

21 M. Polanyi (1958) *Personal Knowledge: Towards a Post-Critical Philosophy*, London, Routledge and Kegan Paul, p.300.

22 M. Polanyi (1959) op. cit., p.36.

23 Ibid., p.26.

24 M. Polanyi (1958) op. cit., p.203.

25 Unlike Freud, Polanyi does not see intellectual and moral endeavour as sublimations, but as drives in their own right. He is certainly not prepared to accept that moral conscience might be 'the interiorization of social pressures'. See M. Polanyi (1958) op. cit., p.309fn.

26 Ibid., p.203

27 Ibid., p.231.

28 W. Dobson (1986) 'The benefits of "marginalisation" ', *New Theatre Quarterly* 2(8), pp.372–3.

29 For an interesting, but not wholly comprehensible, attempt to square this circle, see S. Eriksson and C. Jantzen (1992) 'Still pictures, aesthetic images', *Drama* 1(1), pp.9–12.

30 E.P. Errington (1993) 'Orientations towards drama education in the nineties', in E.P. Errington (ed.) *Arts Education: Beliefs, Practices and Possibilities*, Geelong, Australia, Deakin University Press. Abuse of this kind of knowledge-free empathy is not confined to drama, as historian Norman Davies points out: 'empathetic exercises can only be justified if accompanied by a modicum of knowledge [otherwise] students are sometimes in danger of having nothing but their teacher's prejudices on which to build an awareness of the past'. See N. Davies (1996) *Europe: A History*, Oxford, Oxford University Press, p.3.

31 J. Clark and T. Goode (1991) 'On a road to nowhere' , *The Drama Magazine* July, p.10.

32 G. Bolton (1979) *Towards a Theory of Drama in Education*, London. Longman, p.90.

33 C. O'Neill (1993), from the draft record of proceedings of the *Arts Education Colloquium* 1, (unpublished), University of Melbourne, p.7.

34 H. Fletcher (1995) 'Retrieving the mother/other from the myths and margins of O'Neill's "Seal Wife" drama', *The NADIE Journal* (Australia) 19(2), p.29.

35 G. Bolton (1992) *New Perspectives on Classroom Drama*, Hemel Hempstead, Simon and Schuster Education, p.141.

36 H. Fletcher (1995) op. cit., pp.33–4.

37 J. O'Toole (1992) *The Process of Drama: Negotiating Art and Meaning*, London, Routledge, p.44.

38 T. Eagleton (1983) *Literary Theory*, Oxford, Basil Blackwell, p.128.

39 E. P. Errington (1993) op. cit., p.187.

40 D. Varney (1991) 'Drama education – a re-staging', *The NADIE Journal* (Australia) 15(3), p.20.

41 G. Bolton (1981) 'Assessment of practical drama', *Drama Control* 1, reprinted in D. Davis and C. Lawrence (eds) (1986), op. cit., p.220.

42 D. Varney (1991) op. cit., p.20.

8 CULTURE AND POWER

1 W. Russell (1981) *Educating Rita*, London, Samuel French, scene 7.

2 M. Young (1982) 'Drama and the politics of educational change', in J. Norman (ed.) *Drama in Education: A Curriculum for Change*, Oxford, National Association for the Teaching of Drama/Kemble Press, pp.88–95. For an informed debate about educational knowledge, see M. Young (ed.) (1971) *Knowledge and Control*, London, Collier-Macmillan.

3 R. Williams (1965) *The Long Revolution*, Harmondsworth, Penguin Books, p.172. A full account of Williams' useful theory of cultural formation appears in R. Williams (1977) *Marxism and Literature*, Oxford, Oxford University Press, especially chp.8, 'Dominant, residual and emergent'.

4 Those who think I have misspelled 'Sparticist' here, might like to turn to the English satirical magazine *Private Eye*, in which the political views of Dave and Deirdre Spart were once a regular feature.

5 J. Neelands (1991) 'The meaning of drama', *The Drama Magazine* November, pp.8–9.

6 G. Bolton (1995) in G. Bolton and D. Heathcote, *Drama for Learning: Dorothy Heathcote's Mantle of the Expert Approach to Education*, Portsmouth, New Hampshire, Heinemann, p.4.

7 K. Warren (1993) 'Drama for young children', *Drama* 1(3), p.8.

8 J. Carey (1990) 'Teaching in role and classroom power', *Drama Broadsheet* 7(2), p.5.

9 B. Edmiston (1991) 'Planning for flexibility: the phases of a dramatic structure', *The Drama/Theatre Teacher* 4(1), p.11.

10 H. Fletcher (1995) 'Retrieving the mother/other from the myths and margins of O'Neill's "Seal Wife" drama', *The NADIE Journal* (Australia) 19(2), p.26.

11 B. Edmiston (1991) op. cit.

12 H. Nicholson (1995) 'Performative acts: drama, education and gender', *The NADIE Journal* (Australia) 19(1), p.31.

13 B. Wilks (1975) 'Disciples in need of a discipline', in M. Banham and J. Hodgson (eds) *Drama in Education 3: Annual Survey*, Bath, The Pitman Press, p.96.

14 For this memorable example of the supposed power of improvisation, see B. Way (1967) *Development through Drama*, London, Longman, p.1.

15 C. Geertz (1983) *Local Knowledge*, New York, Basic Books, p.44.

16 Ibid., p.43.

17 Ibid., pp.44–5.

18 J. Clark and J. Spindler (1986) *Education for Change in our Society*, London, National Association for the Teaching of Drama, p.5.

19 Inner London Education Authority (1983) *Race, Sex and Class: 3. A Policy for Equality: Race*, London, ILEA, p.5.

20 D. Hargreaves (1982) *The Challenge for the Comprehensive School*, London, Routledge and Kegan Paul, p.130.

21 D. Morton (1986) 'Other people's stories: GCSE and drama', *Drama Broadsheet* 4(3), p.5.

22 G. Lukács (1971) *History and Class Consciousness*, trans. R. Livingstone, London, Merlin Press, p.52.

23 P. Abbs (1993) 'Backwards forward', *Times Educational Supplement*, 30 April.

9 PRACTICAL AESTHETICS AND DRAMATIC ART

1 E. Said (1993) 'Vultures of culture', *The Times Higher Education Supplement*, 1 January.
2 See M. Arnold (1971) *Culture and Anarchy*, ed. J. Dover Wilson, Cambridge, Cambridge University Press, p.69.
3 R. Williams (1977) *Marxism and Literature*, Oxford, Oxford University Press, p.154.
4 K. Marx (1977) *Selected Writings*, ed. D. McLellan, Oxford, Oxford University Press, p.389.
5 A. Gramsci (1971) *Selections from the Prison Notebooks of Antonio Gramsci*, ed. and trans. Q. Hoare and G. Nowell Smith, London, Lawrence and Wishart, p.263.
6 T. Eagleton (1976) *Marxism and Literary Criticism*, London, Eyre Methuen, p.5.
7 Ibid., p.18.
8 R. Williams (1977) op. cit., p.131.
9 J-P. Sartre (1971) *Sketch for a Theory of the Emotions*, trans. P. Mairet, London, Eyre Methuen, p.57. Existentialism was actually inaugurated by Kierkegaard in the 1840s in opposition to Hegel's idealism.
10 R. Williams (1977) op. cit., p.129.
11 Ibid., pp.130–1.
12 R. Williams (1981) *Politics and Letters: Interviews with 'New Left Review'*, London, Verso, p.159.
13 R. Williams (1977) op. cit., p.132.
14 I am indebted to Paul Willis for this most useful formulation. See P. Willis (1990) *Common Culture*, Milton Keynes, Open University Press, p.21. For a fuller discussion of the grounded aesthetic in relation to drama, see D. Hornbrook (1991) *Education in Drama*, London, The Falmer Press, pp.29–41.
15 Ibid., pp.40–1.
16 R. Barthes (1977) *Image, Music, Text*, ed. and trans. S. Heath, London, Collins, p.157.
17 Ibid., p.159.
18 For a much fuller development of this tripartite structure of making, performing and responding, see D. Hornbrook (1991) op. cit.
19 For a fuller discussion of the significance of dramatic literacy for drama teaching, see C. McCullough (1998) 'Building a dramatic vocabulary', in D. Hornbrook (1998) *On the Subject of Drama*, London, Routledge, Chapter 10.
20 J. Pick (1973) 'Five fallacies in drama', *Young Drama* 1(1), p.9.
21 B. Brecht (1978a) *The Mother*, trans. S. Gooch, London, Eyre Methuen, scene 6.

10 THE DRAMATISED SOCIETY

1 E. Bond (1996) 'Theatre has only one subject: justice', interview with Michael Bogdanov, *The New Statesman* 18 October, p.35.
2 For a more detailed account of the dramatisation of Elizabethan life, see J. Briggs (1983) *This Stage-Play World*, Oxford, Oxford University Press.
3 For a further consideration of this feature of students' drama, see D. Hornbrook (1991) *Education in Drama*, London, The Falmer Press, Chapter 3. See also G. Gangi (1998) 'Making sense of drama in an electronic age', in D. Hornbrook (ed.) *On the Subject of Drama*, London, Routledge, Chapter 9.

4 I refer, of course, to Ronald Reagan and to Margaret Thatcher at her most belligerent at the time of the 1982 Falklands War.

5 R. Williams (1975) *Drama in a Dramatised Society*, Cambridge, Cambridge University Press, pp.15–16.

6 E. Goffman (1969) *The Presentation of Self in Everyday Life*, Harmondsworth, Penguin Books, Chapter 6.

7 Ibid., p.24.

8 G. Bolton (1988) 'Drama as art', *Drama Broadsheet* 5(3), p.13.

9 J. Butler (1990) 'Gender trouble and gender constitution', in S. Case (ed.) *Performing Feminisms: Feminist Critical Theory and Theatre*, London, John Hopkins Press, p.279. For an interesting discussion of some of these ideas, see also A. Franks (1996) 'Drama education, the body and representation', *Research in Drama Education* 1(1), pp.105–20.

10 A. MacIntyre (1981) *After Virtue: A Study in Moral Theory*, London, Duckworth, p.109.

11 For example, see 'Type and archetype', in E. Bentley (1965) *The Life of the Drama*, London, Eyre Methuen, Chapter 2.

12 A. MacIntyre (1981) op. cit., p.26–7.

11 WHAT SHALL WE DO AND HOW SHALL WE LIVE?

1 L. Wittgenstein (1958) *Philosophical Investigations*, trans. G.E.M. Anscombe, Oxford, Basil Blackwell, para. 241, p.88e.

2 See, B. S. Bloom (1964–7) *Taxonomy of Educational Objectives* (3 vols), London, Longman.

3 A. J. Ayer was one of the most lucid exponents of logical positivism. He created something of a sensation in the 1930s with his claim that metaphysical propositions are neither true nor false, but nonsense. See A. J. Ayer (1936) *Language, Truth and Logic*, London, Gollancz.

4 A. Louch (1969) *Explanation and Human Action*, Berkeley, Cal., University of California Press, p.233.

5 Readers will remember that for Humpty Dumpty, a word 'means just what I choose it to mean – neither more nor less'. See L. Carroll (1872) *Alice through the Looking Glass*, Harmondsworth, Penguin Books, Chapter 6, p.116.

6 C. Taylor (1985a) *Human Agency and Language: Philosophical Papers 1.*, Cambridge, Cambridge University Press, p.11.

7 C. Taylor (1985b) *Philosophy and the Human Sciences: Philosophical Papers 2*, Cambridge, Cambridge University Press, pp.22–3.

8 Ibid., p.27.

9 H. G. Gadamer (1975) *Truth and Method*, trans. W. Glyn-Doepel, London, Sheed and Ward, p.258.

10 C. Geertz (1983) *Local Knowledge*, New York, Basic Books, p.31. For an example of this process, see C. Geertz (1973), 'Deep play: notes on the Balinese cockfight', in *The Interpretation of Cultures: Further Essays in Interpretive Anthropology*, New York, Basic Books, Chapter 15. I develop the idea of 'the social text' more fully in D. Hornbrook (1991) *Education in Drama*, London, The Falmer Press, Chapter 3.

11 B. Brecht (1978a) 'In praise of the revolutionary', in *The Mother*, trans. S. Gooch, London, Eyre Methuen, scene 6.

12 See J. Habermas (1974) *Theory and Practice*, London, Heinemann, pp.11–12.

13 E. Durkheim (1961) *Moral Education*, New York, Free Press, quoted in D.

Hargreaves (1982) *The Challenge for the Comprehensive School*, London, Routledge and Kegan Paul, p.108.

14 C. Taylor (1985a) op. cit., p.8.

15 D. Hargreaves (1982) op. cit., p.151.

16 Ibid., p.108.

12 THE DRAMA CURRICULUM

1 P. Abbs (1992) 'Abbs replies to Bolton', *Drama* 1(1) p.3.

2 See B. Bernstein (1977) *Class, Codes and Control, Vol. 3 – Towards a Theory of Educational Transmissions*, London, Routledge and Kegan Paul, p.90.

3 J. Allen (1979) *Drama in Schools: Its Theory and Practice*, London, Heinemann, p.119. John Allen had responsibility for drama in Her Majesty's Inspectorate for eleven years. His 1967 report on drama in schools remains one of the most balanced and illuminating accounts of the field. See Department of Education and Science (1967a), *Drama: Education Survey 2*, London, HMSO.

4 For a much more detailed account of dramatic art in action, see D. Hornbrook (1991) *Education in Drama*, London, The Falmer Press.

5 See A. Kempe (1998) 'Reading plays for performance', in D. Hornbrook (1998) (ed.) *On the Subject of Drama*, London, Routledge, Chapter 6.

6 See also E. Aston and G. Savona (1991) *Theatre as Sign System: A Semiotics of Text and Performance*, London, Routledge; S. Bennett (1990) *Theatre Audiences: A Theory of Production and Reception*, London, Routledge; K. Elam (1980) *The Semiotics of Theatre and Drama*, London, Eyre Methuen; D. Urian (1998) 'On being an audience: a spectator's guide', in D. Hornbrook (1998) op. cit., Chapter 8.

7 G. Bolton and D. Heathcote (1995) *Drama for Learning: Dorothy Heathcote's Mantle of the Expert Approach to Education*, Portsmouth, New Hampshire, Heinemann, p.41.

8 R. Bharucha (1990) *Theatre and the World: Performance and the Politics of Culture*, London, Routledge, p.5 and Chapter 4.

9 Runnymede Trust (1993) *Equality Assurance in Schools: Quality, Identity, Society*, London, Trentham Books, p.28.

10 See S. Brahmachari 'Stages of the world', in D. Hornbrook (1998) op. cit., Chapter 2.

11 See 'The drama laboratory', in D. Hornbrook (1991) op. cit., pp.88–91.

12 G. Bolton (1984) *Drama As Education*, London, Longman, p.161. Bolton seems blind here, not only to what might reasonably be supposed to be *his* vested interest, but also, apparently, to the ways in which painting, literature and music also 'teach us about life'.

13 For the key organising volumes in this library, see P. Abbs (ed.) (1987) *Living Powers: The Arts in Education*, London, The Falmer Press; P. Abbs (1989) *A is for Aesthetic: Essays on Creative and Aesthetic Education*, London, The Falmer Press; T. Pateman (1991) *Key Concepts: A Guide to Aesthetics, Criticism and the Arts in Education*, London, The Falmer Press.

14 *The Arts in Schools*, (1982) London, Calouste Gulbenkian Foundation, p.143. Ken Robinson was a key member of the advisory committee which produced this report, and was also largely responsible for National Curriculum Council (1990) *The Arts 5 to 16: A Framework for Development*, London, Longman.

15 D. Hargreaves (1982) *The Challenge for the Comprehensive School*, London, Routledge and Kegan Paul, pp.152–3.

BIBLIOGRAPHY

Abbs, P. (ed.) (1987) *Living Powers: The Arts in Education*, London: The Falmer Press.

——(1989) *A is for Aesthetic: Essays on Creative and Aesthetic Education*, London: The Falmer Press.

Abrams, M.H. (1953) *The Mirror and the Lamp*, Oxford: Oxford University Press.

Allen, J. (1979), *Drama in Schools: Its Theory and Practice*, London: Heinemann.

Arnold, M. (1971), *Culture and Anarchy*, ed. J. Dover Wilson, Cambridge: Cambridge University Press.

Arts Council of Great Britain (1992) *Drama in Schools: Arts Council Guidance on Drama Education*, London: Arts Council of Great Britain.

The Arts in Schools (1982) London: Calouste Gulbenkian Foundation.

Aston, E. and Savona, G. (1991) *Theatre as Sign System: A Semiotics of Text and Performance*, London: Routledge.

Ayer, A.J. (1936) *Language, Truth and Logic*, London: Gollancz.

Bailin, S. (1994) *Achieving Extraordinary Ends: An Essay on Creativity*, Norwood, New Jersey: Ablex Publishing.

Banham, M. and Hodgson, J. (eds) (1972, 1973 and 1975) *Drama in Education 1, 2, and 3: Annual Survey*, Bath: The Pitman Press.

Barthes, R. (1977) *Image, Music, Text*, ed. and trans. S. Heath, London: Collins Press.

Bennett, S. (1990) *Theatre Audiences: A Theory of Production and Reception*, London: Routledge.

Bentley, E. (1965) *The Life of the Drama*, London: Eyre Methuen.

Bernstein, B. (1977) *Class, Codes and Control, Vol. 3: Towards a Theory of Educational Transmissions*, London: Routledge and Kegan Paul.

Bharucha, R. (1990) *Theatre and the World: Performance and the Politics of Culture*, London: Routledge.

Bloom, B.S. (1964–67) *Taxonomy of Educational Objectives*, 3 vols, London: Longman.

Boal, A. (1979) *Theatre of the Oppressed*, London: Pluto Press. trans, C. and M.O. Leal McBride, London: Pluto Press.

Board of Education (1931) *Report of the Consultative Committee on the Primary School* (The Hadow Report), London: HMSO.

Bolton, G. (1979) *Towards a Theory of Drama in Education*, London: Longman.

——(1984) *Drama As Education*, London: Longman.

——(1992) *New Perspectives on Classroom Drama*, Hemel Hempstead: Simon and Schuster Education.

172

Bolton, G. and Heathcote, D. (1995) *Drama for Learning: Dorothy Heathcote's Mantle of the Expert Approach to Education*, Portsmouth, New Hampshire: Heinemann.

Bowker, J. (ed.) (1991) *Secondary Media Education: A Curriculum Statement*, London: British Film Institute.

Bowskill, D. (1974) *Drama and the Teacher*, Bath: The Pitman Press.

Brecht, B. (1976) *Bertolt Brecht: Poems, 1913–1956*, eds J. Willett and R. Manheim, London: Eyre Methuen.

——(1978a) *The Mother*, trans. S. Gooch, London: Eyre Methuen.

——(1978b) *Brecht on Theatre: The Development of an Aesthetic*, ed. J. Willett, London: Eyre Methuen.

Briggs, J. (1983) *This Stage-Play World*, Oxford: Oxford University Press.

Byron, K. (1986) *Drama in the English Classroom*, London: Methuen.

Caldwell Cook, H. (1917) *The Play Way*, London: Heinemann.

Carroll, L. (1872) *Alice through the Looking Glass*, Harmondsworth: Penguin.

Case, S. (ed.) *Performing Feminisms: Feminist Critical Theory and Theatre*, London: John Hopkins Press.

Centre for Contemporary Cultural Studies (1981) *Unpopular Education*, London: Hutchinson.

Chilver P. (1967) *Improvised Drama*, London: Batsford.

Clark, J. and Spindler, J. (1986) *Education for Change in our Society*, London: National Association for the Teaching of Drama.

Cox, C.B. and Dyson, A.E. (eds) (1969a) *Fight for Education: A Black Paper*, London: Critical Quarterly Society.

——(1969b) *Black Paper 2: The Crisis in Education*, London: Critical Quarterly Society.

Davies, N. (1996) *Europe: A History*, Oxford: Oxford University Press.

Davis, D. and Lawrence, C. (eds) (1986) *Gavin Bolton: Selected Writings*, London: Longman.

Day, C. and Norman, N. (eds) (1983) *Issues in Educational Drama*, London: The Falmer Press.

Department of Education and Science (1967a) *Drama: Education Survey 2*, London: HMSO.

——(1967b) *Report of the Central Advisory Council for Education (England) entitled 'Children and their Primary Schools'* (The Plowden Report), London: HMSO.

——(1977a) *Education in Schools*, London: HMSO.

——(1977b), *Curriculum 11–16* ('The Red Book'), London: HMSO.

——(1984), *Training for Jobs*, White Paper, London: HMSO.

——(1985) *Better Schools*, London: HMSO.

——(1987a) *The National Curriculum 5–16: A Consultation Document*, London: HMSO.

——(1987b) *Speech by the Minister of State at the Annual Conference of the National Association for Education in the Arts*, 28 October 1987, London: HMSO.

——(1988)*National Curriculum: Task Group on Assessment and Testing Report* (The Black Report), London: HMSO.

——(1989) *Drama from 5 to 16: Curriculum Matters 17*, London: HMSO.

——(1990) *The Teaching and Learning of Drama*, London: HMSO.

Dobson, W. (ed.) (1983) *Bolton at the Barbican*, London: National Association for the Teaching of Drama/Longman.

Dunn, J. (1979) *Western Political Theory in the Face of the Future*, Cambridge: Cambridge University Press.

Durkheim, E. (1961) *Moral Education*, New York: The Free Press.

Eagleton, T. (1976) *Marxism and Literary Criticism*, London: Eyre Methuen.

173

——(1983) *Literary Theory*, Oxford: Basil Blackwell.

Education Reform Act 1988, London: HMSO.

Elam, K. (1980) *The Semiotics of Theatre and Drama*, London: Eyre Methuen.

Ellis, J. (1983) *Life Skills Training Manual*, London: Community Service Volunteers.

Errington, E.P. (ed.) (1993) *Arts Education: Beliefs, Practices and Possibilities*, Geelong, Australia: Deakin University Press.

Eysenck, H.J. (1954) *The Psychology of Politics*, London: Eyre Methuen.

Fairclough, G. (1972) *The Play is NOT the Thing*, Oxford: Basil Blackwell.

Finlay-Johnson, H. (1911) *The Dramatic Method of Teaching*, London: James Nisbet.

Fischer, E. (1963) *The Necessity of Art*, trans. A. Bostock, Harmondsworth: Penguin Books.

Fraser, F. and Bartky, S.L. (eds) (1992) *Revaluing French Feminism: Critical Essays on Difference, Agency and Culture*, Indianapolis: Indiana University Press.

Freire, P. (1972) *Pedagogy of the Oppressed*, Harmondsworth: Penguin Books.

Fukuyama, F. (1992) *The End of History and the Last Man*, New York: The Free Press.

Gadamer, H.G. (1975) *Truth and Method*, trans. W. Glyn-Doepel, London: Sheed and Ward.

Geertz, G. (1973) *The Interpretation of Cultures: Further Essays in Interpretive Anthropology*, New York: Basic Books.

——(1983) *Local Knowledge*, New York: Basic Books.

Gellner, E. (1985) *The Psychoanalytic Movement*, London: Paladin Books.

Giles, G.C.T. (1946) *The New School Tie*, London: Pilot Press.

Goethals, M. (ed.) (1982) *Opvoedkundigdrama*, S-Gravenhage, The Netherlands: University of Leiden Press.

Goffman, E. (1969) *The Presentation of Self in Everyday Life*, Harmondsworth: Penguin Books.

Goodridge, J. (1970) *Drama in the Primary School*, London: Heinemann.

Gramsci, A. (1971) *Selections from the Prison Notebooks of Antonio Gramsci*, ed. and trans. Q. Hoare and G. Nowell Smith, London: Lawrence and Wishart.

Groos, K. (1901) *The Play of Man*, trans. E. L. Baldwin, London: Heinemann.

Gutiérrez, G. (1974) *A Theology of Liberation: History, Politics and Salvation*, trans/ed. I. Caridad and J. Eagleson, London: SCM Press.

Habermas, J. (1974) *Theory and Practice*, London: Heinemann.

Hargreaves, D. (1982) *The Challenge for the Comprehensive School*, London: Routledge and Kegan Paul.

Hartnett, A. and Naish, M. (eds) (1986) *Education and Society Today*, London: The Falmer Press.

Health Education Authority (1988) *High Stress Occupations Working Party Report*, London: HMSO.

Heathcote, D. (1980) *Drama as Context*, National Association for the Teaching of English, Aberdeen: Aberdeen University Press.

Heidegger, M. (1978) *Basic Writings*, ed. D. Krell, London: Routledge and Kegan Paul.

Hill, C., Reay, B. and Lamont, W. (eds) (1983) *The World of the Muggletonians*, London: Temple Smith.

Hodgson, J. (ed.) (1972) *The Uses of Drama*, London: Eyre Methuen.

Hodgson, J. and Richards, E. (1966) *Improvisation*, London: Eyre Methuen.

Holderness, G. (ed.) (1988) *The Shakespeare Myth*, Manchester: Manchester University Press.

Hornbrook, D. (1991) *Education in Drama*, London: The Falmer Press.

——(1998) *On the Subject of Drama*, London: Routledge.

174

Husserl, E. (1960) *Cartesian Meditations: An Introduction to Phenomenology*, trans. D. Cairns, The Hague: Martinus Nijhoff.

Inglis, F. (1985) *The Management of Ignorance*, Oxford: Basil Blackwell.

Inner London Education Authority (1983–5) *Race, Sex and Class* (policy documents). London: Inner London Education Authority.

——(1984) *Improving Secondary Schools* (The Hargreaves Report), London: Inner London Education Authority.

Johnson, L. and O'Neill, C. (eds) (1984) *Dorothy Heathcote: Collected Writings*, London: Hutchinson.

Kempe, A. (1990), *GCSE Drama Coursebook*, Oxford: Basil Blackwell.

Kitson, N. and Spiby, I. (1995) *Primary Drama Handbook*, London: Watts Books.

Kogan, M. (ed.) (1971) *The Politics of Education: Edward Boyle and Anthony Crosland in Conversation with Maurice Kogan*, Harmondsworth: Penguin Books.

Lambert, A., Linnell, R., O'Neill, C. and Warr-Wood, J. (1976) *Drama Guidelines*, London: Heinemann, in association with London Drama.

Lambert, A. and O'Neill, C. (1982) *Drama Structures*, London: Hutchinson

Lasch, C. (1980) *The Culture of Narcissism: American Life in an Age of Diminishing Expectations*, London: Sphere Books.

Lawrence, C. (ed.) (1993) *Voices for Change*, London: National Drama Publications.

Lawton, D. and Chitty, C. (eds) (1988) *The National Curriculum*, London: Institute of Education, University of London.

Leavis, F.R. (1930) *Mass Civilisation and Minority Culture*, Cambridge: Cambridge University Press.

Louch, A. (1969) *Explanation and Human Action*, Berkeley, CA: University of California Press.

Lukács, G. (1971) *History and Class Consciousness*, trans. R. Livingstone, London: Merlin Press.

McCaslin, N. (ed.) (1981) *Children and Drama*, second edn, New York: Longman.

McElligott, T. *et al.* (1988) *Report on TVEI*, Assistant Masters and Mistresses Association.

McGregor, L., Tate, M. and Robinson, K. (1977) *Learning through Drama*, London: Heinemann.

MacIntyre, A. (1981) *After Virtue: A Study in Moral Theory*, London: Duckworth.

McLellan, D. (1987) *Marxism and Religion*, London: Macmillan.

Marx, K. (1977) *Selected Writings*, ed. D. McLellan, Oxford: Oxford University Press.

Mendelson, E. (ed.) (1976) *W.H. Auden Collected Poems*, London: Faber and Faber.

Midland Examining Group (1986) *GCSE Leicestershire Mode III Drama*, Cambridge.

Ministry of Education (1963) *Half Our Future* (The Newsom Report), London: HMSO.

Morgan, N. and Saxton, J. (1987) *Teaching Drama: 'A mind of many wonders . . .'*, London: Hutchinson.

Morris, B. (1967) *The New Curriculum*, London: HMSO.

Morton, D. (1989) *Assessment in Drama* (discussion and working document), Leeds: City of Leeds Education Department.

National Curriculum Council (1990) *The Arts 5 to 16: A Framework for Development*, London: Longman.

Neelands, J. (1984) *Making Sense of Drama*, London: Heinemann.

——(1992) *Learning through Imagined Experience*, London: Hodder and Stoughton.

Neelands, J. and Goode, T. (1990) *Structuring Drama Work: A Handbook of Available Forms*, Cambridge: Cambridge University Press.

175

Norman, J. (ed.) (1982) *Drama in Education: A Curriculum for Change*, Oxford: National Association for the Teaching of Drama/Kemble Press.

O'Toole, J. (1992) *The Process of Drama: Negotiating Art and Meaning*, London: Routledge.

Owens, A. and Barber, K. (1997) *Dramaworks*, Carlisle: Carel Press.

Pateman, T. (1991) *Key Concepts: A Guide to Aesthetics, Criticism and the Arts in Education*, London: The Falmer Press.

Pemberton-Billing, R. and Clegg, J. (1965) *Teaching Drama*, London: University of London Press.

Polanyi, M. (1958) *Personal Knowledge: Towards a Post-Critical Philosophy*, London: Routledge and Kegan Paul.

——(1959) *The Study of Man*, London: Routledge and Kegan Paul.

Positive Images: 1985 Conference Publication, (1986) St Albans: Joint Committee (NATD, NATFHE Drama, NAYT, NADECT, NADA).

Read, H. (1943) *Education through Art*, London: Faber and Faber.

Robinson, K. (ed.) (1980) *Exploring Theatre and Education*, London: Heinemann.

Ross, M. (1978) *The Creative Arts*, London: Heinemann.

——(ed.) (1982) *The Development of Aesthetic Experience*, Oxford: Pergamon Press.

Ross, M., Radnor, H., Mitchell, S. and Bierton, C. (1993) *Assessing Achievement in the Arts*, Milton Keynes: Open University Press.

Rousseau, J.-J. (1960) *Politics and the Arts: The Letter to M. d'Alembert on the Theatre*, trans. A. Bloom, Glencoe, Illinois: Free Press.

Rowntree, D. (1977) *Assessing Students: How Shall We Know Them?*, New York: Harper and Row.

Runnymede Trust (1993) *Equality Assurance in Schools: Quality, Identity, Society*, London: Trentham Books.

Russell, W. (1981) *Educating Rita*, London: Samuel French.

Ryle, G. (1971) *Collected Papers, Vol.2: Collected Essays 1929–68*, London: Hutchinson.

Sartre, J.-P. (1971) *Sketch for a Theory of the Emotions*, trans. P. Mairet, London: Eyre Methuen.

——(1972) *Kean*, trans. F. Hauser, London: Davis-Poynter.

Self, D. (1975) *A Practical Guide to Drama in the Secondary School*, London: Ward Lock Educational.

Sennett, R. (1977) *The Fall of Public Man*, Cambridge: Cambridge University Press.

Slade, P. (1954) *Child Drama*, London: University of London Press.

——(1958) *An Introduction to Child Drama*, London: Hodder and Stoughton.

Somers, J. (ed.) (1996) *Drama and Theatre in Education: Contemporary Research*, Ontario: Captus University Publications.

Stanislavski, C. (1980) *My Life in Art*, trans. J. J. Robbins, London: Eyre Methuen.

Stenhouse, L. (1969) *Schools Council Humanities Curriculum Project*, London: Longman.

Taylor, C. (1985a) *Human Agency and Language: Philosophical Papers 1*, Cambridge: Cambridge University Press.

——(1985b) *Philosophy and the Human Sciences: Philosophical Papers 2*, Cambridge: Cambridge University Press.

Taylor, K. (ed.) (1981) *Drama Strategies*, London: Heinemann with London Drama.

Taylor, P. (ed.) (1996) *Researching Drama and Arts Education: Paradigms and Possibilities*, London: The Falmer Press.

Trilling, L. (1971) *Sincerity and Authenticity*, Cambridge, Mass.: Harvard University Press.

Vernon, P.E. (ed.) (1970) *Creativity*, Harmondsworth: Penguin Books.

Wagner, B.-J. (1979) *Dorothy Heathcote: Drama as a Learning Medium*, London: Hutchinson.

Walker, B. (1970) *Teaching Creative Drama*, London: Batsford.

Watkins, B. (1981) *Drama and Education*, London: Batsford.

Way, B. (1967) *Development through Drama*, London: Longman.

Williams, R. (1965) *The Long Revolution*, Harmondsworth: Penguin Books.

——(1975) *Drama in a Dramatised Society*, Cambridge: Cambridge University Press.

——(1977) *Marxism and Literature*, Oxford: Oxford University Press.

——(1979) *Modern Tragedy*, London: Verso.

——(1981) *Politics and Letters: Interviews with 'New Left Review'*, London: Verso.

Willis, P. (1990) *Common Culture*, Milton Keynes: Open University Press.

Witkin, R.W. (1974) *The Intelligence of Feeling*, London: Heinemann.

Wittgenstein, L. (1958) *Philosophical Investigations*, trans. G.E.M. Anscombe, Oxford: Basil Blackwell.

Wootton, M. (ed.) (1982) *New Directions in Drama Teaching*, London: Heinemann.

Young, M. (ed.) (1971) *Knowledge and Control*, London: Collier-Macmillan.

INDEX